*Routledge Revivals*

# Economy, Society & Culture in Contemporary Yemen

First published in 1985, *Economy, Society & Culture in Contemporary Yemen* was written to present a wealth of research and thinking that was new to the field at the time of original publication.

The book covers a wide range of topics, including socio-economic development, agriculture, land use, fiscal policies, emigration, health, education, and politics. In doing so, it provides a close analysis of the situation in Yemen in the 1980s whilst exploring recent developments of the preceding years. It will appeal to those with an interest in the history of Yemen.

# Economy, Society & Culture in Contemporary Yemen

## Edited by B.R. Pridham

Routledge
Taylor & Francis Group

First published in 1985
by Croom Helm Ltd.

This edition first published in 2021 by Routledge
2 Park Square, Milton Park, Abingdon, Oxon, OX14 4RN
and by Routledge
605 Third Avenue, New York, NY 10017

*Routledge is an imprint of the Taylor & Francis Group, an informa business*

© 1985 B.R. Pridham

**Publisher's Note**
The publisher has gone to great lengths to ensure the quality of this reprint but points out that some imperfections in the original copies may be apparent.

**Disclaimer**
The publisher has made every effort to trace copyright holders and welcomes correspondence from those they have been unable to contact.

A Library of Congress record exists under LCCN: 84023102

ISBN 13: 978-0-367-76005-2 (hbk)
ISBN 13: 978-1-003-16515-6 (ebk)

Book DOI: 10.4324/9781003165156

# Economy, Society & *Culture* in Contemporary YEMEN

Edited by
B. R. Pridham

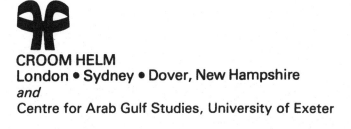

CROOM HELM
London • Sydney • Dover, New Hampshire
*and*
Centre for Arab Gulf Studies, University of Exeter

© 1985 B. R. Pridham
Croom Helm Ltd, Provident House, Burrell Row,
Beckenham, Kent BR3 1AT
Croom Helm Australia Pty Ltd, First Floor, 139 King Street,
Sydney, NSW 2001, Australia

**British Library Cataloguing in Publication Data**

Economy, society and culture in contemporary Yemen.
  1. Yemen — Social conditions
  I. Pridham, B. R.
  953'.3053     HN564.5.A8

  ISBN 0-7099-2093-8


Croom Helm, 51 Washington Street,
Dover, New Hampshire 03820, USA

Library of Congress Cataloging in Publication Data

Economy, society, and culture in contemporary Yemen.

    Papers presented to a symposium held in July
1983 by Exeter University's Centre for Arab Gulf
Studies.
    Includes index.
    1.Yemen – Economic conditions – Congresses.
2. Yemen (People's Democratic Republic) – Economic Con-
ditions – Congresses. 3. Yemen – Social conditions –
Congresses. 4. Yemen (People's Democratic Republic) –
Social conditions – Congresses. I. Pridham, B.R.,
1934-    . II. University of Exeter. Centre for
Arab Gulf Studies.
HC415.34.E26    1985     953'.32     84-23102
ISBN 0-7099-2093-8

# CONTENTS

## TABLES & FIGURES

**Tables**

**Figures**

viii

# PREFACE

This book contains a selection of the papers presented to a symposium on Contemporary Yemen held in July 1983 by Exeter University's Centre for Arab Gulf Studies, in collaboration with the Universities of Aden and San'a'. A first selection has already been published in *Contemporary Yemen: Politics and Historical Background* (Croom Helm, 1984). The general division of topics between the two books is clear enough from their titles, but it should be borne in mind that both consider aspects of a single theme, that is 'Greater Yemen', the geographical area now constituting the states of the Yemen Arab Republic (YAR) and the People's Democratic Republic of Yemen (PDRY). It follows that there must be an overlap between the books in some areas. Education, for example, is examined at length in this volume but its role in nation-building was covered in the earlier compilation; and the reader wishing to understand the nature and importance of tribalism in North Yemen (YAR) will find that its pervasive influence brings it squarely into both books.

The symposium and the books resulting from it rest on the belief that the two Yemeni states can usefully be studied together on two grounds. Not only do the people inhabiting them explicitly share a sense of common identity as Yemenis, but each state achieved its present conformation during the crucial period of the 1960s, exerting in the process an intimate influence on each other. The 1962 revolution which set up the YAR and the withdrawal in 1967 of the British colonial authorities from what became the PDRY have, for Yemenis, a linked importance which transcends mere national boundaries.

It was in the consideration of shared Yemeni experience that the participation of the two Yemeni Universities and of other Yemeni scholars and administrators was particularly valuable. Until very recent years publications on the Yemen have been scarce outside the Middle East, and for helping to fill that gap credit was already due to some of the distinguished participants in the symposium. But the Yemeni point of view has been even less heard in the English-speaking world, and the symposium was the first of its kind in having official participation from North and South. As a result this volume contains invaluable first-hand material from the Yemenis actually involved in the subjects under discussion, as well as the complementary work of outside experts who may well adopt a different viewpoint. At its international symposia, of which this was the sixth, the Centre for Arab Gulf Studies welcomes differing and indeed controversial interpretations of the themes under discussion. Neither the editor nor of course the Centre itself is in any way responsible for the opinions expressed, but both feel a duty not to try to disguise the existence of conflicting views. Needless to say, even the outside experts may disagree; one chapter of this book is a well-argued attempt to refute the customary view (also well-argued in other chapters) that the phenomenon of *qat* is harmful in both economic and social terms.

In the nature of things these two companion volumes cannot claim to provide a systematic coverage of all aspects of Contemporary Yemen. Each chapter, however, represents an expert's insight into his particular field, and no field of importance is overlooked. The editor's role has therefore been minimal; the papers are basically in the form in which they were presented and no attempt has been made to modify one in the light of another.

My thanks go, as before, to Professor M. A. Shaban, the Director of the Centre for Arab Gulf Studies, who chaired the symposium, and to Mr H. G. Balfour-Paul, who planned it and brought it to what was, by common consent, a most successful conclusion.

## NOTE ON TRANSLITERATION

A simplified and uniform system of Arabic transliteration has been used throughout this book. Diacritical marks are not used but, as is usual nowadays, the *hamza* is represented by ' and the *'ain* by '. Both are omitted from initial capital letters. The very few ambiguities which result from the simplification will present no problems to an Arabic speaker. Proper names which are familiar in the English-speaking world, e.g. Aden, have been left in their familiar, not transliterated, forms.

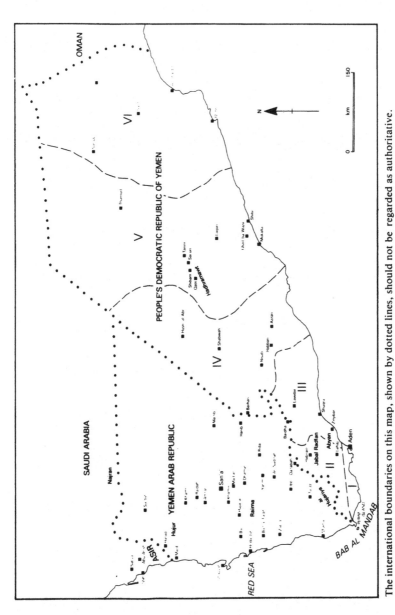

OMAN

VI

PEOPLE'S DEMOCRATIC REPUBLIC OF YEMEN

V

Thamud

Tarim
Sai'un
Shibam
Qatn
Hadhramawt

Ghail ba Wazir
Shihr
Mukalla

IV

Hajar al Abr
Shabwah

Azzan

Nisab
Habban

III

Bashah
Lawdar

Shuqra
Zinjibar
Aden

Ma'rib

Harib

SAUDI ARABIA

Najran

YEMEN ARAB REPUBLIC

San'a

Rada

Dhamar

Jabal Radfan
Abyen
Lahej

II

al
Hujariyah

I

Raima

Hajur

ASIR

RED SEA

BAB AL MANDAB

N
km
0                150

The international boundaries on this map, shown by dotted lines, should not be regarded as authoritative.

PDRY governorates are shown by dashed lines and roman numerals.

# 1 EVALUATION OF SOCIO-ECONOMIC DEVELOPMENT IN THE PEOPLE'S DEMOCRATIC REPUBLIC OF YEMEN

V. V. Naumkin

Many of the chapters in this book discuss questions of the paths, peculiarities, results, problems and prospects of development in the two Yemeni states; to a certain extent this is the book's main theme. Bearing in mind that most of my fellow writers analyse concrete questions of the economic, social, political and cultural life of the Yemeni states, I should like to touch on some general problems and, above all, on problems of appraisal of the results of their development.

In examining the development of the two Yemens, we do not, of course, see them in opposition to each other but, on the contrary, find much that is common to both. Nevertheless, the theme of the book inevitably warrants a comparison of the two states which have chosen different courses of development. In appraising the results of the advance of both states along their chosen roads — the road of capitalist development in one case and the road of socialist orientation in the other, but both of them set on building a developed modern society — it is not enough to fix quantity indices. It should be stressed here that it is not concretely a question of two Yemens. Rather, their experience affords us an opportunity to formulate objective criteria for comparing the two paths of development on a scientific basis.

In such a comparison, consideration should be given to a multitude of diverse factors and circumstances, some of which will be discussed here. We should first note the geographical and demographic factors in the broad meaning of the terms or, in a narrower context, the difference in territory and population. It is not always adequately realised that a country with a more numerous and compact population possesses more possibilities for creating a national economic complex with a modern structure. The creation of a viable economy based on modern means of production requires a minimum of population. Of course, there is no arbitrarily defined minimum; it is mobile and varies with the impact of different factors. There are, moreover, special cases and some exceptions. Nevertheless, under the conditions found in developing countries, a population of a mere 1–3 million creates additional difficulties for development. In this connection it must be noted that, as a result of long colonial domination, the boundaries between different countries of Asia and Africa were in some cases not determined by objective internal ethnic, economic and political processes, but were directly inspired by colonial powers. It is clear that, for the People's Democratic Republic of Yemen (PDRY), its widely dispersed and fragmented population of one and a half million, the existence of just one big city (Aden), and the vast disparity in the level of development between this city and the interior regions which was inherited from colonial times, all created considerable difficulties which can be fully surmounted only in the course of time.

A minimum of population is one of the conditions for the formation of a scientific and technical potential. Any strategy of development has to take this circumstance into consideration. But no less important is another condition — the availability of optimal territory, in both quantity and quality. It is also necessary to stress the quantity indicator, which is important in particular for the prospects of discovering mineral resources (above all, oil and gas). On the whole, a large territory provides more ample opportunities for diversifying the economy. As for quality indicators, their importance is well known, as are the conditions of South Yemen with its small proportion of land fit for cultivation, complex relief, scarcity of water resources, absence of surveyed mineral deposits, poor links between different areas, inadequately developed telecommunications, and so on.

It is also important to consider the paths followed by Afro-Asian countries as they advanced to independence. The number of countries whose peoples attained national independence through a long liberation struggle and the use of armed methods is rather limited. This course inevitably entails a certain destruction of productive forces and damage to the human factor (both material and spiritual), the consequences of which can be overcome only with time. The four years' national liberation struggle of the people of South Yemen (PDRY) was its means of attaining independence. It also served as a potent means of national-ethnic consolidation. Considering that the level of this consolidation in a recent past was extremely low (up to the Second World War there was practically no patriotic movement in the country), this circumstance is significant.

At the same time, a war of liberation, like any other war, incurs damage to the productive forces.

There is one more aspect that must be taken into account in appraising development. It is important to ascertain how rapidly a country freed from colonialism has been able to restore the level of productive forces reached before liberation. This is of great theoretical significance, since many countries, for quite understandable reasons, have spent long years in restoring it. Nevertheless, this factor is not of particular relevance for South Yemen: in the colonial period its interior regions were at an exceptionally low level of development, while Aden, with its ample supply of resources spent by the mother country on the upkeep of its base, was a centre of consumerism rather than a source of development. None the less, some aspects of socio-economic life (oil processing, the re-export trade, port activity) were quite advanced. Due both to objective causes (Britain's loss of interest in the operation of the refinery, the closure of the Suez Canal, competition on the part of other ports of the region, the refusal of a number of regimes to co-operate with South Yemen) and to subjective causes (the extremist mistakes criticised and then rectified by the Yemen Socialist Party (YSP) itself), even the restoration of the old level was a complex task. It was all the more difficult for a country which lived through numerous plots and became the target of subversion from outside (the activity of mercenaries and the threats of imperialist reactionary forces which necessitated high defence expenditure) and from within (sabotage by a section of the civil servants).

The effectiveness of a development structure can be verified only when it reaches the old (pre-revolutionary) level after overcoming the destructive element inevitably contained in the break-up of the old pattern of life and transferring the national economy to new lines of development. Nor should we forget that, under present conditions, the building of modern enterprises and their capacity operation require a long period of time — anything up to ten years. In other words, the question of the effectiveness of production in the PDRY can be raised only in the 1980s. Any comparison which disregards the time factor is unjustified.

Furthermore, the reorganisation of the structure — and in South Yemen it was radical and thorough-going — involves certain difficulties, including financial and economic ones. The task of reorganisation may be facilitated in countries with oil earnings or in a country such as Egypt where all cultivable lands are irrigated. In any case, when appraising the degree of success of the development of a particular country, we .cannot operate with the data of the reorganisation period, for the socio-economic effect of the implemented measures can make itself felt only some time later. The supporters of the revolutionary path of social development are well aware that the results of the changes which occur in developing countries at the stage of transition to the road of socialist orientation do not automatically follow in the wake of political events marking this transition.

An equally mistaken approach to the appraisal of results is when account is sometimes taken of just the quantitative indicator of the development of the productive forces. The field of study is often confined to material elements of the productive forces, with the use of figures indicating volume of output, and so on. According to the scientific socialist conception, the human factor is no less significant. Thus the analysis of the results of socio-economic development must be accompanied by an analysis of changes in the conditions of life and work, gains in education, the health service, culture, and so on. This social aspect must also include, in the author's view, the degree of people's activity and their role in production, as in social and political life. In this field the PDRY has already scored undeniable successes (we shall deal with them below).

In short, it would be a gross error to study the results of economic activity 'independently', in isolation from all that is considered 'purely social'. Armed with isolated, individual facts, people sometimes try to prove the inefficiency of the road of development chosen by the Afro-Asian countries which are advancing along the lines of a radical reshaping of the established system of relations, that is, a break-away from the capitalist system, leading to freedom from dependence. The human factor, however, must figure as an element of the socio-economic structure in its own right.

The question of appraisal is also complicated by the absence of comprehensive statistical information on countries of the Arabian Peninsula and the Arabian Gulf which would cover a wide range of questions: the available statistical data need reworking; the existing statistical system does not register concealed relations; a number of questions remain beyond the boundaries of polls, and so on. It is necessary to create a system of comprehensive statistical coverage of processes developing in the two Yemens and in other countries of the Arabian Peninsula and the Arabian Gulf, bearing in mind that those processes under way in all countries of the region are no doubt closely interconnected.

This is not to say that South Yemen, like any other state using the socialist experience in solving problems of development, is looking for compliments. The intention here is only to emphasise the importance of a scientific approach to appraisals. On the basis of a retrospective analysis of the experience of South Yemen and a comparative analysis of development of the two Yemens it is, perhaps, possible to raise a broader and more general scientific problem. A study aimed at elevating one country and downgrading the other can hardly be called scientific.

In the light of the foregoing, we now touch on some results and problems of the socio-economic development of the PDRY. The most acute problem is that of the food supply for the population. From the previous regime the republic inherited a very undeveloped system of agriculture with an archaic pre-capitalist structure, an almost complete absence of modern farming machinery, and water shortages. The reorganisation of the entire system of socio-economic relations in agriculture, the abolition of the system of feudal exploitation and the creation of new forms of farming — co-operative and state-operated — required much time, involved considerable difficulties and, moreover, were accompanied by a number of mistakes pointed out by the YSP leadership itself. However, already during the First Five-Year Plan (1974–78), agricultural output, according to official PDRY statistics, increased by 32 per cent. The planned volume of investments amounting to 20.8 million dinars (YD) was topped by 100 per cent (YD 43.3 million or 22 per cent of total investments). The co-operative and private sectors each contributed 40 per cent of the value of agricultural commercial output, the other 20 per cent coming from the state sector. Although agricultural output (with the exception of raw cotton) was rising despite the unfavourable weather conditions, crop yields remained low, as before (thus, wheat yields in the country as a whole averaged 14–16 quintals/ha), and the PDRY failed to make any substantial advance in solving the main task confronting it, that of achieving self-sufficiency in food supplies. Grain production covers less than half of domestic requirements and domestic production of meat, milk and eggs meets just 10–15 per cent of the country's needs. In 1978 the PDRY imported 100 per cent of the rice, sugar and tea it consumed, 75 per cent of the wheat and 70 per cent of the fats and vegetable oil. It was spending YD 22–25 million annually on food purchases abroad. Cattle-breeding made a slow advance, but poultry output grew rapidly owing to the building of modern farms. In particular, egg production multiplied more than eightfold.

Among successes achieved in agriculture are the development of new lands and the improvement of the irrigation system. Here the use of foreign aid and foreign experience is highly important for the PDRY. In particular, with Soviet assistance, the republic has built nine water-intake dams and about 100 km of irrigation canals, and 70,000 ha of land have been irrigated and brought into cultivation. Current construction projects include central workshops for the repair of agricultural machines, a new dam and the building of the Ministry of Agriculture and Agrarian Reform. In the Hadramawt a large contingent of Soviet hydro-geologists, drillers, soil specialists and agronomists is working. Soviet specialists, jointly with their Yemeni counterparts, have established the size of the water resources of the Hadramawt Valley, compiled soil maps, carried out economic feasibility estimates for building state farms (today the province already has six state farms built with Soviet assistance) and made recommendations for creating industrial enterprises and infrastructure facilities in the province. The new land development in the Hadramawt may turn the province into the country's granary. In other regions too the building of water-intake dams, the drilling of artesian wells, the building of canals and the organisation of farms carried out with Soviet assistance are helping to solve the serious problem of raising agricultural output.

In connection with this problem, it is worth mentioning one aspect of the social policy of the YSP which is at the same time a component part of its economic policy. Back in the 1970s the PDRY government took measures to maintain the level of domestic prices of consumer goods in order to protect the people from the effects of world price-rises. In particular, the state compensated for differences in the prices of flour, rice, tea, milk, fish, vegetables, medicines, tomatoes, home-made fabrics, electricity, books and children's clothes. It had to bear a burden of additional expenditure which in 1977 reached YD 6.4 million and in 1978 (the last year of the First Five-Year Plan) over YD 7 million (according to the estimates of the First Congress of the YSP). Subsequently, as economic conditions deteriorated, the state continued to allocate subsidies to maintain stable prices for food and primary necessities. Expenditure on this reached YD 7.8 million in 1979 and 16.5 million in 1980. The Second Congress of the YSP, which met in October 1980, pointed out that the state was also losing over YD 27 million annually as a consequence of disparities between the world prices of oil and oil products and their domestic prices, though the latter were raised too.

The problem of employment in the PDRY was extremely complex. The reshaping of the entire economic system in the post-colonial period, the shortage of specialists, the flight of some skilled personnel abroad, the scarcity of land resources, agrarian overpopulation, the deficit of funds, and so on, all adversely affected the situation in this sector. But as early as in the course of the First Five-Year Plan, employment increased. As the First Congress of the YSP pointed out, the total number of those employed rose by 135,000 after 1969, reaching 399,000 in 1976. From 1973 to 1976 the growth was 76,000. Special note was taken of the growth of employment in material production: from 1973 to 1976 the number of those employed in agriculture and fishing increased by 29,000, in manufacturing by 6,000 and in construction by 13,000. In 1978 the total workforce reached 411,000. But the structure of manpower at that time largely reflected the difficulties in the economic sphere. About 70–75 per cent were employed in the non-productive sphere and about 20 per cent in agriculture. By 1978 the industrial proletariat numbered less than 10,000, or 2 per cent of the employed. This problem is constantly kept in focus by the party and state-leadership of the PDRY, who strive to transfer as much labour as possible to the production sphere.

At present, when new enterprises are emerging apace, more and more attention is given to the training of skilled workers, in particular through a network of vocational schools, courses and professional training centres. The projects built with the assistance of socialist countries envisage the training of local workers and technical personnel in different specialities. The continuing movement of labour to neighbouring Arab states, though limited in scope and financially profitable for the state, causes labour deficits in a number of branches. It may sound paradoxical, but the PDRY is compelled to use foreign labour on a small scale (on projects built by foreign capital or with the assistance of capitalist countries).

Overall, a successful solution to the problem of employment is ensured by a well-thought-out strategy of development, economic planning, and a social policy pursued by the YSP in the interests of the broad working masses.

Speaking of the most complex problems of development in the

PDRY, we cannot but mention the so-called 'demonstration effect'. Both Yemens border on rich oil-producing countries with the highest *per capita* incomes in the world. There is no need to demonstrate the ease with which these countries have attained prosperity and the complexity of development against this background for a country which has not yet surveyed its resources of oil and other minerals. It is all the more important therefore to stress that, for many people, the social gains of the PDRY have a greater appeal than the material affluence in some countries with conservative regimes: social benefits often carry more weight. In the PDRY much attention is justifiably given to promoting relations with other countries of the region, but it can hardly find acceptable the model of Arabian integration proposed by a number of these countries: a Yemeni workforce plus the money and other resources of Arab countries.

As can be seen from the analysis of processes developing in the life of Arabian states, the model advocated by the PDRY implies several aspects of relations. First, integration on the basis of equality and co-operation, in which financial and economic aid is extended to South Yemen by individual states and inter-Arab organisations. In this context special mention should be made of relations between Kuwait and South Yemen, which can be seen as an inspiring example. Second, there is the participation by South Yemeni labour in the economic activity of the rich oil-producing states within limits which are not prejudicial to the national interests of the PDRY. Third, there is the activity of South Yemeni entrepreneurs beyond the frontiers of the country who take a part in developing the national economy. In recent years the PDRY has taken a number of well-known measures aimed at developing this co-operation, which is a source of significant receipts. According to an official government spokesman, in 1982 remittances by South Yemeni nationals abroad reached YD 155,392,380 (over $450 million). In the first three months of 1983 alone, South Yemeni emigrants remitted about YD 27 million to the PDRY. The success in attracting funds from South Yemeni entrepreneurs for the development of the country is evidenced by the creation and gradual expansion of the share of the mixed sector in the country's economy. By the end of the First Five-Year Plan this sector was producing 16 per cent of industrial output.

PDRY policy lays great emphasis on normalising relations with all states of the region, including Oman. In this connection, it is worth touching briefly on the basis principles of the PDRY's foreign policy. In 1975 the Sixth Congress of the National Front adopted a programme stating that at the basis of its foreign policy orientation lay two principles — internationalism and peaceful coexistence. The practical embodiment of the principle of peaceful coexistence can be seen in the PDRY's relations with the countries of the region, which are an important component in ensuring socio-economic development. As regards the deviations from this principle (made in the 1970s by representatives of the extremist wing and then strongly criticised by the ruling party, which got rid of adventurists in 1978), they originated not from the theory of scientific socialism but from the ideas of European and Afro-Asian neo-Trotskyites. The PDRY and the YSP constantly declare their readiness to develop relations with all countries of the region. The principle of internationalism, in particular, implies the support which the PDRY extends to national liberation movements. The YSP has, for example, long-standing, close and friendly relations with the Palestine Liberation Organisation (PLO). We can also point to the PDRY's co-operation with socialist Ethiopia.

The PDRY leadership justly rests its hopes on the development of fishing in the country. The development in the near future of the rich fish stocks of South Yemen will go a long way to build up the financial and economic potential of the republic. So far, these stocks are far from being fully exploited. Fish catches and marine products obtained in 1978 amounted to about 150,000 t, or half of the potential amount, according to experts. Fishing was done by the state-sector fishing fleet, fishing co-operatives, the private sector and also foreign (Japanese) and mixed (Yemeni-Soviet and Yemeni-Iraqi) companies. Foreign and mixed companies, whose catches of fish and sea products were just above 8 per cent of the total volume, accounted for 65 per cent of their value. This is due to the fact that these companies caught the most valuable types of fish and sea products (langoustes and squid), using the most modern vessels and fishing tackle. The state and the private sectors contributed about 80 per cent of all catches, but in terms of value this constituted slightly over 20 per cent, for they netted chiefly fish species of low value. At present the efforts of the country are directed towards developing national fishing. It is creating a modern fishing fleet and building fishing ports, refrigerator capacities and processing enterprises, and training national personnel. In this field South Yemen is actively co-operating with the Soviet Union. The republic would have rosy prospects indeed if it also had oil and gas resources. This is why large-scale geological survey projects are under way in the country, including aerial geophysical mapping and drilling of experimental wells.

One of the most formidable problems facing the PDRY is that of investments. In the 1970s, 75–85 per cent of all investments were provided by foreign financial aid and credits. As the Second Congress of the YSP pointed out, during the First Five-Year Plan 22 per cent of budget allocations came from domestic sources and the remaining 78 per cent were covered by foreign aid and credits. Of these, 61 per cent were supplied by socialist countries, 21 per cent came from Arab countries and funds, 6 per cent from international organisations and funds and 12 per cent from other sources of financing (material aid and various forms of solidarity). The Directives on the Second Five-Year Plan (1981–85) stipulated the need to take resolute measures to mobilise internal resources and cut the budget deficit. The Plan envisages an increase in receipts from internal sources of up to YD 128 million, of which YD 84 million are to be provided by state sources, 26 million by bank credits and 18 million through self-financing of state institutions. Naturally, the solution of this task requires great effort, an emphasis on savings, a rise in productivity and better performance by the state apparatus.

In this chapter we cannot review all the results and problems of the socio-economic development of the PDRY. We should simply note that we have a new and interesting experiment before us. It is noteworthy for its mature conception of socio-economic development in complex conditions, formulated by the YSP which guides the entire life of the country. This conception is characterised, on one hand, by reliance on the state and co-operative sectors in the economy (the share of the state sector in GNP is to rise from 52 per cent in 1978 to 76.1 per cent in 1985) and, on the other, by the preservation of the private capitalist sector and also by the development of small-commodity production in a number of branches (trade, transport, and so on). In 1981 a law on foreign investments was passed; this provided some benefits for investors who, in particular, could draw profits from an enterprise over several years. It can be said that the leftist excesses of the early 1970s have now been finally overcome. The negative attitude towards the service economy, justified in the years immediately after the revolution, has given way to a more sober view of development strategy, according to which port activity, the re-export trade, and so on, are given prominence in the economic structure.

As already pointed out, the prospects for the country's socio-economic development are inseparable from the advance in socio-political development. The PDRY, which has introduced almost universal schooling for children (of this more will be said in other chapters), has thereby made a breakthrough in raising the living standards of the population. The health service and social security are developing and the state is carrying on housing construction. Under the Second Five-Year Plan YD 46 million have been allocated for building 5,570 flats, although this will not provide a complete solution to the housing problem.

The growth of the social activity of working people is promoted by the establishment of a system of elective people's councils at all levels and by the perfection of mass public organisations. It is indicative, for instance, that the South Yemeni regime has not hesitated to arm the people (a very rare phenomenon in developing countries), whose broadest sections have for many years served actively with the People's Militia, guard units and People's Defence Committees. The conscious mass support of the working people for the ruling regime and its policy testify to the effectiveness of the road it has chosen.

The aim of this chapter has not been simply to praise the PDRY. The task is, rather, to raise the problem and to outline the questions that must be elucidated in order to arrive at a scientific, sober approach to the phenomena under consideration. In this respect the political vanguard of the PDRY, seriously preoccupied with the development of the country as it is, merits the highest commendation and support.

# 2 PROBLEMS OF DEVELOPMENT PLANNING IN THE PEOPLE'S DEMOCRATIC REPUBLIC OF YEMEN

Ahmed Ali Abdulsadiq

The People's Democratic Republic of Yemen (PDRY) is located in the south of the Arabian Peninsula, and extends over 336,000 sq. km, including the islands of Socotra (3,500 sq. km) and Perim (300 sq. km). Geographically, the mainland may be divided as follows: (a) the coastal zones in the south, about 1,200 km long and 12–25 km wide; (b) the highlands and plateaus of the interior; (c) the northern desert to the north of the Hadramawt; and (d) the green valleys (wadis), scattered between the highlands, with seasonally rain-fed streams which, when dried up, leave some underground water for human and agricultural use.

The climate is tropical but rainfall is irregular and scanty, with averages ranging from only 50 mm in the coastal area to about 400 mm in the highlands. The coastal area is hot and humid but in the inland mountainous region the weather tends to be mild.

Deserts and wasteland cover about 65 per cent of PDRY territory. Thus, the population is considerably scattered. Long distances separate the major towns and other settlements, a fact which makes the costs of infrastructure, transport and other services extremely high. The population is estimated at about 2 million (mid-1982), and the density at less than 6 inhabitants per sq. km. The country is generally poor in natural resources. It lacks permanent water streams, and agricultural production is limited to only 0.3 per cent of the country's surface; no significant mineral deposits suitable for commercial exploitation exist. The PDRY's major strengths are its considerable fishery resources, the excellent harbour of Aden and a talented labour force, of whom a significant number are working abroad and transferring remittances to their families residing in the country.

Democratic Yemen achieved independence in 1967 after nearly 130 years of British colonial rule, and since then has achieved substantial progress on both the economic and social fronts. Adopting a socialistic orientation, the government introduced drastic reforms

12

in order to change the country's former colonial-traditional economic and social structure. Before independence, South Yemen's economy had a dualistic nature. The modern sector was based almost entirely on servicing British rule, with its substantial military base and government in Aden, the port of Aden with its associated activities and Aden refinery. The internal parts of the country were largely rural areas where the population had been engaged in traditional activities such as agriculture, fishing and pasturing. These areas had witnessed meagre or no positive changes in economic and social life during the colonial era. The main reforms introduced to change the country's economy included the nationalisation of foreign and major economic and financial entities and foreign trade, plus agrarian reform. As a result of those measures a strong public sector has emerged and now dominates in all major sectors of the country's economy.

The agricultural sector at present includes 50 state farms occupying a total area of 12,000 ha. Besides the public sector there are 52 productive co-operatives extending over a total area of 141,000 ha. Out of a total area of 231,000 ha, comprising the cultivable land of the PDRY, the share of the socialist-oriented sector is 153,000 ha or 66 per cent. In the fisheries sector the occupation of about 13,000 private fishermen has been reorganised towards the development of a large state-owned fleet directed by the Ministry of Fish Wealth, fishing co-operatives and various joint ventures.

Prior to independence the industrial sector was limited to Aden refinery and small industrial units located in Aden. During the period of development-planning, significant progress was made in establishing a number of light and consumer-goods industries. The public sector played the key role in industrial-sector development. Recently (1980) the contribution of the public sector to industrial output has been 60 per cent, the private sector 24.7 per cent, the joint sector 13.8 and the co-operative sector 1.5 per cent.

Relying on a strong public sector with a dominant role in social and economic development and the management of the economy, the PDRY has vigorously pursued a strategy of developing the economy within the framework of a socialistic orientation. The main objectives of development in PDRY have been: (a) to raise the living standard of the people, to satisfy their basic needs for food, essential consumer goods, drinking water, employment and health care; (b) to develop the productive capacity of the economy, especially in agriculture, fisheries, industry, transport and power;

and (c) to raise the educational standards of the people, emphasising technical and primary education. The institutional reforms have paved the way for the strengthening of planning capabilities and influencing the government's policies and regulations. Consequently the PDRY's political framework underpins the government's efforts toward comprehensive economic and social planning.

Establishment of adequate planning institutions started immediately after independence. Since then, and especially after 1969, both the scope and the size of the planning apparatus have substantially increased. The planning machinery is now highly centralised in the hands of the Ministry of Planning, for both the preparation and the implementation of national development plans.

The Ministry of Planning operates in close collaboration with two sets of planning units: one established in all sectoral Ministries and public enterprises and the other established in the governorates. These units are responsible for the preparation of primary inputs in the planning process, namely the investment projects. The regional and sectoral planning units differ from each other in that, whilst the former are only responsible for the social projects, the latter are responsible for the productive projects as well as for the co-ordination of the social projects when they fall within their purview, as in the case of the Ministry of Education or the Ministry of Health.

The sectoral planning units are responsible for the preparation and implementation of the draft development plans and programmes in their respective fields. Their responsibility includes the collection of relevant data on past performance and the present situation in the light of an assessment of sectoral targets and priorities for the national development plans; identification, formulation and appraisal of projects; preparation of annual investment plans and sectoral production plans in the case of agriculture, industry and trade; and monitoring of project implementation.

In view of the establishment of planned economic and social order in the country, the need for proper, accurate and reliable statistical data cannot be over-emphasised. Two organisations are now responsible for the collection of basic data: the Central Statistical Office (CSO) is responsible for the collection and analysis of data needed for development planning, including the population census, field surveys, socio-economic and demographic research and related studies; and the Civil Registration Office (CRO) in the Ministry of Justice is responsible for the registration of births, deaths, and so on, and the maintenance of the population register. In addition, each governorate has a statistical unit under the supervision of the CSO. There is also a statistical unit in each Ministry technically responsible to the CSO.

Development planning in the PDRY began with the Three-Year Development Plan (1971/72–1973/74), followed by the First Five-Year Plan, which covered the period April 1974 — December 1978. The Second Five-Year Plan was launched in January 1981.

The Three-Year Plan was mainly an investment programme. The main targets were to build the material and technological base of the economy. About 60 per cent of the total expenditures was spent on developing the infrastructure of the economy and land reclamation, whereas only 26 per cent of total investment was spent on industrial, agricultural, fisheries and communications projects and 14 per cent for social services. During the First Five-Year Plan, more emphasis was placed on developing the productive sectors of the economy, especially manufacturing, fisheries and agriculture.

Despite severe constraints such as a low base of natural resources, geographic disadvantages, harsh climatic conditions, a small domestic market and low *per capita* income, the PDRY has achieved significant economic and social development in the past decade. This is mainly attributable to an acceleration in investment through a concerted mobilisation of domestic and foreign resources, planning attitudes and governmental policies and regulations.

To meet the rapid increases in public expenditures, the government has taken major strides in mobilising domestic as well as external resources. The main instrument used in mobilising domestic resources is taxation. Tax revenues rose from 12 per cent of GDP in 1969/70 to about 20 per cent in 1979. Resources were also mobilised for development through the transfer of retained profits of public enterprises, salary contributions to the Development Fund and self-financing of public entities. To supplement domestic resources, the government has secured external assistance from bilateral and multilateral sources.

Total public-sector investment up to 1980 had amounted to about 340 million dinars (YD), or $950 million. High levels of investment in the productive sectors have accelerated the rate of economic growth, and GDP (at 1977 constant prices) grew at an average annual rate of 8 per cent. In spite of this impressive record of performance, the PDRY faces a formidable challenge in its long-term social and economic development. The major constraints are those of limited

known natural resources, unfavourable climate and rugged topography, an undiversified export base and limited domestic market,
and a shortage of technical and managerial skills.

A limited potential area suitable for cultivation — less than 0.7
per cent of the PDRY's land surface — and the scarce availability
of irrigation water are the major constraints to rapid agricultural
progress in the country. In future, the possibility of horizontal
expansion of cultivation is limited by availability of water. The
vertical development of agriculture, through increasing yields per
hectare and improved cropping intensity, offers the best prospects
for the PDRY. A serious problem is that of post-harvest losses,
which are around 15 per cent in the case of cereals and considerably
higher in the case of fruits and vegetables. Measures to reduce these
losses could significantly improve domestic supplies and save
imports. Development of storage facilities and construction of
feeder roads connecting the main producing centres have to be considered in the agricultural programme.

Fishery is by far the most promising sector of the country's
economy, with substantial unexploited potential. The investment
programme resulted in a rapid growth of output and exports, which
reached their peak of 160,000 t and 29,000 t  respectively in 1977.
However, the fishery sector has so far developed only a part of its
potential. It is estimated that less than one-third of the substainable
yield of fish resources is presently utilised. Horizontal expansion of
large-scale fishing seems to have outstripped the country's capacity
to provide qualified and trained personnel for its management. Any
further expansion of a large-scale fishery sector and its efficient
management will therefore depend crucially on the availability of a
large number of qualified Yemeni technicians and managers.

The manufacturing sector played a relatively minor role in the
early years of independence. During the period of planned development (since 1971) significant progress has been made in establishing
a number of light and consumer-goods industries. These are agro-
based industries such as foodstuffs and cigarettes, textiles and
leather products, some import-substituting industries such as paints
and plastic products, and light ship-repairing. PDRY mineral
resources have not been fully explored. The potential of the extraction industry, quarrying and mining depends on the results of
explorations yet to be carried out. Long-range prospects for the
industrialisation of the PDRY are limited. This is mainly due to the
very few known resources for industrial processing and the small

size of the domestic market. There are only a few agricultural live-stock and mineral resources that can sustain rapid long-range indus-trialisation.

Structural problems in the economy include a meagre resource base and an increased need of imports for consumption, domestic production and development. An accelerated rise in the prices of imported foodstuffs, petroleum, fertilisers and capital goods affects the balance of payments, which is characterised by a growing trade deficit and a heavy dependence on workers' remittances and foreign aid. The trade deficit is estimated at YD 221 million for 1980. Export earnings are equivalent to slightly over 3 per cent of GDP and cover less than 5 per cent of the value of retained imports. Fish has recently replaced cotton as the leading export item, as a result of substantial investment in modern fishing.

A major strength of the PDRY's external sector is its positive invisible earnings dominated by remittances of Yemeni workers abroad, nearly 87 per cent of net invisible earnings. Net invisibles from other sources reflect the growing activities mainly of Aden port and Aden oil refinery. An increasing level of disbursement from bilateral and multilateral sources, together with workers' remittances, has enabled the PDRY to cover its import require-ments, for both consumption and development, as well as to strengthen the foreign-exchange reserves. However, the large inflow of foreign loans led to a rapid accumulation of external debt. Debt-service obligations are projected to increase steadily in coming years, which will exert pressure on the balance of payments.

A possible balance of payments strategy might aim at achieving: (a) the sustained expansion of export earnings from agricultural, fishery and manufacturing products by widening and diversifying the export base; (b) expanding and strengthening net invisible earnings; and (c) securing import substitution in selected consumer and intermediate goods primarily based on local raw materials. This is not only suitable in order to reduce the trade deficit but is also appropriate for the maximum utilisation of productive resources and the attainment of greater self-reliance. The Second Five-Year Plan (1981–85) initiates important steps to achieve these targets.

The major goals of agricultural development in the Plan are to attain self-sufficiency in fruits and vegetables, to meet as much as possible of the country's needs in food grains and to increase cotton production 140 per cent by 1985, in order to cover the needs of the domestic textile industry and to expand the country's export capacity.

Since the main constraints on rapid agricultural progress are the shortage of irrigation water and low productivity, the agricultural investment programme contains 31 projects, including irrigation schemes, identification of water resources, exploitation of reclaimed lands, development of wadis, construction of silos and storage facilities, improvement of seeds, and establishment and development of workshops for agricultural machinery. The Plan aims to raise agriculture's contribution to GDP from YD 17.4 million in 1980 to YD 26.9 million in 1985.

The Second Five-Year Plan also envisages raising the share of manufacturing in GDP from YD 16.1 million in 1980 (7.3 per cent) to YD 30.8 million (8.7 per cent) in 1985, reflecting a growth rate of 13.8 per cent annually. However, against an increase of YD 14.7 million in the contribution of manufacturing to GDP during the period of the Plan, investment in this sector is planned to be only YD 19.6 million, indicating a capital-production ratio of only 1.33. This reflects government policy, which gives emphasis in the development of this sector to the utilisation of idle capacity and improvement of productivity rather than to the sector's horizontal expansion. Investment in this sector goes to the modernisation of existing industries such as soap, salt, oxygen gas, textiles, plastics, cigarettes, canned fish and others. Most of these industries aim to provide the basic needs of the population and depend more on the utilisation of local raw materials.

The fishery sector not only provides the country with the necessary protein, but also contributes the bulk of the country's commodity export. The Plan emphasises both vertical and horizontal expansion and aims at raising its contribution to GDP from YD 12.6 million in 1980 to about YD 19.1 million (at 1980 constant prices) in 1985. The horizontal expansion requires investment expenditures of about YD 33 million during the period of the Plan.

As a result of the government's planning efforts, the social structure of the PDRY has changed radically during the past decade. Health conditions are those of a typical developing country: a low life-expectancy of 45 years, a high death-rate of 19 per 1,000 and a high infant mortality rate of 114 per 1,000. The Second Five-Year Plan, like the First, emphasises preventive as well as curative aspects of health care. Between 1973 and 1978 expenditures on medical services averaged around 5.5 per cent of total government expenditure. In much the same period the number of hospital beds rose from about 1,278 to around 3,000 in 1980. At present there are 29 hospitals, 17 medical centres, 263 medical units, both static and mobile, and 91 clinics throughout the country. In spite of this progress, health conditions still need to be improved. The number of physicians, 1.1 per 10,000, is inadequate. Hospitals must be well equipped and provided with additional facilities and qualified staff. Several widespread diseases such as dysentery, malaria and others have to be fully controlled.

In the education sector, the emphasis in the Second Five-Year Plan is on basic education. The number of students enrolled at all levels of formal education rose from about 110,000 in 1970 to about 282,000 in 1978 at an average annual growth-rate of 10.9 per cent. In addition to formal schools there are now about 446 adult literacy centres (with 44,000 participants) and a limited number of vocational training institutes, where total enrolment in 1981/82 was about 4,140.

Despite the above-mentioned development efforts, the severe constraints already described will inevitably continue to influence the PDRY's development in the future. Consequently, the country's major problems of future economic growth must be overcome on the basis of optimum utilisation of available resources and maximisation of their potential through effective planning efficient management and further mobilisation of internal and external resources. The achievement of those objectives depends on the improvement of planning methodology and procedures.

Notwithstanding the strenuous efforts to build up and improve the planning machinery, there is still wide room for improvement. Long-term planning in major sectors such as manpower, transport and power is lacking. This is particularly important because of the long gestation period involved in the identification, preparation and implementation of investment programmes in economic and social infrastructure.

A macro-economic framework was lacking when the First Five-Year Plan was prepared. This resulted in the emergence of certain investment projects which were not necessarily related to each other. Furthermore, the relative priorities and alternative benefits from certain projects were not examined. In the Second Five-Year Plan some form of macro-economic framework has been employed. The macro-elements of the plan include the growth-rate of the population, the growth of GDP by sector, the required investment to achieve the planned rates of growth of the economy, trade and balance of payments, the requirements of external resources, and government revenues and expenditures. However, the technical basis of the macro-framework still needs to be strengthened.

Another field of planning that requires further consolidation is the appraisal and evaluation of projects. The consequences of ignoring this are quite common among many developing, as well as least-developed, countries and include the emergence of oversized projects, wrong locations and lack of complementary facilities. Unfortunately, dependence on foreign consulting firms does not solve this problem because their findings still need to be checked and co-ordinated with other sectors of the economy. At present this gap is covered through multilateral and bilateral technical assistance in various fields.

To remedy the situation, and in order to strengthen the planning process, the government is considering the establishment of a planning research institute as a source of consultancy services, a centre for training in specific aspects of planning and qualified to provide back-stopping and supporting functions.

**Conclusion**

Economic development in the PDRY during the post-independence period has improved the infrastructural base and the productive capacity of the economy, has helped to establish a range of consumer-goods industries, and has made progress towards equalising incomes and meeting the basic needs of the population. The current Five-Year Plan seeks to build further on these gains, thereby underlining the impression that the basic objectives of development planning in the PDRY have remained unchanged throughout. Unless additional resources can be discovered in the future, the best way of achieving the development objectives is to maximise the utilisation of available resources. The best results might be gained through efficient planning, good co-ordination of economic policies and improvement of management capabilities. The Yemen Socialist Party and the government of the PDRY are fully aware of these matters.

**General References**

Ahmed Ali Abdulsadiq, 'Planning of the development of truck

transport in the People's Democratic Republic of Yemen',
unpublished PhD thesis, Institute of National Economy, Kiev,
1982: in Russian.

Economic Committee for Western Asia, *Directions and Perspectives of Development in Selected Countries of ECWA Region*
(Beirut, 1978), pp. 5–31: in Arabic.

International Bank for Reconstruction and Development, *People's Democratic Republic of Yemen: a review of Economic and Social Development* (Johns Hopkins Press, Baltimore, Md., 1979).

Ministry of Education, *Situation of Vocational Training in PDRY*
(Aden, 1983), pp. 2–12: in Arabic.

Ministry of Planning, *The Three-Year Development Plan for
1971/72–73/74* (Aden, 1971): in Arabic.

_____ *The First Five-Year Plan for 1974–78* (Aden, 1974): in Arabic.

_____ *The Revised Second Five-Year Plan for 1981–85* (Aden, 1981):
in Arabic.

_____ *A Substantial New Programme for Accelerated Development
of People's Democratic Republic of Yemen* (Aden, 1981),
pp. 4–76.

V. N. Purmistrov, *People's Democratic Republic of Yemen:
Economy and External Trade* (Nauka Press, Moscow, 1981),
pp. 5–31: in Russian.

G. V. Smirnov, *Theory and Methodology of Planning in Developing Countries* (Progress, Moscow, 1978): in Russian.

# 3 AGRICULTURAL DEVELOPMENT IN THE YEMENI TIHAMA: THE PAST TEN YEARS

Martha Mundy

## Introduction

This chapter discusses the changing character of agriculture in the Yemeni Tihama over the past decade.[1] The sketch is necessarily brief and broad: it explores in a preliminary manner the basic questions raised by the present transformation of agriculture in the Tihama.[2]

In the wake of the rise in oil prices in 1973 and the subsequent construction boom in the Arab oil states, the economy of the Yemen Arab Republic (YAR) has become ever more closely integrated into that of its rich neighbours. Along with this, Yemeni agriculture has been transformed. What this process entails is by now well known: the mass migration of young men to work in the oil states, huge sums of cash wages repatriated, increased interest by the industrial world expressed in large aid programmes, spiralling consumer demand and ever growing imports. Such imports include not only the automobile and the cassette recorder but, first and last, grain — grain which is as much the product of high-energy industrial procedures as any consumer durable.

Yemeni farmers have seen the terms of trade for their staple agricultural products decline swiftly. This has been true for grain since the early 1970s and for cash-crops such as cotton and sesame since the late 1970s.[3] As the structure of local wages and of consumer aspirations has become tied to that of industrial nations through the economies of oil finance, the grain produced locally by ecologically efficient but labour-intensive methods of cultivation has not been able to compete with that produced by high-energy, mechanised agriculture. This is all the more so when the latter, unlike the former, is produced under conditions of ecological bounty and political protection. In the face of this silent revolution Yemeni farmers have reacted well, developing high-value, fresh produce for the growing consumer markets. With *qat* in the mountains and melons and vegetables in the Tihama, truck-farming is the order of the day.

Qat is a wonder cure for an agricultural economy where the bases of peasant production have been swept away but where the demand for labour in the centres of oil finance remains most selective. For the rural household qat has no rival. It has no price on the international market; indeed, its price and demand seem to keep pace with every Saudi rial crossing the border. (Qat permits both conviviality and conspicuous consumption: with it, past and present meet effortlessly.) Yet on the production side, qat does not necessarily require costly intensification in machinery, imported inputs or labour. And for whatever reason — perhaps its extremely short shelf-life plays a part here — its marketing has remained labour-intensive, decentralised, and little subject to monopoly trading.

The farmers of the Tihama have no hope of finding such an enviable crop. Qat does not grow in the Tihama and for them the general rule holds true: higher-value produce means higher-energy agriculture, with all that that entails both socially and ecologically. In the Tihama, then, the switch to high-value fresh produce requires what the switch to qat only invites: costly machinery, other imported inputs and considerable restructuring of labour patterns. In order to grow vegetables and melons in the furnace of the Tihama, one must have access to and control over irrigation water at the wrong half of the year (roughly October to March) when surface water is scarcest. In short, one must draw on ground water. In the 1970s a large new zone of lift-pump farming developed in the Yemeni Tihama. This development has not supplanted the older forms of wadi irrigation; rather, the areas of pump expansion lie on the fringes and to the west of the older core of intensively irrigated wadi lands.[4] But if the new pump-farming zones and the old wadi centres appear at points distinct, they continue to form one social system. This being so, before turning to recent change we should examine briefly the older forms of production and irrigation against which this new technical division has arisen. This may allow us better to understand what is at stake in the present pattern of development.

**The Older Agricultural Systems**

The old core of settlement and production in the Tihama lay around the large spate-irrigated wadis of Risyan, Zabid, Rima, Surdud, Mawr, Siham and Jizan (the last in what is now Saudi Arabia). Agriculture in the wadis depended upon the diversion of spring and

summer spate floods by means of temporary deflectors and barrages. But the pattern of wadi flows is not uniform: we have to
distinguish the major floods from more manageable small floods,
recession flows, and the small but cumulatively important base
flows. Although base flow at any one time is often very low, it
represents a large proportion of annual flow in most major wadis
(e.g. 60 per cent or more). Indeed, the major disputes over water
concern access to base flows and recession flows (flows which can be
diverted entirely by a single deflector). Of the three wadis of which
the author has some knowledge, Zabid was the only one where there
was a formal agreement — and a formally undisputed agreement
— about the division of rights to such flows.

Although in each wadi we find a number of striking anomalies in
the distribution of water (resulting either from the historical development of settlement and hence the recognition of prior rights, or
from a more recent concentration of political and economic power
in the hands of a particular group), we can nevertheless distinguish
several general types of irrigated land in every wadi. First, there are
the relatively small but intensively irrigated lands, which enjoy regular access to base flow and small floods. Such lands (A) may receive
as many as nine waterings annually; they lie in the eastern part of the
wadis, relatively close to the foothills. The second category comprises lands which are irrigated several times each year, perhaps
three times or more. Such lands (B) lie comparatively close to the
wadi bed and have access to small floods, perhaps to some base
flow, and certainly to recession flows. The third major zone (C)
comprises lands which receive a regular irrigation or two in all but
the very worst years. Such lands are irrigated by the major spring
and summer floods. Lastly, there are lands (D) irrigated only irre-
gularly in years of large floods. This is by far the largest category of
land in the wadis. Some such major zones of irrigated land are found
in all the wadis. There are important variations, however, between
the various wadis in the flow patterns (dimensions of base flow,
length of spates, peak period, etc.) and so too in the relative size of
the different zones of irrigated land.

Both the timing and the total volume of the spates vary markedly
from year to year and the existing systems reflect this: they aim at
maximum utilisation of a capricious and violent flood pattern. The
irrigation system in a wadi is composed of a number — perhaps as
many as 20 on a side — of independent diversion structures, each of

Figure 3.1:    Agricultural Calendar for the Wadi Mawr Area[a]

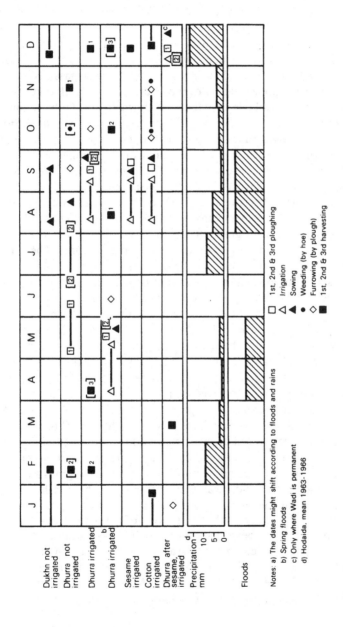

Notes: a) The dates might shift according to floods and rains

b) Spring floods

c) Only where Wadi is permanent

d) Hodaida, mean 1963-1966

□  1st, 2nd & 3rd ploughing
◁  Irrigation
▲  Sowing
●  Weeding (by hoe)
◇  Furrowing (by plough)
■  1st, 2nd & 3rd harvesting

Source: H. Escher, draft report, vol. 1, on Wadi Mawr, p. 18, reproduced in B. Mitchell, H. Escher, and M. Mundy, *A Baseline Socio-Economic Survey of the Wadi Mawr Region* (The World Bank, Washington, DC, 1978). p. 41.

which feeds a primary canal. The deflectors divert a portion of the spate floods, and their distribution corresponds to the differing patterns of flows in a way that allows water to be extracted at some point or another along the wadi. Made of stones, tree trunks, brush and sand, the diversion structures are washed out by high floods and demand both continual repair during the flood season and a major annual overhaul. The high spates wash over and bypass diversion structures in the upper reaches of the wadi, with the result that flood waters become available to deflectors downstream. Only in some western areas, where flood velocities are generally lower, are semi-permeable barrages built up right across the wadi bed in the hope of diverting the whole of the flow into a canal or side channel. However inefficient the individual diversion structure may appear, the system as a whole may achieve an efficient utilisation of flows: low flows are diverted in the upper reaches and high flows in the lower reaches.

Once within the primary canal the velocity of water remains high, as water diverted rises gradually from the wadi bed and continues into what becomes a comparatively steep sloping channel. There are few subsidiary canals feeding the fields. Basin irrigation is practised; water is let into one field and after that field is filled, the bunds are breached so that water may pass into the next block of fields. Water passes from field to field in large quantities as the bunds are breached. Farmers seek to distribute water quickly since they have no way of storage and the spates are often of very short duration. The quantity of water applied to a field differs between the major zones of land (A to D), the height of the bunds being inversely related to the frequency of irrigation.

Basin irrigation means that planting occurs after irrigation. A farmer may plough before irrigation to open the topsoil but he will plant only a week or ten days after irrigation when the field is dry enough to work. The major crops under irrigation are sorghum (several varieties of red and white, important both for grain and for fodder) and cotton and sesame as cash-crops. There is hardly a season when all the fields of the wadi are idle, since planting of different zones varies with the timing of irrigation and aga:. according to the number of irrigations applied to sorghum: the local varieties of sorghum could produce a second ratoon and even a third of fodder under irrigation. The chart of the agricultural calendar prepared by Escher in 1974 for Wadi Mawr and reproduced at Figure 3.1 gives an idea of the long agricultural calendar for a wadi system as a whole.

Altogether, the systems of wadi irrigation have proven ecologically stable and efficient. No report, to the author's knowledge, has mentioned soil salinisation as a problem in the wadi-irrigated zones. The gradual depositing of silt by basin irrigation resulted in long-term deepening and improvement of the soils, endowing them with excellent properties of infiltration and water retention. The overall efficiency of water distribution, achieved with the violent and erratic spate flows, has made it difficult to justify massive reshaping of such systems with imported technology and outside investment. There is little modern technology specifically designed to utilise such difficult — or marginal in relation to high technology — sources of water. When measured in simple cost-benefit terms against the performance of the existing systems, the benefits promised by individually more efficient diversion structures remain rather limited.

The wadi systems produced large surpluses, which played a central role in the national economic order before the oil era. Such efficiency in the application of water and such high rates of surplus production were achieved by a fine division and an intensive application of labour. In the central irrigated areas, hierarchical control over the workforce was dazzling. Where irrigation was most assured the claims on production were most dense: at the level of the system as a whole there was a clear correspondence between intensive irrigation, large holdings of land, tenant farming as the primary form of farming unit, and centralised control over the distribution of water on a single canal. By contrast, where risks were greater and irrigation less certain, ownership was more likely to be in the hands of the cultivators. The 'natural democracy' of the high spates, which sweep through the deflectors in the central landlord zones, provided farmers in zones C and D with irrigation in good years. Such farmers in turn developed strategies against the risks of bad years: migrant work in winter harvesting, livestock production and a claim, established by inheritance or marriage, on plots of land dispersed in several areas.

In Mawr a decade ago the classic agreement between landowner and sharecropper was a two-way division of the grain after the share of the harvesters and threshers and the *zakat* (tithe) had been taken off the top.[5] The landowner assumed no further costs, except in so far as he might also have provided the sharecropper with the oxen with which to work the land and which the sharecropper kept under a separate 'sharecropping' arrangement for the landlord. Very often the landlord employed several agents both to keep an eye on the agricultural work generally and to supervise irrigation: the irrigation agent often became a powerful intermediary, since not only did he effectively control irrigation on the channel but he also mobilised labour and material for its upkeep. Only in the event of a major failure of crops or the destruction of a diversion structure might the sharecroppers or the irrigation manager appeal to the landlord directly. Otherwise the maintenance of the diversion structure and channels was the responsibility of the farmers, each according to the land he held.

The sharecroppers of the central irrigated zones were but one part of the rural workforce: indeed they appeared almost as the established elders of local society, often with their own fields in less well-irrigated zones. Rights to sharecrop the best land were passed from father to son. And not infrequently one heard accounts of how the land had long been in the family but that the title had been wrested one fateful day by the up-and-coming landlord.[6] The central irrigated lands were densely populated and almost every sharecropper had a regular labourer of free or slave origin who worked with the family. Beyond such regular labour, harvesting often required further day-labour, often migrant. Labourers were paid in kind for work in harvesting grain and sesame and in kind and cash for picking cotton. The latter was almost exclusively the work of women and children. As for grain, men did the cutting and transporting of the stalks, but the harvesting of the grain itself was carried out by large teams of women organised along lines outside the domestic economic unit.

In short, landlords and irrigation managers directed the work of a large number of sharecroppers and their power could in practice extend beyond the ranks of the sharecroppers of the central irrigated zones. Even seemingly peripheral and only occasionally irrigated areas were tied to the central zones through the movement of farm families during periods of slack (or need) in their home areas. Ecological efficiency rested not only upon tried and complex techniques of water management but also upon the movement of labour to where the crops stood and the work waited. Indeed, workers moved not only within one wadi but also between wadis since the timing of irrigation often varied markedly between the wadis. The 'fixed' proportions assigned for tasks in harvesting would slide according to the demand for labour. Although differences in the standard of living between an established sharecropper and a simple labourer were not all that great, in a bad year the livelihood of the labourer or the farmer without irrigation at home was simple indeed.

Such systems were built about grain. Day-labour was paid in kind, landlords were paid in kind, taxes were paid in kind. Farmers might sell some grain after harvest and might cultivate cotton or sesame as a cash-crop — although landowners were more enthusiastic about this than most farmers — but the basic mode of savings against adverse times was livestock. Milk products were the major source of protein in the rural diet. Farming families invested grain and fodder in livestock and almost all families, save the very poorest threshers, held some sheep, goats or cattle. Such livestock was, however, more an insurance against bad years than a form of wealth convertible into land. As mentioned, the more prosperous share-cropping farmers of the central irrigated areas often did not own most of the cattle they kept. Limited cash income meant, as in so many peasant societies, that many farming families had debts, often with a local trader. A number of the major landlords themselves began as traders.

This description is both idealised and general. There were in fact marked differences between the major wadis in the complexity of the physical infrastructure of irrigation and of the social structures of land-holding and surplus extraction. Thus, if one compares the great southern wadi of Zabid with that of Mawr in the north, one finds the structures more complex and developed in the south than in the north.

## Changing Patterns in Agriculture

### The Background

Although local economic history remains undocumented, the broad lines of change are clear enough. Following the opening of the Suez Canal, Yemeni markets opened slowly during the late-nineteenth century to finished industrial products. After a period of true marginality to the imperial powers and to the routes of world trade, Yemen again lay on the map. First the Ottoman rulers and then, after an interregnum, the Imamic government extended central power along the coast. In both cases, officials took a direct interest in the development of irrigated agriculture on a labour-intensive and highly extractive basis. For example, Ottoman officials acquired large estates in less developed areas of the Tihama and, much later, the supervisor of Imamic lands in the Tihama, al-Jabali, introduced new seeds and pumping equipment to distant landlords. More generally, it seems that the consolidation of large holdings during the past century was tied, first, to the extension of central state control and, second, to the increasing importance of cotton as a cash-crop and to the changes occurring in the processing and marketing of cotton in the late Imamic period. The latter corresponded to a shift from production for local craft-weaving to production for export, tied in turn to the increasing imports of finished cloth through Aden and other ports. The areas planted in cotton appear to have expanded during the later years of the Imamate and this growth continued well into the 1970s, aided at that point by a rise in the price of cotton along with that of other primary products. Yet, as is well known, it was a leap in the price of yet another primary product, oil, that in turn spelt the end of a way of life until then still very closed in upon itself.[7]

*The Past Decade: Pump Farming*

The first few pumps were introduced in the Tihama in the late Imamic period but it was not until the 1970s that substantial areas came to be irrigated by lift-pumps. Until the mid 1970s the selection of crops on land irrigated by lift-pumps differed only little from that common on land irrigated from the wadi flows. Cotton and sesame formed the major cash-crops, followed by tobacco, with only small areas given to vegetable and fruit production, especially in the winter season. By far the largest area was sown in sorghum (and some millet or maize) as families continued to rely upon domestic grain and fodder production. The initial impetus for the development of lift-pump irrigation in the Tihama was simply the large returns still going to those who controlled the supply of water.[8] For the most part, the funds for this development seem to have been generated within the agricultural sector; the first wave of investors included substantial landowners (especially in the north, where the horizons of landowners were more exclusively limited to agriculture), a number of local managers of big estates (especially in Zabid) and important farmers (notably in Rima). Medium trading finance also played some part, although in general during this period funds appear to have been moving out of agriculture and into trading at a higher level. Foreseeing the way of the future the major landowning families of the Southern Tihama, who had long had links with trading circles, worked to establish themselves in the growing import sector in Hodaida. Profits were to be made more from importing pumps than from running them and, by and large, the green revolution was left to the local managers.

From the middle 1970s, however, the circle of those investing in pumping equipment began to widen, following the increase in funds brought back by workers abroad and the relaxation of loan rules in the Agricultural Credit Fund, which had been established a few years earlier with funds from the World Bank. In more western zones, where land-holdings were less concentrated than in the central eastern wadi areas, a number of substantial farmers came to buy pumps. This was most notably true in Wadi Rima but also true to a lesser extent in Zabid.

The changes entailed in the development of pump farming are many. Throughout the Tihama, farmers, most especially in the old irrigated centres, lament the shortages of labour at harvest time. The movement of young men to work abroad, to the town or into the army clearly plays a part here. But that is not all. Most agricultural workers (who were formerly migrant) have now settled, often in the pump-farming zones, and small farmers who likewise might have moved with the harvests do so no longer. Today, labourers may not always be employed but they can make ends meet without migrant agricultural work so long as they have a brother, father or son sending back money from outside employment. So too, women need not work for people outside the family, but only in the fields which the family may have under cultivation.

As before, land lies servant to water, but where before the two were joined by the farmer's labour, now they are more clearly divided by the new technology. Where the pump-owner is agent for the landlord — as is often the case in Zabid — the relations with the sharecropping cultivator need not change fundamentally, though doubtless the relation of the sometime manager to the absent land-lord may alter. But where the pump-owner is a more successful farmer among smaller neighbours, one finds considerable restruc-turing of holdings about the new source of water. The smallholding farmer finds his bargaining power little better than that of an ordi-nary labourer willing to sharecrop land for the pump-owner. The pump-owner can set the terms, offering, for example, better terms for cash-crops than for grain crops. The smallholder has less interest in such crops since they draw him more closely into the calculations of the pump-owner, calling for greater risk and more labour, regardless of whether the pump-owner provides expensive inputs such as pesticides. With such crops, moreover, the smallholder can rarely handle the marketing himself. By the same token, the pump-owner is no longer concerned with the upkeep of the common diversion structures. Without the support of the bigger farmers, on whom the lion's share of the work used to fall, the smallholders and sharecroppers in western areas find it more difficult to maintain structures which might, in any case, provide only a single irrigation or two.

The shift to higher-value vegetable and melon crops since the late 1970s, a process speeded by a decline in the international price of cotton, has encouraged the adoption of imported technology and so too the stratification of farmers according to their control over the new technology. Although the overall proportion of land devoted to cash-crops in the winter season does not appear to have changed much, vegetables and melons have come to replace cotton, sesame and tobacco on lands unaffected by salinity. This has speeded the introduction of new techniques. Tractors, which in basin irrigation were used only for pre-planting cultivation, can be used for ridge-and-furrow ploughing for pre-irrigation planting of vegetables. The imported vegetable seeds invite their other companions: pesticides, fertilisers, herbicides. Such inputs are rendered all the more essential by the unexpected consequences of another import entering Hodaida: new pests and plant diseases. The new knowledge and labour discipline required for the efficient utilisation of such technology in an ever more difficult environment gives the big entrepreneur an edge over the small pump-owner. This is especially so since the latter is more likely to farm in an area of recent pump expansion where ground water is less plentiful, and where costs in what is fast becoming a race for a falling water table are likewise greater.

In the course of the 1970s the number of lift-pumps increased over tenfold. By 1980 the water table was falling markedly, credit was being used to finance the deepening of wells, and the regulation of water extraction was becoming imperative. The flooding of high-energy technology into the fragile environment of the Tihama is not proving an easy matter. Short of strong central regulation, the signs now point to a future reduction in the numbers of those with titles to the new forms of agricultural capital after the recent expansion in their ranks. Yet if profits lie as much in importing technology as in its application, regulation of its application promises to be difficult.

## The Past Decade: the Spate-irrigated Zones

As funds have flowed into pump farming, they have bypassed the old forms of irrigated agriculture. The burden of investment in such structures lies with the farmers of the area, land-holding and share-cropping alike, while those with funds have placed them in more promising forms of investment: trading, urban real estate and, in agriculture, pumps and tractors. Farmers continue to rely upon oxen and manpower in maintaining the diversion structures; to date there has been very little mechanisation. This cannot be for purely technical reasons since on the major holding of state land in the Tihama, where the state manager assumes responsibility for mainte-nance of the diversion structure, bulldozers are used. The reasons lie rather, first, in the economic conditions of those directly responsible for maintaining such structures — for example, their limited indi-vidual capital and the virtues of keeping oxen for the small farmer (e.g. their reproduction occurs outside the cash nexus, yet oxen provide cash income when sold or let out for ploughing); and second, in the general principle upon which the disbursal of agri-cultural credit rests, the notion of an individual owner.[9] Almost all loans for agricultural credit are granted to an individual (or at most to two brothers), although the individual in question may draw on family resources well beyond his own to provide his part of the funds and surety against the loan. For example, a mother's land is pledged against a loan for a tractor in the name of her son.

One interesting change is that title to the new forms of capital seems to lie more exclusively in the hands of men than did title to older forms of property. This change should be considered in the context of two intertwined processes: first, a general mobilisation and reduction in complex claims on land (and on the labour of others beyond the immediate household) in favour of individual title to the new forms of capital; and second, a concomitant emphasis upon the conjugal household as the proper sphere of women's work. Such transformations clearly affect different strata in different ways, being bound up with wider economic changes. Such changes include: the cessation of wide-scale migrant agricultural work in which tasks were organised along sex-specific lines outside the household; the new forms of migrant labour and the clarity of the sexual division of labour on which they are built (where the man earns the cash wage away and the woman raises the family 'at home'); and, lastly, the sharply individuating character of the new agricultural capital.

Economic relations within agriculture have changed following the decline in the relative market value of agricultural produce, the departure of formerly migrant labour to other zones, and the partial monetarisation of wages in agriculture. Such changes have made it impossible to sustain the previous levels of agricultural rent. The once thorough and onerous state tithe, with its four seasons of tax collection, is now but a shadow of its former self. In principle, moreover, a portion of what is now collected goes for local development. The proportion of the crop due to the landlord has also begun to fall. By threatening to withdraw from cultivation, sharecroppers have won reductions in the share formally accorded the landowner, from one-half to one-third in some central irrigated areas. Although the level of direct rents has dropped, agriculture is increasingly subservient to the towns: farmers pay rents to urban landowners, albeit at lower levels, yet there is little internal investment in irrigation works. Through their control of the booming import trade, moreover, the towns and their inhabitants stand on the right side of a global structure of prices set against local producers of agricultural staples. Given the level of prices for grain and cotton and the rising costs of wage labour, it is not difficult to understand why, in spite of the existence of large holdings and the introduction of tractors, there has been virtually no internal movement towards more capital-intensive methods and larger units of production in the old wadi zones. Rather, the sharecropping family remains the basic unit of production in the irrigated areas. The reasons for this are both social and technical.

Given the present structure of prices and wages, it appears unlikely that large-scale, mechanised farming of grains and traditional cash-crops could prove profitable. In such circumstances, by contrast, the sharecropping family possesses considerable strengths. It does not seek to sell large quantities of grain; rather it aims, first, to provide for the basic needs of the family in grain and, second, to invest fodder in livestock. Animal production provides both valuable milk products for family consumption and also stock, which fetches good prices in the livestock markets of the Tihama. The Tihama markets are now national livestock markets, as butchers come from all the major towns of the mountains. The sharecropping family can afford to remain in farming since its domestic budget is geared not only to providing subsistence for family members on the land, but also — for the more fortunate — to producing young male labour for work abroad or in other sectors where men earn higher cash wages. The farming family forms a unit structured not only about farming production but also about the (re)production of wage labour for work outside the farm sector. If measured by the cash value of their agricultural production, the remuneration of family members working on the land appears very low compared to cash wages in other sectors, but the converse of this is that women's labour is little in demand and poorly remunerated in other sectors. Inevitably, such systems are built around the difference between the wage a woman might command and that which a man commands or, in other words, around a definition of women's work as work within the framework of the household economy.

On the technical side, the developed basin irrigation systems and the high level of uncertainty concerning the timing of irrigation in many parts of the wadi system have discouraged those who, a decade ago, may have dreamt of large-scale mechanisation. More generally, the very complexity of farming techniques and of social relations in the central areas of wadi irrigation has rendered their wholesale replacement by imported techniques of high-energy agri-culture a risky proposition and their piecemeal transformation a difficult job.

Lest this vision of large-scale mechanised agriculture be thought purely fanciful, it should be noted that the agricultural extension services promoted by the major development agencies have had little to offer farmers except those seeds that have been developed to perform well in just such mechanised, high-energy agriculture. Season after season, extension workers faced the embarrassing prospect of promoting the Sudanese sorghum, *qadam al-hammam*. This sorghum is excellent for mechanised farming, being easy to machine-harvest (i.e. short with low fodder yields) and bearing very high grain yields under optimal conditions. But such virtues are vices to the small farmer and, not surprisingly, his wife rejects the grain as tasting like cement: the farmer, after all, seeks maximum fodder yield and an ensured grain yield, albeit low, to allow for family needs in what are rarely optimal conditions. The case was only slightly different with the form of maize promoted: the farmer had to balance possibly much higher grain yields under optimal conditions (more water, longer growing season) versus a lower assured yield under sub-optimal conditions (less water, shorter growing season) with the existing maize stock.

The provision of 'optimal conditions' is in fact possible only in small areas of the Tihama wadis: the lands with assured irrigation (zone A and some of B). If agricultural development was to take place in the wadi zones, the areas of assured irrigation had to be expanded. There was never any secret to this, and by the late 1960s development agencies, first East European, then Western, began to work on schemes for the technical improvement of the irrigation systems. Until recently the almost unquestioned assumption in such work was that the starting-point was technical improvement, that such improvements should be made at the top level of the systems, and that thereafter the rest would follow suit. There are some four basic visions of such technical improvements, although, properly speaking, the fourth is more of a dissenting voice.

The first solution proposes large-scale watershed management in the mountain catchment areas. Since the basic problem in the present high-risk irrigation systems derives from the nature of existing flow patterns, greater predictability of irrigation would demand large-scale watershed management in the mountain areas, so as to store portions of the run-off for predictable use. Both for technical reasons (problems of siting retaining structures; problems of silting; problems of evaporation losses) and for economic reasons, such solutions have not been pursued in any detail. They require very large investment and a long period for implementation, to be counted in decades not years.

Since the first approach provides few solutions in the short term, the planners face the fact that regulation is feasible essentially only for those flows which are already reasonably well managed by the traditional systems: the base flow, the recession flows and the small floods. The second solution, then, simply replaces the traditional, repeatedly renewed diversion structures with more permanent concrete structures. To replace every diversion structure with a masonry equivalent is an exceedingly expensive proposition. For this reason, the number of such more permanent structures tends to be reduced on the drawing-board to far less than the previous number of off-take points. This in turn requires considerable changes in the pattern of water distribution at the next level down: within the canals and across fields. The problem of the fit between change at the higher level of the system and at the lower levels of water distribution is a complex one, rarely considered in detail by the engineer, who is more concerned with the technical efficiency of the particular diversion structure and the carrying load of the widened primary canal. In principle such concrete structures diminish some of the risks since they are not washed out, as are traditional structures, by high floods. Likewise, they require less labour in maintenance from farmers. But then they are far less flexible; they draw farmers ever more into the cash nexus, since the tax for their maintenance is levied in cash; and their maintenance requires, in turn, more foreign expertise. The results of the experiment in Wadi Zabid have yet to be determined fully.

The third solution is again that of foreign engineering technology, but in this the number of the diversion structures is reduced to one. The proposal is for a single, large structure which can be overtopped by high floods but which controls all base, recession and small flows. As for the most unmanageable high floods (perhaps some 15 per cent of annual flows in southern wadis), they are simply to flow over the structure and be extracted by conventional means downstream. No provision is made for them. By definition this solution provides new means for the extraction of flows at present used in the intensively irrigated zones (zones A and B), traditionally the areas of the largest land-holdings. By diverting the bulk of the flow at a single point, the system will allow for far more central power over the distribution of irrigation water than was previously possible. Yet no radical change in the distribution of water is envisaged. The underlying assumption is that existing water rights will simply be observed. If this is in fact to happen, it will be necessary to overcome both technical problems and economic pressures, in a situation where further intensification (further inequality of distribution) has suddenly become possible. On the technical side, the changes in the pattern of flows entering the major canals will require adjustments at the lower levels of the system, if present patterns of distribution are to be maintained. As described above, there are few secondary canals in the present system; large blocks of water move from field to field, and existing field layout is related to average flow patterns. On the social and economic side, to ensure that present water rights are observed will demand strong management. Such management must possess special strengths: intimate knowledge of existing patterns of distribution and farming, understanding of the new technology, powers of persuasion, uncorruptibility and effective social power. Management — or, more generally, social relations — is critical here: it is unlikely to come right simply as an afterthought once the new structure has been put in place. More than the other proposals, this solution promises greater intensification in a limited area. Thus, even if present distribution patterns are largely maintained, no provision is to be made either for the most difficult flows (economically the most 'marginal' water) or for the farmers least likely to survive in agriculture — those who have only irregular irrigation at present.

The fourth type of solution comprises a number of proposals advanced by those worried over questions such as the suitability and durability of large concrete structures and the problem of technical dependence they present, the social and ecological implications of a solution of the third type for peasant farming, or the problems of management to be faced in more unified systems. Proposals of this type urge the consideration of simpler technology, and advocate the provision of assistance to groups of farmers to improve and maintain shorter-lived diversion structures. Such approaches appear to accept that Yemen's place in the international economy means that farming families will remain on the land so long as some support is offered the small and medium farmer. This judgement rests on the assumption that large-scale industrialisation and full social integration into the oil economies remain unlikely in the foreseeable future. Such conceptions admit that in order to support small and medium farmers it is necessary not to intensify production in limited areas still further, but rather to redistribute some portion of the more easily controlled flows so as to provide an assured two irrigations to a larger number of farmers, at the expense of those now enjoying six or more irrigations a year. Such policies seek to maximise global production rather than to increase yields within more limited and intensively farmed areas.

Such an approach represents a break from technological visions of agricultural development. In order to be implemented, it would require a major commitment to the agricultural sector; this is unlikely within the present economic environment. For good reasons, the mere mention of redistribution of water rights or of changes in sharecropping agreements sends shivers down the spine of the lonely administrator battling in the heat of the Tihama, regardless of whether he has heard of a precedent for a more egalitarian distribution.

We have come to the heart of the matter: what kind of development (or salvage operation) is possible in the wadi zones of the Tihama? If Yemen is now above all a producer of male labour and a market for industrial products produced elsewhere, how can one best ensure the continuity of some agriculture and the social and economic health of a farming population in the era of oil and thereafter? The question is not for an outsider to answer but rather for those most directly concerned. As a privileged outside observer, I have sought only to clarify what has already occurred and what, in turn, the present choices may represent.

## Notes

1. By the Yemeni Tihama is meant those areas of the Red Sea coastal plain that lie within the borders of the Yemen Arab Republic.

2. This chapter represents an exploratory essay rather than the results of finished research. Although I have been interested in social change in the Tihama for a number of years, I have worked only briefly in the Tihama, both times as a consultant for development projects, first in Wadi Mawr in 1973–74 and later in Wadi Rima in 1980. Distance has allowed me here to skim over many major shortcomings in my knowledge — a distance compounded by the fact that I came to write this chapter in Jordan, where I had neither my own field material nor other reports to hand. The little I do understand I in fact owe to others: Huriya al-Mu'ayyid, Taher Ali Saif and Brigitta Mitchell for the earlier period, and Ahmad Ali Hummad, Ibrahim al-Dumi, Abd al-Halim Abdallah and others for the later period. I also owe a great deal to the written work of the engineer Leo Silva and the agronomist J. B. Williams on Wadi Rima. Such persons are, however, in no way responsible for the views expressed here.

3. Cf. the essay by J. C. Swanson, *Emigration and Economic Development: the Case of the Yemen Arab Republic* (Westview Press, Boulder, Colo., 1979), where the implications of worsening terms of trade for grain agriculture in the mountains during this period are discussed.

4. Just as there are large differences in flow patterns in the various wadis, so too there is great variation in the quality and relative location of ground water, expecially between the better endowed southern wadis of Zabid and Rima and the great northern wadi of Mawr.

5. Cf. B. Mitchell, H. Escher and M. Mundy, *A Baseline Socio-Economic Survey of the Wadi Mawr Region* (The World Bank, Washington, DC, 1978).

6. Although large holdings of land were characteristic of the zones of intensively irrigated land, a number of farmers might also hold title to plots on a channel. Farmers retained a sense of village and regional solidarity but the local political associations of farmers ('tribal' identities) rarely had the weight they did in many mountain areas, where smallholding was the dominant form of land tenure. Such associations were here cross-cut by the vertical division of labour. Such local political structures or identities remained more important in areas which had been less developed earlier in this century and where the consolidation of big landholdings followed the entry of outside groups or agencies. An example is Wadi Rima, where the Zaraniq were defeated by the central state in the late 1920s.

7. The Tihama was the last of the major zones of the YAR to send its youth in great numbers to work in Saudi Arabia. In the early 1970s the local economic systems were binding, farming families held less capital than in many areas of the mountains, and agricultural wages were only half what they were in most areas of the mountains.

8. Cf. ECWA/FAO Joint Agricultural Division, 'The transfer of technology and investment policy design: a case study in rural poverty', in A.B. Zahlan (ed.), *Technology Transfer and Change in the Arab World* (Pergamon, Oxford, 1978). The authors discuss the returns accruing to the different factors of production (landowner, sharecropper, labourer, and pump-owner) in pump-farming in Wadi Zabid. They state that all the 268 lift-pumps existing in Wadi Zabid at the time of writing were owned:

by an entrepreneurial class which previously acted as intermediary between the absentee land-owners and their tenants (p. 325) . . . As the new technology was capital-intensive, it decidedly remained beyond the reach of small owner-operators. Similarly, the State tenants had neither the will nor the capacity to invest in lift-pumps. The benefits of the new technology went exclusively to the large farm sector managed by the intermediaries now turned pump-owners. . .

The result was disparate patterns of growth . . . The disparate patterns of growth tended to reinforce historic income inequalities. The family incomes of owner-operators and State tenants remained unchanged at 1,000 and 2,250 Rls, respectively, a natural outcome of near-zero growth in this sector. On the other hand, in the large farm sector which monopolized growth, significant changes took place in income distribution . . . Overall, the new technology helped the owners of capital to increase their share of total disposable income from 43% to 58% at the expense of a corresponding fall from 57% to 42% in the incomes of the wage-earners. (p. 326).

9. It is of course easy enough to understand the administrative virtues of such a procedure!

# 4  LAND USAGE AND ITS IMPLICATIONS FOR YEMENI AGRICULTURE

Horst Kopp

The fame of the 'Arabia Felix' of ancient times is based particularly upon the variety of agricultural products in south-west Arabia. In contrast to 'Arabia Deserta' — and basically thanks to the influence of the monsoon — a highly specialised rural culture could evolve which, up until the recent past, was hardly affected by external factors. This fact demands particular emphasis, especially when one remembers that south-west Arabia[1] belongs to the Sahel Zone, where desertification problems are extremely grave. Population pressure, imported technology and an incorrect appraisal of the natural potential have triggered off disastrous processes everywhere in this marginal, tropical, semi-arid, wet-dry climatic zone. This chapter deals mainly with the examination of the following two problem-complexes:

(1) Given the natural geographical factors, which form of agrarian technology permitted the realisation of Yemen's agricultural potential up to the heyday of Arabia Felix?
(2) How have the recent changes in socio-economic conditions affected the agricultural area of the Yemen Arab Republic (YAR)?

To begin with, it is necessary to outline the peculiarities of Yemen in comparison with the other countries in the Sahel Zone:

(1) Yemen is chiefly a mountainous country, with a high relief intensity.
(2) In contrast to other countries in the Sahel Zone, the exploitation and development of the area began very early; an advanced civilisation with a high population-density was already present during ancient times.
(3) Apart from the urban trade centres along the frankincense route, Yemen is basically a rural society; nomadism has remained unimportant up to the present day.[2]

41

(4) Since the Islamisation process, if not before, south-west Arabia has had a marginal position with no outside connections; there was no European colonial influence and thus the socio-economic structures and traditional agrarian technology have been subjected solely to inherent development processes.
(5) Yemen has become accessible only since the end of the civil war in 1970. A relatively large amount of capital was made available soon afterwards, with the result that since then diffusion processes have rapidly taken their course. As will be shown, a completely new assessment of the natural potential has become necessary through the transformation from a subsistence to a market-oriented economy.

In order to answer the question posed at the beginning of this chapter, it is, first of all, necessary to examine the spatial effect of economic man and the development possibilities offered by the natural potential.

The five landform units in Yemen run parallel to the meridians and are ordered, from west to east, as follows:

(1) The 20–40 km-wide coastal lowland of the Tihama, stretching along the Red Sea and consisting mainly of fluviatile deposits.
(2) The deeply dissected western mountain zone, reaching heights of up to 3,600 m.
(3) The central zone, consisting of individual high plateaus between heights of 1,800 and 2,500 m.
(4) The eastern mountain zone, characterised on the one hand by high relief intensity and on the other by plateaus.
(5) The eastern plain, reaching heights of up to 1,000 m.

Solely from the point of view of relief, zones 2 and 4 are the most difficult to exploit because of the steep slopes and the inaccessibility of isolated massifs.

The most important stipulation for agricultural use is climate, especially the thermal and humid conditions. As can be expected in such latitudes, tropical thermal conditions predominate, i.e. the daily temperature fluctuations are larger than the annual fluctuations. The relief also affects absolute temperatures: the frost limit is to be found at about 2,200 m; in the Tihama lowland, on the other hand, it is very hot all the year round. The cultivation of certain plants is thus restricted to certain altitudes, so these thermal variations caused by relief permit the cultivation of completely different plants within relatively short distances.

In a semi-arid region rainfall is, however, much more important. Although Yemen has two rainfall maximums (in the spring and late summer), if one views the year as a whole a distinctive dry period, virtually devoid of precipitation, can be identified. Even during the rainy season, precipitation usually takes the form of short, heavy rain-storms, thus resulting in great spatial and temporal variability and precipitation uncertainty, which is once again reinforced by relief. Annual rainfall, on the basis of the long-term average, permits normal cultivation only in parts of the mountains of the south and west. Elsewhere irrigation is a necessity. The kind of rainfall and the clearance of the dry forest which formerly covered the entire country have led to increased surface drainage, with the result that the majority of the valleys are water-carrying for short periods only (*sail*). Perennial rivers (*ghail*, pl. *ghuyul*) are to be found only in the middle stretches of the large westward-flowing wadis. Increased surface drainage means that there are few springs and that ground-water regeneration can take place only very slowly. The low precipitation levels and their general uncertainty play a decisive role in potential utilisation.

Traditional agrarian technology has, however, adapted itself excellently to these unfavourable conditions, probably through a long-lasting process of challenge and response. The most important aspects in this respect are terrace formation and the levelling of agricultural land. The rainfall occurring during heavy storms is collected on the terraces, so that after such a storm the area looks like a lake landscape. The carefully built terraces, which can also be found in the flat basin plains, have a soil-conserving as well as a water-collecting function, i.e. they effectively curb erosion, especially on the steep slopes. Of the agricultural land, 95 per cent is either terraced or levelled. However, the amount of rain falling on these surfaces guarantees a harvest in only a few areas. Well-adapted systems of dry-farming add a degree of certainty in these regions. The principle of rainwater-harvesting is, however, much more widespread: the excess surface water is fed specifically from neighbouring parcels of land which are not used for agricultural purposes to other fields, thus providing more water and sediment. The collection areas and the areas under cultivation are excellently matched in size to the respective local levels of precipitation.

The *sails* which flow episodically in the valleys are diverted to the bordering fields through dams of varying sizes. This principle is particularly widespread in the Tihama, with the result that virtually no water from the large westward-flowing wadis reaches the Red Sea. Most favourably situated are those areas lying along a ghail, although in such cases it is usually only small parcels of land in the narrow valleys which can be used for agriculture. In the traditional agrarian system, well-irrigation was limited almost entirely to house gardens.

The indigenous agrarian technology was so well adapted to local conditions that over wide stretches of the country the harvests were fully guaranteed, and the soil-conserving character of these methods permitted continuous sorghum cultivation without the necessity of organic fertilisation.

The socio-economic structure of Yemen's traditional agrarian society can be described as follows:

(1) We are concerned here with a tribal peasantry as described by de Planhol, with a pronounced, territorially defined tribal organisation.
(2) The dominating subsistence economy led to an under-developed urban structure; the main trade centres were rural markets. The cultivation of grain for bread (sorghum) was predominant everywhere, irrespective of the varying natural conditions in the different parts of the country.
(3) The transport network was based entirely on beasts of burden and was thus little developed.

The population distribution in 1975, at which time the traditional structures were little changed, reflects almost completely the distribution of rainfall. Irrespective of relief, the humidity conditions are, therefore, *the* limiting factor as far as agricultural potential is concerned. By employing such simple, labour-intensive farming methods, the limited amounts of rainfall and soil have been used optimally and, in the long-term, effectively by the Yemenis. Apparently, however, the limits of efficiency were reached relatively early, a fact which is emphasised by the terracing of extremely steep slopes with very poor soils. The possibilities for spatial extension must have been exhausted, and intensification based on the traditional methods could only be achieved slowly, if at all. The resulting population pressure brought about not only bitter tribal feuds over land but also the strict enforcement of the *juwara* law[3] and the tradition of emigration in southern Arabia.

It is thus necessary to qualify the term 'Arabia Felix'. The impressive picture of terraced, densely populated mountain landscapes is solely the result of excessive population pressure and the Yemeni farmer has been living on the breadline for a long time. Because of the country's isolated position, agricultural innovations which might have led to increased productivity could not gain a foothold. The isolation policy followed by the last Imam intensified the problem as, during this period, improvements, especially in the agricultural sector, were being achieved elsewhere. This might be another reason for the success of the 1962 revolution. The Yemeni farmers hoped that they could achieve better yields from their small parcels of land with the help of improved seeds, fertilisers and pump irrigation.

In summary, it can be said that with the help of highly specialised manual methods, economic man adapted himself excellently to the conditions present in this area. A decisive role was undoubtedly played by the historical settlement processes, about which little is known. It is possible to distinguish between two development phases, although they must be regarded with care:

(1) To begin with, the centres of civilisation were situated in the east on the margins of the Rub' al-Khali. Later they were to be found in the highlands. The colonisation of the western and southern mountain areas followed from here. Clearance and terracing processes were thus diffused in a downward direction, which must be regarded as advantageous with respect to the water supply and protective measures against erosion.
(2) The second colonisation phase, which followed later, began in the Tihama and extended into the large valleys. This phase was initiated by other ethnic groups and took place under different natural conditions, with the result that pronounced differences can still be seen today between the 'Tihamis' and the 'Jabalis' (mountain-dwellers). In many regions there still exists a large settlement void between the two groups.

It can thus be assumed that increased surface drainage was caused by extensive forest clearance in the mountainous areas which, in turn, allowed extensive *sail* irrigation in the Tihama. This is just one example of how man has influenced the complex ecosystem in south-west Arabia. Since, however, this process (as is often the case), evolved slowly, the population was able to adjust to the changes without fundamentally altering the farming methods. In general terms, one can say that until the recent past Yemen had a man-made ecosystem which lived in harmony with the available agrarian technology.

Since the revolution in 1962, and particularly since 1970 when the civil war came to an end, the fundamental socio-economic conditions in Yemen have been radically altered. The complete opening up to the world market and to every kind of innovation, the changed geo-political situation in the Horn of Africa, the closeness of financially powerful but under-populated oil countries and the creation of a modern national state based on economic growth are the decisive parameters of this transformation. The consequences in the agricultural sector are as follows:

(1) Through massive labour migration, Yemen has been freed from a historical plague: the population pressure has eased and has now resulted in a lack of labour and subsequently an enormous increase in its cost.

(2) Private investment, especially in the consumer-goods sector, has been made possible through the capital brought into the country by returning foreign workers. Despite this, and thanks basically to the government's liberal trade policy, the prices for agricultural products, especially grain,[4] have been little affected by the general upward price trend.

(3) The administrative infrastructure, which is still in the initial development stages, has remained financially weak and incapable of steering the enormous economic boom.

(4) Owing to a general lack of information and the factors mentioned above, the large amounts of development aid flowing into the country remain generally ineffective.

(5) There has been a rapid improvement in the transport network, whereas the educational sector still lags behind.

Within a period of scarcely ten years, the spatial consequences of these processes have become obvious. In those areas where the use of agricultural machinery is virtually impossible, where increased yields can be achieved only through increased labour intensity, where there is no question of pump irrigation — in other words, where increased yields cannot be achieved quickly — land has been abandoned. Between 1975 and 1980, 7.5 per cent of the area under cultivation in Yemen was abandoned and most of this land lay in the carefully terraced mountainous areas. During the same period, grain production fell by 14 per cent, with the result that at present more than half of the grain needed to meet the demand for bread has to be imported. Terrace decay in the mountains usually signals the start of an irreversible process. The resulting changes in drainage patterns are far-reaching. A maximum of four harvests per year can be achieved in the middle stretches of the valleys. However, disastrous floods which destroy the crops and wash away the fertile soils are occurring with increasing frequency. The control of these floods is difficult even in the Tihama where ground-water regeneration is restricted, thus allowing increased drainage to the sea.

The over-exploitation of the remaining forest areas and over-stocking, which have been brought about by increased timber and meat prices, have also contributed to the changes in the drainage patterns. Increased production has been achieved at the cost of permanent damage to the ecosystem. The interference with the ground-water supply through the rapid expansion of pump irrigation[5] is even more serious. This irrigation method is particularly widespread in the Tihama and in the high plateau areas, where it is hoped that increased yields can be achieved more rapidly. The results are impressive: between 1975 and 1980 vegetable production rose by 43 per cent, fruit production by 35 per cent and potato production by 72 per cent. Although there is no exact information concerning the amount of ground-water potential, new wells are constantly being bored. The only governmental guideline for this problem was released in 1981 and stipulates that at least 50 m must lie between neighbouring wells. However, even this lamentably inadequate measure can be implemented only in the vicinity of the capital. The most frequent method of irrigation practised is basin irrigation. The water is fed to the fields by means of earth channels; this results in vast losses through evaporation and either too much irrigation is undertaken or it comes at the wrong time during the growth cycle. According to the most recent information,[6] most of the ground water is fossil: during the last 2,000 years no ground-water regeneration worth mentioning has taken place. The drawdown rates are already frighteningly high. Although conditions in the Tihama are generally more favourable, the over-exploitation of ground water could also lead to problems here, particularly as much water is squandered in this area (sorghum cultivation on sandy soils).

The concentration of highly productive agricultural land in the high plateaus and in the Tihama has resulted in a displacement of the potential labour supply and has thus contributed to the regional disparities. In those areas where pump irrigation has been intro-duced, the old irrigation methods (i.e. rainwater-harvesting and *sail* irrigation) have been abandoned relatively quickly. This means that more fertilisation has to be undertaken, thus increasing costs which can only be carried by intensive cultivation.

Modern development in the agrarian sector in Yemen is completely under the influence of a factor which cannot be expressed in numbers — the phenomenon of *qat*. The areas under qat and the yields achieved are not taken into consideration by the official statistics. It is safe to assume, however, that between 1970 and 1980 the percentage of agricultural land under qat rose from 2 to 7 per cent. The increased private income is used mainly to meet the higher demand for qat. The yield per unit of land is ten times higher than that achieved through intensive vegetable cultivation. Especially in the vicinity of the urban markets and on the best soils qat is virtually a monoculture. The use of fertilisers is worthwhile and higher wages can be paid.

In summary, owing to the changed socio-economic conditions, a new assessment of the natural potential has been undertaken. In favourable areas, short-term increases in yields can be achieved. However, the abandonment of the mountain areas and of many traditional farming methods has brought about alterations in the drainage patterns and soil systems which, in turn, means that even these favourable areas are endangered in the long run. The capacity of the agricultural potential has become less and less important through the introduction of modern technology. A market-oriented agricultural economy, practising the over-exploitation of resources, has grown out of a farming economy based on the retention of the natural equilibrium.

What could the future hold? First, it must be recognised that the processes described here are still active and are anchored in the medium-term development planning in Yemen. At present, prestige irrigation projects are given priority[7] and virtually nothing is being done for the mountainous areas. Short-term economic targets dominate over the long-term conservation of the ecosystem when the problem of sustained production is being considered.

On the other hand, a few encouraging aspects can be found in the present situation. Although the transformation process described here is of a highly dynamic nature, it is still very much in its initial stages. The rural way of life and ties with the soil cannot be extinguished within one generation; thus the villages are still grow-ing and, although the prices for agricultural products are low, terrace farming is still being practised. The capital earned abroad is often used to balance out the deficits arising from indigenous farm-ing. Yemen's agricultural products are highly regarded on the home markets and, although of a lower quality, are usually more expen-sive than imported goods. The Yemeni peasants are willing to accept innovations and control a relatively large amount of capital in com-parison with their counterparts in other Sahel countries. Through the years they have developed an understanding of ecological con-nections. Finally, the markets for Yemen's agricultural products are to be found not only at home but also in the neighbouring, finan-cially strong oil countries.

The transport network in Yemen has undergone extensive deve-lopment, with the result that market-oriented production can be undertaken virtually everywhere. These changes mean, however, that more interest has to be taken in the ecological consequences of such land use. The majority of the rainfall occurs in those mountain areas in which the present planning systems show little interest. The development of new methods of cultivation which are on the one hand economically profitable and on the other ecologically accept-able must, therefore, be given priority in these regions. Orchard cultivation, fodder crops to allow more intensive pastoral farming, and re-afforestation could complement each other, depending on the site. Success demands not only the implementation of knowhow from the industrialised countries, but also greater efforts within Yemen's educational system. The frightening transformation of the former Arabia Felix into an Arabia Deserta can be checked only if such measures are implemented immediately.

## Notes

1. This chapter deals solely with the national territory of the present Yemen Arab Republic and is based on information from Horst Kopp, *Agrargeographie der Arabischen Republik Jemen* (Erlanger Geographische Arbeiten, Sonderband 11, Erlangen, 1981).

2. According to the 1975 census, only about 1 per cent of the total population can be considered as fully nomadic. Cf. Hans Steffen, *A Contribution to the Population Geography of the Yemen Arab Republic* (Beihefte zum TAVO, B 39, Wiesbaden, 1979).

3. This law prohibited the sale of land to non-tribal members. It was first dealt with by Walter Dostal, 'Sozio-ökonomische Aspekte der Stammesdemokratie in Nordost-Jemen', *Sociologus*, no. 24 (1974), pp. 1–15.

4. The trade price index rose from 1975/76 ( = 100) to 212 in 1980/81. In the case of grain, however, it rose to 138 (207 for meat and 252 for vegetables). Yemen Arab Republic, Central Planning Organisation, *Statistical Year Book 1981* (San'a', 1982).

5. This is all too obvious when one examines the number of imported pumps: 1970: *c.* 1,400; 1976: *c.* 6,000; 1980: *c.* 10,000 (Steffen, *A Contribution*, and private research).

6. Studies carried out by Dr E. Jungfer (Erlangen) concerning the San'a' Basin (not yet published).

7. Including the economically absurd rebuilding of a dam at the site of ancient Ma'rib. The Abu Dhabi Fund has already given $210 million for preparatory work.

# 5 IRRIGATION AND LAND USE IN THE MA'RIB REGION

Ueli Brunner

## Introduction

The agriculture of the Ma'rib region depends wholly on the *sail* of Wadi Dhana, which waters a catchment area of not less than 10,000 sq. km. It reaches as far west as the Dhamar Basin. Nevertheless, the catchment area lies mainly on the dry eastern escarpment of the Yemen highlands and therefore the mean annual rainfall is very low, at an estimated 300 mm. The run-off is considered to be 7 per cent,[1] so one can expect an annual flow of more than 200 million cu. m. However, there are as yet no measurements of the run-off. Guided by signs on bushes and rocks at the borders of the wadi, the author took three cross-sections of the rather high spring-flood of 1982. They vary between 250 sq. m. in the steeper and 500 sq. m. in the flatter part of the wadi course. We may assume that the peak flow of the *sail* reached the level of almost 1,000 cu. m/sec. Because of the gravelly wadi bed, a large part of the *sail* normally seeps into the Pleistocene alluvial fan, the storage material for the ground water. The aquifer lies at a depth of about 40 m, so it can be reached by a well. The local precipitation is unknown, but it will be less than 100 mm/year; clearly it is not enough to allow cultivation without irrigation. This means that land use in Ma'rib is very closely related to irrigation, and can be discussed as part of the latter. The continually very dry climate is not the only problem faced by the peasants in Ma'rib. The soils too, consisting mostly of sands or basaltic lava, prejudice a rich yield. The main subject of this chapter is to show how the people of Ma'rib have managed to handle the *sail* for agricultural purposes over the course of time.

## The Situation in Ancient Times

In pre-Islamic, i.e. Sabaean, times, Ma'rib was a very wealthy city, earning a large part of its income as the major centre of the incense trade. Thus it could levy taxes on that famous product and supply the caravans with food for their long journey to the Mediterranean Sea. The food was of local origin, produced in the two fertile gardens on either side of Wadi Dhana. They were supplied with water by the famous Great Dam of Ma'rib which closed the gorge in the Jibal Balaq.[2]

The Great Dam had a length of 680 m, leading from the well-built South Sluice on the slope of the Jabal Balaq al-Awsat to the similar North Sluice on the opposite rocks of the Qibli. In the middle part, its height reached more than 16 m and in some parts the water's edge was protected by unhewn lava and limestone rocks.[3] On the north side of the wadi two fine examples are preserved.

Although the Great Dam stretched over the entire wadi, it was nevertheless a diversion rather than a storage dam. Its main purpose was to raise the water to such a level that it could flow into the distant fields, which were several metres above the wadi floor. Furthermore, the storage capacity would have diminished rapidly because of the heavy silt load which came, and continues to come, down with every *sail*, and which lies in the order of 2.5 million cu. m/year.[4] The Great Dam initially had a capacity of about 55 million cu. m. This means that it would fill up within less than a century. But there is evidence that the dam has lasted for more than a millennium. Therefore the whole system must have been prepared to handle the *sail* directly without retention. This was managed by big outlets on both sides of the dam. In the South Sluice, one led into a basin from which the main canal was fed. If too much water came into the basin, a secure overflow directed it to the wadi downstream. We find a similar arrangement at the North Sluice. The huge wall connecting the Jabal Balaq with the North Sluice acted as an overflow. To the right, two outlets diverted the water into a basin from where it flowed into the well-preserved main canal. This canal can be detected over 1.1 km to the south-western end of the North Oasis, where it ended in the round main distributor. It shows 15 outlets which led to secondary canals.[5]

These secondary canals ran across the North Oasis mostly from south-west to north-east. On their alignments, at right angles, stood distributors for smaller, tertiary canals. Small distributors in the canal border diverted the water into the prepared fields (Figure 5.1). Sometimes there also existed a masonry structure which led the water from one field to the next. The level of its gap indicated the height of the flooding in the field, which seems to have been around

60 cm.[6] The excess water was directed back to the wadi by means of well-built drops. This was necessary because of the danger of erosion on the steep margins of the oases.

Figure 5.1:   Example of the Ancient Irrigation and Land-use System in Ma'rib from the Western Part of the South Oasis

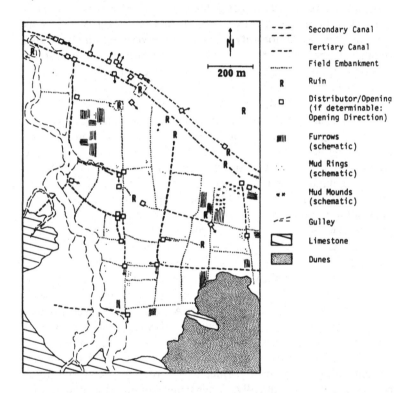

| | |
|---|---|
| - - - | Secondary Canal |
| - - - | Tertiary Canal |
| ........... | Field Embankment |
| R | Ruin |
| □ | Distributor/Opening (if determinable: Opening Direction) |
| ▥ | Furrows (schematic) |
| | Mud Rings (schematic) |
| ▪ ▪ | Mud Mounds (schematic) |
| ≈≈ | Gulley |
| ▨ | Limestone |
| ▧ | Dunes |

Source: U. Brunner, 'Die Erforschung der antiken Oase von Marib mit Hilfe geomorphologischer Untersuchungsmethoden' in *Archäologische Berichte aus dem Yemen* (Zaberndruck, Mainz, 1983), vol. 2, p. 102, fig. 31.

Nevertheless, the whole system faced many severe problems. First, the heavy sediment load of the *sail* has to be considered. The coarse sediments were deposited in the basin of the episodical lake of the dam. Only finer sediments, mostly silt, reached the fields. The North and South Oases silted up quite rapidly at a rate of 1.1 cm/year.[7] The silt was also used to prepare new fields on the rocky lava strips. Small escarpments were built by collecting loose stones. In years with sufficient water, these fields were flooded, so the fertile silt accumulated. Eventually the oases would rise to a level which was too high for the existing dam, so the dam had to be built higher if the system was to fulfil its function.

Another problem lay in the exceptionally large *sails* that occurred from time to time. In such instances, destruction of the dam was possible. There are records of at least five such disasters within the last 300 years or so of the existence of the Great Dam. Yet it seems that the dam failed not only because of the very big *sails*, but also because of the lack of maintenance of the whole irrigation system. Local thunderstorms, slides in the steep slope of the dam, or silting up of primary canals could severely weaken the catchment of the irrigation arrangement.

To co-ordinate and conduct all this maintenance work, a powerful authority was needed. In the early times, until about 500 BC, these were the Mukarribs; later on the Kings of Saba'. Only in the fifth and sixth centuries AD did the central power move from Ma'rib to the highlands. Thenceforth the supervision became less and less efficient, although in AD 450 20,000 people helped to rebuild the dam, after it had been partly washed away.[8] At the beginning of the seventh century AD the final collapse of the Great Dam took place and, because of the lack of a firm central power, it has not yet been rebuilt.[9]

In former times mainly grain crops were cultivated. According to van Beek, teff,[10] millet, barley and oats have been identified as seed impressions on clay vessels of South Arabia. 'Other useful plants include broom-corn, grape, cumin, flax, garden sorrel and sesame.'[11] Furthermore, there exists evidence of palm plantations. They are indicated by mud mounds and mud rings on the barren ancient oases. They show former trunks of trees which had been planted partly systematically. Other structures on the ground can be identified as ancient furrows, originating from ploughing for cereals. Some bush or tree crops needed irrigation throughout the year; for this and for household purposes wells were used, some of which still exist. The gross area irrigated by the Great Dam in Sabaean times was around 9,600 ha[12] (Figure 5.2). It seems to have been sufficient to supply about 30,000 to 50,000 people.[13] An unknown area of fields may also have been irrigated by simple diversion dams below the two oases.

Figure 5.2:   Development of Cultivated Land in the Ma'rib Region

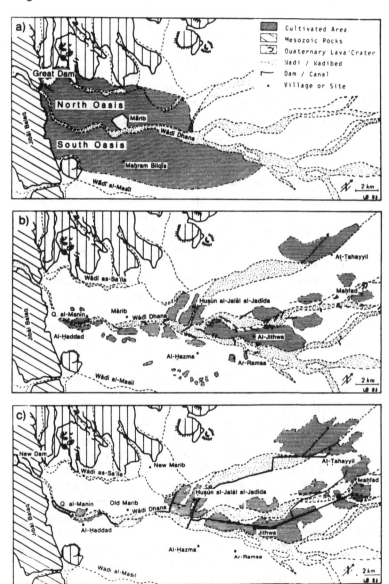

a)  Sabaean situation (after Brunner, p. 61 fig. 23; see Note 3).
b)  Situation in 1973 (after Schoch, p. 125, fig. 3; see Note 5).
c)  Future situation, planned irrigated areas only (after Electrowatt, vol. 5, fig. 22; see Note 16).

**The Present Land-Use Pattern**

After the collapse of the Great Dam, the two oases on either side of Wadi Dhana were too high for *sail* irrigation. This led to the well-known exodus of people to foreign countries. Only a minority tried to stay in the region, and there is no reliable information as to what these people did. However, it is possible that, in search of irrigable land, they moved downstream to the north-east where they found suitable land at the border of the sand desert, Ramlat al-Sab'atain. Since the soils were not as good as the ones they had formerly known, they later took the chance to move back near the old sites, when the *sails* had eroded wide terraces into the ancient oases.

The irrigation practices will not have changed greatly up to the present day. The *sail* is caught by an earth diversion dam which leads into the wadi at an acute angle. Such unstable diversion dams were often washed away, but they could be easily rebuilt by the community; they protected the fields against destruction by a big *sail*. The diverted water flows either into a channel (Figure 5.3) or directly into a huge empoldered field. Sometimes an unprotected opening in the embankment leads to another, mostly smaller field. The field must be covered by more than 0.5 m of water, so that the crops, which are always planted after the irrigation, can grow on the retained soil moisture. This irrigation method gives a high fertility to the soil, due to the heavy silt load which is brought by the annual *sails* and afterwards sedimented in the basins. On *sail*-irrigated fields *dhurra* and wheat or barley are mostly grown.[14]

Some bunds also exist in the smaller wadis, such as Wadi as-Sa'ila and Wadi al-Masil. Their function is to retain some water to increase the growth of bushes and grasses as food for the grazing stock. This extensive land use is highly dependent on local rains which are very scarce and do not occur every year. On the basis of aerial pictures taken in 1973, Schoch measured a *sail*-irrigated area of 3,900 ha in the Ma'rib region.[15] Of this land about 2,000 ha produced at least one yield every year and the remaining 1,900 ha are flooded episodically only in years with a big *sail*.

A comparison of the present irrigated area with the Sabaean one shows clearly that the natural water resources are no longer fully used (Figure 5.2). Nowadays quite a large part of the *sail* flows into the desert. This means that, given the amount of available water, the irrigated area in the Ma'rib region could be enlarged. A severe problem facing the present irrigation is the wide fluctuations in volume

Figure 5.3:    Present *Sail* Irrigation System South-east of Husun al-Jalal al-Jadida

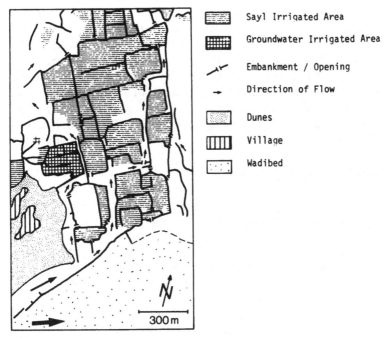

| | |
|---|---|
| Sayl Irrigated Area |
| Groundwater Irrigated Area |
| Embankment / Opening |
| Direction of Flow |
| Dunes |
| Village |
| Wadibed |

Note: The water is caught in the wadi by a diversion dam. The irrigation ensues mostly from field to field.
Source: Sketch map on basis of aerial pictures taken by Aero-Precisa, Beirut, in December 1973.

and time of the occurrence of the *sail*. In wet years all the prepared fields can be irrigated and a high yield results, whereas in a dry year only the preferred fields upstream will get some of the scarce water. Even there, the insufficient flooding of the fields leads to rather low yields.

A more reliable source of water for the farmers consists of wells. There is a widespread aquifer in the quaternary fan at a depth of 25–50 m. Within the stable ancient silts, it can be reached with an unprotected hole. The ground water is pumped up mostly by Japanese diesel engines. Fields irrigated by ground water can be cultivated all the year round. The principal crops grown are wheat in winter and sesame and a little maize in summer. Lucerne as a perennial crop is cultivated all the time[16] and may reach six to eight yields a year. Furthermore, in some garden-like fields, grapes, vegetables, citrus fruits, figs and *qat* are cultivated, mostly for home consumption.

It is not therefore surprising that the incoming money from labourers abroad and from the local border trade has led to an enormous spread of diesel-driven ground-water pumps. Electrowatt[17] estimates that in 1977 about 160 working pumps existed, irrigating an area of some 636 ha. A more recent study[18] estimates that the number of wells has been growing at a rate of 20–35 per annum. As a result, the area irrigated by ground water is expanding by some 100 ha a year, and is now double that in 1977. This process can be observed very clearly in the margin of the ancient fields. For centuries these terraces were too high for any irrigation and their barren surface still showed the structure of the Sabaean land-use pattern. Only in the last few years has cultivation started. Broad zones on the terraces, mostly along the main wadi, have been flattened by bulldozers and taken into cultivation. During the author's fieldwork it was found that old tracks are cut off by new fields every year, and the detour necessary to get to a particular site gets progressively longer. Even families from other tribes have started migrating to Ma'rib to profit from what they believe to be the region's inexhaustible ground-water reservoir.[19]

Meanwhile, the first signs of an over-use of the ground water occurred. Near Qaryat al-Manin a 1977 hand-built well became dry in 1980 and a deeper one had to be dug just beside it. Other hand-sunk wells suffered the same fate. The fact is that the excavation of a well becomes difficult as soon as it strikes ground water. It can rarely penetrate deeper than 1 or 2 m below the ground-water level. This means that all hand-dug wells are affected by small fluctuations of the aquifer surface as they occur from a wet to a dry year. An examination of the rainfall statistics of San'a'[20] for the last few years shows the very dry Sahel drought at the beginning of the 1970s, followed by a rather wet period in the mid-70s; 1979 and 1980 were again very dry. 1982 and 1983, for which there are as yet no data available, seem to be rather wet.[21] The above-mentioned well near Qaryat al-Manin was built under favourable climatic conditions and dried out in the second year with low rainfall. But what will happen if a series of dry years follows? Will the aquifer be sufficiently recharged to be able to cope with the never-ending demand for ground water? As mentioned above, the first indications seem to suggest negative answers to these questions.

Another problem that has become more prevalent in recent years is the fertility of the soils. Through *sail* irrigation, the fields receive a layer of fine sediments full of nutrients with every flooding. As demonstrated by the success of Sabaean agriculture, these sediments had maintained the fertility of the soil for centuries. This natural manure does not occur in a field irrigated by pumps and the result is that 'the soils get tired', as the tribesmen say. The yield diminishes and the field finally has to be given up. This process can be observed especially in perennial qat cultivations.

Most farmers with a pump of their own work only for themselves. They do not depend on their neighbours because they are almost self-sufficient; they produce what they need for their families and their livestock. This is the case for an average farm-size of about 4 ha. Owing to the enormous need for new land, some fighting over the location of farm boundaries has occurred. (In 1976 an estimated population of 13,000 people inhabited the Ma'rib region.[22]) More co-ordination is necessary between those farmers who depend on *sail* irrigation. Only the construction of the main diversion dam in the wadi must be undertaken by the local community; the rest is the duty of the farmers. The distribution of the *sail* is strictly ruled by Islamic law: first, the area upstream may drink, then the one below, and so on.

## The Proposed Development of the Region[23]

For several years there have been plans to improve agriculture in the Ma'rib region. The principal goal of the project is to enlarge the cultivated area and to provide water for irrigation all the year round. Furthermore, the project includes the establishment of a simple infrastructure for the region, mainly roads. The improvement of agriculture would be made possible by a 38 m-high and 600 m-long dam across Wadi Dhana in the upper part of the gorge of the Jibal Balaq. This earth dam would cause an artificial lake with a maximal storage capacity of 398 million cu. m. An outflow of 25 cu. m/sec. would leave through the bottom outlet to the former wadi bed. In its natural course, it would run downwards to the diversion embankments. These would divert the water to primary canals which would feed the main branches. All these structures would be financed by the governmental project fund. All further work of the second system would be undertaken by the local farmers. In this way it is hoped that the project would ensure the support of the local tribes. Farm units consisting of five farms would cover an area of 70 ha. Altogether it is expected to control 6,304 ha of irrigable land, including almost all the 4,472 ha hitherto cultivated; this would result in an increase of about 50 per cent. The more secure water supply promises a higher crop-intensity, so one can expect a doubling of the annual yield in the Ma'rib region. The crops proposed are the same as today: sesame and maize in summer, wheat in winter and lucerne, vegetables and fruits all year round. The project description features a comparatively high degree of profitability. The possibly improved aquifer recharge would provide further indirect benefits from an increase in ground-water abstraction.

In assessing the impact of the project on the region, the following points should be taken into consideration:

*Advantages:*
— Controlled use of water resources
— Higher yields due to permanent irrigation
— No flood hazards
— Controlled development of the region
— Establishment of a road network
— Possibility of being able to protect archaeological sites

*Disadvantages:*
— Danger of social unrest due to forced migration of tribes
— High costs
— Diminution of the liberty of local tribes
— Possible occurrence of infectious diseases (malaria, bilharzia)
— Possibility that farmers may plant high-return industrial crops (qat, cotton) instead of grain for their basic needs

The Ma'rib Dam and Irrigation Project is one possible proposal for the development of the region. Whether it will reintroduce the former Sabaean wealth to the region depends heavily on whether the new irrigation system, once established, will be maintained in good working condition or not.

## Conclusions

(1) All intensive agriculture in the arid climate of the Ma'rib region relies upon irrigation. By far the most limiting factor is the water

quantity, as well as its distribution in time. All other natural resources of the region, such as climatic conditions, soils, topography and water quality, may be considered as sufficient-to-good.

(2) The ancient irrigation system seems to have reached the upper limit of the potential agricultural area, with its extension of almost 10,000 ha. A strong central power controlled this wonderful irrigation scheme and ordered — if necessary — thousands of people to repair any damage. The system was based mainly on direct *sail* irrigation without big retention basins; only special plantations were sustained by ground-water irrigation.

(3) The present picture shows a cultivated area only about two-fifths of that of Sabaean times. Thus the natural water supply is not all used. In the last few years special efforts have been made to profit from the rich aquifer. The area irrigated by pumps is expanding very rapidly, whereas the *sail* irrigation is stagnating. A continuous expansion of lift-pumps will endanger the hitherto sufficient ground water.

(4) The development of the region as proposed would diminish the danger mentioned above, thanks to the reinforcement of the *sail* irrigation by means of the storage dam and the permanent network of diversion structures, canals, branches and distributors. Furthermore, the permanent flow in the wadi would recharge the aquifer all the year round. The comparison of the planned irrigated area with the Sabaean situation shows that the agricultural potential of the Ma'rib region would not be over-stretched by the project (Figure 5.3).

## Acknowledgements

Without the help of Prof. Dr J. Schmidt, head of the German Archaeological Institute in San'a', I should never have had the opportunity to study the irrigation practices in the Ma'rib region during three field trips lasting altogether more than five months. These stays provided the basic information for this chapter. I should like to express my special gratitude to him.

The government of the Yemen Arab Republic (YAR) granted me permission to visit the Ma'rib region, for which I am deeply grateful.

I enjoyed the permanent support of the Department of Geography at the University of Zurich, which has conducted many successful research projects in the YAR.[24]

Special thanks are due to Prof. Dr H. Weiss, who carefully corrected the English draft.

Last, but not least, I am greatly indebted to Electrowatt Engineering Services Ltd in Zurich, who supplied me with material and always offered me substantial information about their experience in Ma'rib.

## Notes

1. Electrowatt Engineering Services Ltd, *Marib Dam and Irrigation Project*, Annex VII: Hydrology (Zurich, 1978), p. 41.
2. In the last few years new archaeological research has been going on in Ma'rib. Under the direction of Prof. Dr J. Schmidt, the German Archaeological Institute financed several field trips. The main subject was an inventory of the relics of the Sabaean civilisation as a whole. This was made by a survey with aerial pictures as well as a ground search. Special efforts were made to increase the understanding of the history and function of the Sabaean irrigation system. First results were published in *Archäologische Berichte aus dem Yemen* (Zaberndruck, Mainz, 1982/83), vols. 1/2.
3. U. Brunner, 'Die Erforschung der antiken Oase von Marib mit Hilfe geomorphologischer Untersuchungsmethoden' in *Archäologische Berichte*, vol. 2, p. 57.
4. Ibid., p. 47.
5. R. Schoch, 'Wasserbauten auf der Nordoase' in *Archäologische Berichte*, vol. 1, p. 26.
6. Brunner, 'Die Erforschung', p. 90.
7. Ibid., p. 90.
8. In the inscription GI 554 = CIH 540, line 71/72, a crowd of 20,000 people is mentioned as coming to repair the Great Dam.
9. Brunner, 'Die Erforschung', p. 116.
10. A variety of millet, today used for bread only in Ethiopia; in all other countries as a fast-growing forage plant.
11. G. van Beek, 'The Land of Sheba' in J. B. Pritchard (ed.), *Solomon and Sheba* (Phaidon Press, London, 1974), p. 44.
12. Brunner, 'Die Erforschung', p. 90.
13. Ibid., p. 106.
14. Swiss Technical Co-operation Service, *Final Report on the Airphoto Interpretation Project* (Central Planning Organisation, San'a'/Department of Geography, University of Zurich, 1978), p. II/131.
15. R. Schoch, 'Die antike Kulturlandschaft des Stadtbezirkes Saba' und die heutige Oase von Ma'rib in der Arabischen Republik Jemen' in *Geographica Helvetica*, no. 33/3 (Berne, 1978), p. 126.
16. Electrowatt Engineering, *Marib Dam*, Engineer's Report, vol. 6: Project Descriptions (Zurich, 1981), p. 26.
17. Electrowatt Engineering, *Marib Dam*, Annex III: Agriculture (Zurich, 1978), p. 26.
18. Electrowatt Engineering, *Marib Dam*, Engineer's Report, vol. 6: Project Descriptions (Zurich, 1981), p. 27.
19. At the southernmost end of the North Oasis a man from Arhab and his family bought an area of about 300 m × 600 m from a member of the Bani Ashraf.

20. The *Statistical Year Books* (Central Planning Organisation, San'a', 1972–82) give the following data for San'a' for the twelve years:

| | | | |
|------|----------|------|----------|
| 1970 | 158.0 mm | 1976 | 154.2 mm |
| 1971 | 111.4 mm | 1977 | 335.6 mm |
| 1972 | 116.5 mm | 1978 | 166.5 mm |
| 1973 | 163.1 mm | 1979 | 95.9 mm |
| 1974 | 236.5 mm | 1980 | 98.6 mm |
| 1975 | 384.7 mm | 1981 | 166.8 mm |

21. In 1982 the spring *sail* of Wadi Dhana may have been a five-year highwater with a maximum discharge of about 1,000 cu. m/sec.

22. Swiss Technical Co-operation, *Final Report*, p. II/142.

23. All the following facts are extracts from Electrowatt Engineering, *Marib Dam*.

24. For example, H. Escher, 'Wirtschafts- und Sozialgeographische Untersuchungen in der Wadi Mawr Region' in *Beihefte zum Tübinger Atlas des Vorderen Orients*, Reihe B (Wiesbaden, 1976), vol. 23; Swiss Technical Co-operation, *Final Report*; H. Steffen, 'A Contribution to the Population Geography of the Yemen Arab Republic' in *Beihefte zum Tübinger Atlas des Vorderen Orients*, Reihe B (Wiesbaden, 1979), vol. 39; R. Schoch, 'Land-Cover Studies and Crop Average Estimates from Aerial Photography and Satellite Imagery' in *Remote Sensing Series* (Department of Geography, University of Zurich, 1982), vol. 5.

# 6 ECONOMIC ASPECTS OF THE QAT INDUSTRY IN NORTH-WEST YEMEN

Shelagh Weir

There is considerable concern in official circles and among development economists at the great expansion in *qat* cultivation which took place in the Yemen Arab Republic (YAR) during the 1970s. This expansion was in response to the substantial national increase in qat consumption and the inflation in qat prices which took place during the same period. Before the civil war of 1962–70 only a relatively affluent, mainly urban, minority were regular, frequent qat consumers, but during the 1970s qat consumption spread throughout the population and for the first time became a majority practice. In the early 1970s the average price of a bunch (*rubta*) of qat was about 4 rials (YR) (less than $1). By 1979/80 increased demand had pushed up the price of a rubta to an average of YR 45 ($10). Most consumers were by then buying between three and eight bunches a week and many were buying much more. The increase in qat consumption and qat prices was clearly linked to the substantial rise in disposable incomes, due mainly to the great influx of cash remittances from the vast numbers of Yemenis who took up temporary employment in Saudi Arabia from the early 1970s. A large proportion of the money repatriated by these migrant labourers was being spent on qat.

Many officials believe that the huge national expenditure on qat and the high proportion of prime agricultural land devoted to its cultivation are retarding Yemen's economic development by diverting cash from productive investment, and by obstructing the officially promulgated aim of working towards greater national self-sufficiency in food production. In the author's view, these and various other assumptions which have been made about the negative effects of both the consumption and production of qat require greater scrutiny and debate than they have yet received. But so far the debate has been hindered by the dearth of information on all aspects of qat. In particular, very little is known about the structure of its production, or of the effects on regional economies of the expansion in its cultivation and the influx of high revenues from its sales. This chapter is intended as a contribution to this area of knowledge. Drawing on information collected during 14 months' fieldwork in a qat-trading community in Razih, a highland province in north-west Yemen, the chapter will (a) outline the salient features of the local qat industry and (b) describe some of the positive economic effects qat production has had in the area. It will show that qat has helped to promote and sustain agriculture, and has stimulated and helped to finance certain technological innovations and infrastructural developments.

The community to be discussed lives on the highest slopes of a steep mountain, which will be called by the fictitious name of al-Jabal. It lies at an altitude of about 2,100 m on the western edge of the Yemeni highlands close to the international border with Saudi Arabia. Below the mountain to the west stretches the hot dry Tihama plain which borders the Red Sea; to the east extend the rugged mountains of the highland massif; and about 50 km as the crow flies beyond this craggy terrain lies the high flat central plateau of Yemen and the walled town of Sa'da.

The population of al-Jabal is about 4,500, of whom some 900 live in the largest settlement on the mountain known as the *madina* (town) of al-Jabal. The madina consists of about 70 multi-storeyed stone houses clustered along a ridge near the summit of the mountain, and has at its centre a large open market-place with the main mosque of al-Jabal on its edge, both surrounded by dozens of small shops. The madina is the economic, social, religious and political centre of al-Jabal. The remainder of the population lives in over 30 small scattered hamlets perched on rocky outcrops overlooking the terraces. Until the late 1970s, when al-Jabal was first linked to the outside world by motor tracks, all travel and transportation was on foot or on donkey and camel-back along the myriad of narrow tortuous paths which wind through the mountains.

The community of al-Jabal constitutes a political unit or *qabila* (tribe) which is internally administered and externally represented by a *shaikh* and tribal elders. Al-Jabal together with a mountain to its north, occupied by a tribe of about 1,000 people, comprise the main qat-producing areas of Razih. Because of its geographical location and altitude, the upper slopes of al-Jabal are blessed with relatively high rainfall (an estimated annual average of 700–1,000 mm) and — equally important for agricultural production — the mountain is frequently bathed in humid mists which reduce evaporation from the soil. It is therefore exceptionally green and fertile compared with either the Tihama or the mountains further east which receive far less rain. The mountain is so steep that agriculture would be impossible without terracing and, above an altitude of about 1,300 m (corresponding to the zone of maximum rainfall), the slopes are clothed in row upon row of beautifully constructed stone-walled terraces. Only the most precipitous slopes are unterraced and these are one important source of fodder for domestic animals. A minority of households keep one or two cattle and three or four sheep. Domestic livestock production has always been limited by the scarcity of fodder and the lack of land suitable for grazing on the steep mountain-sides. All fodder is collected by hand by the women and brought to the animals in the settlements.

In addition to qat, the main crops cultivated in al-Jabal are coffee, banana, summer sorghum, and winter wheat and barley. There is also some interplanting of legumes, and there are a few scattered fruit trees — peach and papaya on the upper slopes and lime and citron further down. All crops except banana are exclusively rain-fed or irrigated by surface run-off water. Most banana is grown in dense plantations in narrow clefts and steep valleys containing small permanent springs which allow some controlled irrigation of the terraces.

Al-Jabal is situated in a strategic position between the Tihama and the highlands on a major trade route between the two regions which passes through the mountainous province of Razih and eventually connects with the central plateau north of Sa'da. The market of al-Jabal is therefore important not only for the exchange of local produce, but also as an entrepôt for cash-crops exported from the western highlands to the coast and abroad (skins and coffee), for foreign commodities imported at the Red Sea ports, and for grain and fruits traded west from the eastern highlands and plateau regions. Today it is the largest and most vigorous of a network of weekly markets spanning southern Razih and the adjacent Tihama.

On account of its strategic position and resources, al-Jabal has always had a diverse economy based on a combination of subsistence and commercial agriculture, small-scale domestic livestock production, commerce and petty trading, and the provision of transportation services. All these activities remain part of the local economy but their scale and relative importance have changed. The major factors for economic change have been the out-migration of local men to work in Saudi Arabia and their cash remittances; and the greatly increased financial returns on qat. As al-Jabal is situated close to the Saudi border, migration for work is not considered a long-term undertaking; men return quite frequently and many spend only part

of the year abroad in order to save capital for specific projects. Much
of the money earned abroad is channelled to older men in the form of
bride-prices, or is spent on establishing shops or other enterprises, or
on home improvements such as household cisterns. In April 1977
over 30 per cent of adult men (over the age of 15) were temporarily
employed in Saudi Arabia, mainly as unskilled construction workers.
From December 1979 to January 1980, when the author's second
census was conducted, only 10 per cent were working abroad. This
reduction must be partly acccounted for by the increased opportunities for employment locally, especially in the qat industry and in
the burgeoning commercial and transportation sectors.

The population density of al-Jabal is very high: between 100 and
200 persons/sq. km in relation to the entire mountain, and over
750/sq. km in relation to the intensively cultivated upper slopes
where all the settlements are concentrated. This very high population
density is closely related to the agricultural productivity of the mountain and to its commercial importance. People were attracted to relatively prosperous areas of Yemen such as al-Jabal during famines and
at times of political unrest elsewhere in the country.

Because of the size of the population in relation to cultivable land,
there is great pressure on land, holdings are relatively small, and a
large minority of households — over 30 per cent — own only one
small terrace or no land at all. (In al-Jabal landownership is not a
condition for full *qabili* (tribal) status as elsewhere in tribal Yemen.)
Terraces vary in size and shape, but most fall within the range of
0.02–0.1 ha in area. The average size of a terrace is about 0.05 ha.
Most households with agricultural terraces own between 0.15 and
0.5 ha of land. Anything more than this amount is considered a very
large land-holding by local standards. Perhaps 5 per cent of households own as much as 1 ha of terraced land. (Unterraced fodder land
is also privately owned.) Because of the scarcity of land, and the high
proportion devoted to the cultivation of cash-crops, al-Jabal imports
much of its grain and other food requirements, and this was probably
always the case, to some extent, in the past.

The qat industry was of much less importance in al-Jabal before the
civil war than during the 1970s. Only a few families were involved in
qat trading, and a far smaller proportion of the terraces was given
over to its cultivation. Some of the qat produced then was for local
consumption — mainly by the wealthier members of the community, as the phenomenon was not then as widespread in al-Jabal or the
surrounding areas as it is today. The rest was exported — mainly to

Sa'da, over two full days' travel from al-Jabal by donkey, where it was consumed by government officials stationed there or by members of the local urban elite.

In early 1977 (when the author first arrived in al-Jabal) qat was already the major crop in terms of the revenues it attracted and it was planted on approximately 15 per cent of the terraces. By 1980 the area planted with qat had roughly doubled and qat occupied about 30 per cent of the cultivable land on the upper slopes of the mountain.

By 1980 a very large proportion of the local workforce was involved in some capacity in the qat industry. Most people who owned terraces which received sufficient rain to support qat were growing at least some trees, and many men were intermittently employed to hoe and plough between the trees, and to apply fertiliser and insecticides. Some smallholders choose not to market their qat themselves and instead sell it on the tree to qat traders, and many men were involved in the qat trade as pickers, packers and transporters. This work is also intermittent as qat is sold only when it is ready for harvesting, and new marketable leaves are produced only after rainfall. However, al-Jabal often gets rain throughout the year, including the winter months which are dry in most of Yemen; people expect to harvest their qat three times a year from each tree, and even four times if the earth is worked and fertilised frequently and there is abundant rainfall. People also harvest their qat at different times. There was therefore some work available in the qat industry throughout the year, though mostly in the periods immediately following heavy or prolonged rainfall.

Qat is traded by small-scale, family-based enterprises consisting of brothers or a father and his sons working in partnership for a share of the profits. Extra personnel are hired on an *ad hoc* basis as and when the extra labour is needed; these workers are often also relatives. During the qat-harvesting period in early 1980 about 15 per cent of the adult men of al-Jabal were working in such family trading units, and many more were employed to pick and pack qat when family labour was insufficient. Some qat trading units owned their own donkeys or motor vehicles and took their own qat directly to market, but the majority hired transportation — almost entirely from local men.

This does not exhaust the categories of people involved one way or another in the local qat industry. In addition to landowners, agricultural labourers, qat traders and their employees and qat transporters, a number of people supply essential materials to the qat trade. The most important of these materials are banana stems. The people of al-Jabal pack their qat for market in sections of banana stem which are stiff and moist and therefore help to keep the qat leaves fresh and protect them from damage during transportation to market. The stems are carried from the plantations to the al-Jabal market, or directly to the homes of the qat traders, on donkey-back or, when the slopes are too steep for donkeys, on the backs or heads of men or women. Sometimes the carriers are the owners of the banana who want to make the maximum profit and so undertake the arduous task of carrying the extremely heavy stems to cut out transportation expenses. The income from selling banana stems is far in excess of that formerly earned by selling the fruit.

With the rise in the price of qat and the expansion of cultivation, theft became a major problem. A thief could pick and make off with thousands of rials' worth of qat at night in a matter of minutes. After the completion of a motor track from the Tihama to the top of al-Jabal in 1979, local traders began importing wire-mesh fencing, and most of those who owned qat terrace in vulnerable positions (especially those adjacent to the track) enclosed them with this fencing. It also became essential to guard the qat as the time for harvesting drew near; galvanised iron sheets, which were already being imported in substantial quantities to build shops, were also used to construct guard huts on the terraces. The same material was also used extensively to build huts for packing qat for market, since many traders did not have room in their houses for this purpose. It can be seen that the expansion of the qat industry generated work and income for a wide range of people in the local population.

It is impossible to be precise about the manner in which revenues from qat are distributed because of the great variability of inputs on the part of landowners and traders, and the fluctuations in the price of qat in the market-place. However, Figure 6.1 gives a rough indication of the way the cake is divided.

As Figure 6.1 illustrates, the main beneficiaries from qat revenues are the landowners and traders. According to figures collected by the author during the early 1980 qat-harvesting season, the greater proportion of gross revenues — between 50 and 70 per cent — went to the trader, but the greater net profits were made by the landowner as his expenses were lower. However, this calculation does not take into account any capital expenditure on land. It is likely that these proportions vary considerably in the long term, as there are considerable fluctuations in market prices from one harvest to the next, depending on the quantity of qat produced in other areas and when it is marketed.

Figure 6.1:    YAR: The Distribution of Qat Revenues

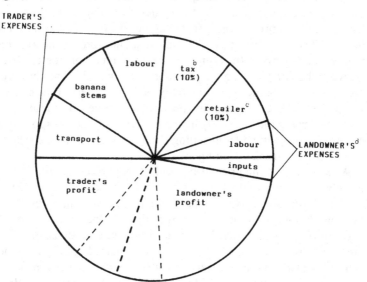

Notes: a.   The fixed cost of a hut in which to pack qat and electricity costs for night work are not included.
b.   The tax can be levied on production, but is more often extracted at the market.
c.   Apart from taxes, this is the main part of qat revenues which remain outside the producing area.
d.   Capital outlay on land and fixed costs such as fencing and guard hut are not taken into consideration.

Although qat growers and traders are among the wealthiest members of the community, the expansion of the qat industry has not resulted in their accumulating large land-holdings (as happened in the past in the coffee trade), nor has the qat trade become the monopoly of a few big merchants (as also happened with coffee). One of the effects of the high financial yields from qat has been to increase the investment value of land. This factor, combined with the great increase in general prosperity and cash incomes, has resulted in a widespread reluctance to sell land and less need to do so. (During famines in the past much land was sold just to buy food.) Little land therefore comes up for sale and when it does the prices are enormous. Eight terraces of small and medium size sold between 1979 and 1981 fetched from $4,000 to $25,000, or the equivalent of between $200,000 and $600,000 a hectare. No one, however wealthy, is in a position to accumulate land at such prices even were it readily available.

Gerholm speculated that the qat trade in Haraz, also in the western highlands of Yemen, might become dominated by big merchants after the development of modern transportation facilities. For then, he reasoned, Harazi qat, which was only sold locally in the mid-1970s when he was there, could be sold in more distant markets and would fetch higher prices. As transportation expenses would be high, those with substantial capital to risk would monopolise the trade.[1] However, there is no sign of this happening in al-Jabal.

Qat trading in al-Jabal certainly favours those with substantial capital to risk but this is not mainly because of the high cost of transportation. It is not necessary to own a vehicle to be a qat trader as space in vehicles owned by others can be hired. But even if a trader owns his own truck, the cost of buying the qat from the landowner soon exceeds the cost of buying and running a vehicle. It is in qat transactions that the greatest capital investment is made and the greatest financial risk taken. For qat is bought on the tree and the price is negotiated and the money paid before the trader takes the qat to market; and although the amount agreed is based on the most recent prices fetched in the market, prices can plummet if there is a sudden glut.

The key factors which determine the character of the qat trade and which act as constraints on the development of large-scale capitalist enterprises dominated by big merchants are the high perishability of the product and the impossibility of predicting the state of the market. Qat must be sold within one or two days of picking or its leaves wilt and its value can drop to well below the price paid on the tree. The main aim of the trader is therefore to sell his consignment as quickly as possible after he arrives at the market and at a price which will yield him a profit. Until he has reached the market, however, he cannot forecast whether high prices fetched recently will be maintained or whether, as happens, other traders will also have rushed their qat to market to benefit from them, causing them to fall because of the resultant excess of supply. If the trader arrived with several truckloads of qat at such a time, not only would he be in danger of being unable to sell his qat before it wilted, but he would also contribute to the drop in prices by swelling supplies still further. In such circumstances where reliable and up-to-date information is so hard to acquire, trading could be revolutionised by the introduction of a telephone network. Fundamental changes would also come about were refrigerated trucks available.

It will be evident that the best strategy for a trader aiming at an unpredictable market with a highly perishable product in which he has invested considerable capital is to buy and market it in relatively small quantities. He is thus less vulnerable to a single gigantic loss. This is the strategy employed. The maximum quantity of qat which is normally marketed by a single trading unit on each occasion is one truckload. In some cases qat sufficient to fill more than one truck is bought in one purchase but this is picked, packed and sent to market in separate smaller consignments on different days. Such large purchases are, however, the exception. The author never encountered any speculation in qat, a custom which could also theoretically lead to monopolisation of the qat trade by big merchants. To her knowledge, all qat is bought when ready for harvesting, when both buyer and seller can see the quantity and quality of new leaves the trees have produced, and when they both have as good an idea as possible of the price the qat is likely to fetch two days or so later when it reaches the market.

There are thus major disincentives facing any trader who might have the capital and inclination to expand the size and scale of his enterprise. Therefore, although trading units vary in size according to the quantity of qat being prepared for market on a particular day, they never exceed a maximum of about six or seven persons as this is roughly the number of people necessary for picking and packing a single truck-size consignment in a day.

The profits to be made from qat cultivation are so great that there is no difficulty in understanding why landowners were planting the crop wherever they could in the late 1970s. In al-Jabal qat is traded in packages called *gurufs* which contain a number of branches of qat tied in small bunches and packed in sections of banana stem. Yields and sales are always discussed in terms of gurufs. One guruf is roughly equivalent to two bunches or rubtas of qat — one rubta being the quantity of qat most individuals consume in any one day.

In al-Jabal approximately 3,500 qat trees are planted to the hectare, yielding about 2,000 gurufs of qat at each harvest. In a year when the average price of a rubta of qat in the market is, say, YR 50 (which was the case in 1980), the market value of the qat from 1 ha of land, if it yielded two harvests, would be YR 400,000 (approx. $90,000) and if it yielded three harvests (which is common), YR 600,000 (approx. $130,000). If we relate these figures to a typical individual land-holding of 0.2 ha and assume it is planted entirely with qat, the market value of the qat on that land in 1980 would have been about YR 80,000 (approx. $17,000) if it yielded two harvests, and YR 120,000 ($26,000) if it yielded three harvests. These figures give some indication of the enormous revenues from qat in a year when al-Jabal received good rainfall and the price of qat remained high. In years of low rainfall, however, it may not be possible to harvest the qat more than once, although the crop which is harvested might fetch a higher price in the market because of the shortage of supply. It should be remembered that the above figures do not represent the gross income to the landowner but the total cash revenues generated from specific areas of land — these being distributed among the various categories of person involved in the qat industry as indicated in Figure 6.1. If we assume the landowner's gross income is about 30 per cent of the total price his qat fetches in the market, then his gross income on 0.2 ha of qat land in 1980 would have been approximately $5,000–7,800. Of this about 85 per cent is net profit. These notional figures conform with data collected by the author on the actual incomes of several landowners for the year 1979/80. The net profits of a landowner can of course be much greater, perhaps twice as much, if he markets the qat himself, but then the financial risks are also greater.

What effects are the high revenues from qat sales and the expansion of qat cultivation having on cropping patterns and on agriculture in general in al-Jabal? One of the major criticisms levelled at qat is that it is supplanting coffee in those areas where both trees are cultivated. Qat and coffee thrive in the same ecological conditions, but qat is the hardier crop and can survive short frosts and prolonged droughts better than coffee. Although both trees are planted on the same mountain-sides, and are often interspersed on the same terraces, qat can often be found cultivated at a higher altitude than would be possible for coffee. Because of the widespread assumption that coffee trees are being uprooted throughout Yemen to make way for qat, it is important to emphasise that there was no evidence of this happening in al-Jabal. In areas where coffee is being replaced by qat on the terraces, it is probable either that the coffee is planted in marginal ecological conditions and harvests were poor, or that the higher labour-input required by coffee makes it economically prohibitive to continue cultivating it — especially for those farmers with limited family labour upon which to draw. There is a need for close studies of the local social and economic environment in each of the areas where coffee production has recently been reduced in order to elucidate the particular factors involved in each case.

In al-Jabal there are still important incentives for cultivating coffee although they are probably more social than economic. Coffee is still a lucrative cash-crop, even though the international trade in Yemeni coffee has greatly declined, because the demand within Yemen and Saudi Arabia has increased and prices have risen. In February 1980 coffee beans were selling in the local Jabali market for SR 25 ($7.5) a kilo (Saudi rials are the main local currency), and the coffee husks from which Yemenis brew a popular national beverage (*qishr*) were fetching SR 25 for a measure of about 2 l. Coffee is therefore still an important cash-crop in al-Jabal, and a proportion is exported from the area. However, the profits on coffee for the landowner are several times less than those on qat, so it cannot continue to be cultivated entirely for financial reasons.

There are several reasons why coffee remains an important crop in al-Jabal despite the competition from qat. The Jabalis have always had a diverse economy, and most men derive their incomes from cultivating a range of crops and engaging in more than one occupation. It is therefore possible that they are conscious of the prudence of agricultural and economic diversification: their survival and that of their community has depended on it for centuries, punctuated by frequent droughts and political upheavals which disrupted trade. They are also aware that the demand for qat and high qat prices are linked to high incomes and could therefore easily decline if the demand for Yemeni labour in Saudi Arabia decreased (as it already showed signs of doing in 1980). Even though the local demand for coffee might also decline in such circumstances, it would be difficult for a Yemeni to imagine a radical reduction in coffee consumption — whereas the spread of qat consumption is very recent and every adult can recall when it was an almost exclusively urban phenomenon. There would probably have to be a major long-term slump in coffee consumption, both locally and nationally, before Jabalis would uproot a tree which takes six years from planting to bear fruit.

A further incentive to coffee cultivation is its prestige value, both as a crop and as a drink. When strangers arrive in al-Jabal the local people point out their terraces of coffee and qat, bursting with pride at the greenery. Coffee is an important expression of hospitality towards a guest, and is a form of 'conspicuous display' of wealth and generosity when it is brewed from the bean (*safi*) rather than the cheaper husk (qishr). Coffee is also of considerable importance in formal presentations. Government officials are sometimes presented with bags of beans when they visit al-Jabal, sacks of coffee are given as political tribute to local tribal leaders and coffee is a standard present to take to one's host when visiting outside the area.

The expansion of qat cultivation in al-Jabal has not, therefore, been at the expense of coffee; it has been entirely at the expense of grain. It must be emphasised that this change in cropping ratios does not represent, at the local level, a fundamental shift away from subsistence agriculture. Agricultural economists estimate that it takes between 1 and 2 ha of well-watered land to yield grain sufficient to support one six-person family. Thus it is clear that few households in al Jabal (which at present average 6.6 persons) have the potential to be self-supporting in grain production. Unless the community was once much smaller than today, it must always have had to import most of its grain requirements from the surrounding areas.

The people of al-Jabal have probably always grown as many cash-crops (banana, coffee, qat) as they could market or consume themselves, and grown grain on the rest of the terraces to minimise what they had to buy in. Grain, specifically the main crop of summer sorghum, was grown as much for its value as fodder and fuel as for its food value. The leaves of sorghum are stripped shortly before the grain is harvested and they are fed to sheep and cattle. After the grain harvest the long stalk is cut in half and the top half is fed to cattle while the lower half is uprooted and used as fuel in domestic ovens. Until the late 1970s sorghum was a vital resource in al-Jabal because of the limited fodder sources near the settlements, and because of the enormous distances women had to climb up and down the mountain to collect firewood. The nearest source of fuel is 1,500 m below the settlements, and fetching wood was by far the most arduous and time-consuming task women performed.

Recent changes have reduced the value of sorghum leaves and stalks as sources of fodder and fuel. Since the completion of a motor track between the Tihama and the summit of al-Jabal in 1979, wood has been trucked up the mountain from the coast and women no longer have to collect it on foot. In addition, domestic livestock production within the community of al-Jabal has decreased partly as a consequence of the rise in prosperity. Although meat consumption has greatly increased, most meat is imported on the hoof from the Tihama. Cattle were (and to a lesser extent still are) kept for their products more than for their meat; this is now less necessary as dried milk and tinned butter are available in the local market. The new conditions have therefore undermined the incentive to keep animals. Animals were always a high-risk investment: there are many diseases endemic in Yemen, and it has become increasingly expensive to provide shelter.

Wheat and barley were always crops of secondary importance to sorghum — they were cultivated in order to utilise the sorghum terraces productively during the winter months but were probably not vital to the livelihood of most landowners. Now the cost of labour has increased to such an extent that the production of these grains is hardly worthwhile and sorghum terraces are often left bare during the winter.

The high cost of labour is the major disincentive to any grain production, not only in al-Jabal but throughout Yemen. In 1980 the average daily wage in al-Jabal for an unskilled worker (such as would be employed to plough and hoe) was SR 60–100 ($18–30), depending on season, and only a little less in non-qat-growing areas of Yemen. Sorghum, especially, requires a high work-input; each terrace needs to be ploughed or hoed several times both before and after sowing, and there is manuring, thinning and replanting of shoots, weeding and finally harvesting to be done (although the latter task is largely the work of unpaid female family members). A landowner with small capital reserves, no animals and insufficient family labour obviously has little incentive to grow sorghum and every reason to prefer qat, which has low labour requirements compared with all other crops and a high market value, and is therefore much more profitable.

The reduction in sorghum cultivation and the virtual demise of wheat and barley in al-Jabal are not therefore to be attributed entirely to the expansion in qat production. All three crops are of less economic importance than before, for reasons unconnected with the competition from qat on the terraces and in the market-place.

It is possible, furthermore, that qat may actually be helping to sustain what grain production is still taking place in al-Jabal. Many of those who are still growing sorghum are able to afford the high wages for labour because they also grow qat. Qat revenues may therefore be helping to finance grain production. Or to put it another way, those who are cultivating qat are making more than enough money to finance even today's soaring levels of consumption and can therefore afford to maintain a terrace or two of sorghum. A financial incentive to do so is the very high price of locally produced clarified butter (*saman*). Cattle are no longer important for subsistence but have become an important cash-crop in the new affluent conditions.

Qat is certainly helping to sustain the production of banana in al-Jabal. There is every reason to believe that the Jabalis would have stopped growing banana after the construction of the motor track from the Tihama, when imported (Del Monte) bananas flooded the local markets. Most Jabali banana is grown in deep clefts and steep narrow valleys watered by small permanent springs, and requires regular irrigation. These areas are especially vulnerable to the torrents of water which cascade down the steep mountain-sides after heavy rain and banana terraces therefore require considerable maintenance and repair. These factors make banana a very labour-intensive crop and expensive to cultivate. Banana is also relatively perishable and has none of the compensatory prestige or monetary value of qat and coffee. However, the ecological chance that makes al-Jabal suitable for the cultivation of both qat and banana has probably saved the latter from extinction as a local crop. This is because of the vital importance of banana stems as packaging materials for qat. In 1980 banana stems were being sold in the local Jabali market for between SR 50 and SR 200 ($15–60) each, depending on size. By then the fruit had become so unimportant that the stems were often cut down before the bananas had grown.

Qat production has had some important beneficial effects not only on agriculture in al-Jabal, but also on the agriculture of the surrounding mountains and the adjacent areas of the Tihama. These areas are ecologically unsuitable for the cultivation of qat or coffee, but they can and do support grain, vegetables and fruit. It is from these areas that the people of al-Jabal and its neighbouring qat-producing mountain buy a significant proportion of their food. Even though imported wheat is cheaper than Yemeni grain, many people prefer the latter for its flavour and colour, and for making traditional dishes such as sorghum porridge (*'asid*). (There is also an element of prestige in serving sorghum bread and porridge to guests, which may be another factor sustaining Jabali sorghum production.) There are a number of highly valued vegetables and fruits produced locally for which there is no competition from imports: fenugreek (*hulba*), the beans and leaves of which are both important components of the local diet, parsley (*hilf*), leek tops, spring onions, white radishes, various legumes, peaches, apricots, limes and lemons. In addition, large quantities of grapes and pomegranates are traded into al-Jabal from the central plateau area to the east. In short, the wealthy qat-producing communities of the western highlands provide an important market for produce from a wide area.

In many areas of Yemen manpower shortages due to the out-migration of men to work in Saudi Arabia, combined with the consequent high cost of labour at home, have caused a serious decline in agriculture. Many fields and terraces have been abandoned because the revenues from the crops which can be grown on them are insufficient for family requirements and to subsidise expensive maintenance. This often has an irrevocably disastrous effect on agriculture — especially in areas of terraced cultivation. Terraces are inundated by the torrential summer rains, the retaining walls collapse and precious soils are swept down the mountain-sides. It is difficult to imagine that such terraces could ever be reconstructed. This kind of erosion has not taken place in al-Jabal nor in much of the surrounding area. The terraces of al-Jabal are beautifully maintained and have not been allowed to fall into disrepair because their owners have powerful incentives to maintain them and the means to do so.

In addition to its beneficial effects on agriculture, the qat industry has also played a part in the improvement and development of certain important local facilities. The vital importance of trade in al-Jabal, and particularly of the qat trade, provided a powerful stimulus for a major self-help development project which had fundamental repercussions on all sectors of the local economy and everyday life — the construction of the motor track from the Tihama to the settled area at the top of the mountain. At the time this ambitious plan was initiated, in 1978, a government/Local Development Association-sponsored track was under construction which was intended to link the plateau region north of Sa'da in the east with the Tihama below al-Jabal in the west, passing through the mountainous province of Razih. However, work on the eastern section had stopped at the border of Razih, a day's walk from al-Jabal, and work on the Tihama section, which had started at about the same time, had taken the track only as far as the lower slopes of al-Jabal before it also ceased. The people of al-Jabal were extremely impatient for a motor link with the outside world and were frustrated at the lack of progress with the official tracks. They therefore decided to try to complete the track from the Tihama themselves. This would give them access to the Red Sea ports of Yemen and Saudi Arabia, with which they conducted much of their trade; of particular importance would be improved access to the major qat market of Hodaida.

The construction of the track up the mountain from the Tihama was a difficult and expensive undertaking because of the extremely steep and rocky terrain and the high cost of hiring a bulldozer and driver — SR 200 ($60) an hour. The work was financed by collecting money from each adult male in the tribe according to traditional tribal custom whereby each man is obliged, as a formal condition of tribal membership, to contribute financially to certain communal enterprises defined in customary law. These occur mostly in the politico-legal domain — for example, inter-tribal litigation or blood-money payments. It was therefore of great interest to see these centuries-old mechanisms being activated for this modern purpose.

The work on the track proceeded slowly, with frequent hold-ups because of disputes over the route it should take and shortages of funds. Each time the money ran out, often every few days, another collection was made. Finally, after about 18 months, the track reached the settlements at the top of al-Jabal. The construction of this track at local initiative and expense must be counted a tremendous logistical, organisational and financial achievement. By Western standards the track is very unsafe, but it works — vehicles can, albeit with difficulty, get up and down it — and the local people are delighted with it despite its perils. They also have a vested interest in its maintenance as they built it — they do not regard this as the responsibility of a distant government bureaucracy. Whenever there are landfalls on the track, subscriptions are levied from the tribe to pay for their removal.

After the track was completed, the people of al-Jabal negotiated a financial deal with the neighbouring qat-producing tribe to allow this tribe to build a feeder track into its territory from the upper section of the al-Jabal track. The shaikhs of al-Jabal argued quite reasonably that their community should receive some financial compensation for their enormous financial investment in getting the track up the mountain in the first place. The completion of the al-Jabal track provided the impetus for a flurry of road-building on the part of the other Razih tribes, and within two or three years the whole territory was covered by a network of narrow feeder tracks serving all the major settlements. The track from Sa'da finally reached al-Jabal in 1981 to complete the east-west link through the mountains.

The establishment of a motor link with the Tihama, which was both motivated and financed to a significant extent by the qat industry, had important effects on the local economy. It boosted the qat industry itself by providing the traders with quicker and easier access to the major qat market of Hodaida at a time when national demand for qat was high and prices were rising. (The gradual approach of the track from the east also affected qat trading as it reduced the distance the crop had to be transported on donkey-back, and made the qat market of Sa'da increasingly accessible.) The advent of motor transport also resulted in a dramatic increase in commercial activity generally, and a wide range of foodstuffs and other commodities could now be imported more cheaply. Large heavy equipment, which it had previously been impossible to import, could also be hauled up the mountain.

Dozens of Jabali men invested qat profits and money earned in Saudi Arabia in building shops. These were constructed from sheets of galvanised iron, which could now be imported more easily and cheaply than when they were carried up the mountain on camel-back. Between 1977 and 1980 the market nearly doubled in size: in 1977 it had contained about 70 businesses (already a great increase on the early 1970s); by 1980 there were 130. Many of these were open every day, not only on the two main market-days. (It should be noted here that there is no stigma attached to petty trading in al-Jabal as there is elsewhere in Yemen, and the majority of the shopkeepers are Jabalis of 'tribal' status.) Possibly a number of these shops were uneconomic and will be reduced to a more realistic number after any substantial fall in the qat and remittance income which is helping finance them, and in accordance with the more modest consumption levels which would result from a widespread reduction in disposable incomes. It should be emphasised, however, that — at a period when men from many other parts of Yemen were staying long periods abroad, or were seeking employment and constructing new lives in the towns — the men of al-Jabal still felt they had a major social and economic stake in their own community. The ownership of a shop in the market has, after all, important social as well as financial consequences, for it is a place to spend the day and converse with a constant flow of people, and a base for establishing a wide range of relationships. The importance of these less commonly acknowledged aspects of shopkeeping and commerce for the community of al-Jabal can be gauged from the fact that in 1980 about half the adult male population was engaged in some aspect of trade or the provision of services based in the market-place.

The advent of motor transport meant that the days of donkey and camel transport were more or less over, except for short hauls, but the men of al-Jabal transferred to motor vehicles with enthusiasm and confidence. By 1981 no fewer than 20 per cent of adult men owned motor vehicles — mainly four-wheel-drive Toyota pick-ups — and a high proportion were employed in transporting people and commodities up and down the mountain and to other parts of Yemen.

The increase in financial prosperity and improved transportation facilities engendered a number of improvements in the quality of life of the people of al-Jabal — which is not to deny that many problems were also created. A number of the commodities and foodstuffs which became more easily and cheaply available, or which were imported for the first time, made life easier, more comfortable and more healthy — for example, mattresses, blankets, clothing, cooking utensils, buckets and fresh fruit. A number of large generators were imported by local men and within a few months every settlement was electrified. During the day-time some of these generators were used to run flour mills. Motorised flour mills had been introduced in some settlements in the 1950s, but now every family had easy access to one and the laborious grinding of grain on stone hand-mills, a female task, became a thing of the past. The most radical changes, especially for women, were the importation of firewood by truck, and the construction of household cisterns. The two most arduous female chores were thus alleviated at a stroke. Women no longer had to climb down the mountain to fetch firewood, and the storage of water near their homes greatly reduced the quantity of water they had to carry up from springs way below the settlements. Cisterns are a good example of an expensive capital investment made at a period of relative affluence which should continue to benefit the community if the present economic boom comes to an end.

The economic conditions which obtained in Yemen during the second half of the 1970s were almost certainly temporary; the unprecedented affluence experienced by most Yemenis was only a fleeting moment of plenty, and may by now be nearly over. The demand for Yemeni labour from Saudi Arabia has already greatly diminished with the mass importation of cheaper labour from East Asia. Yemen can therefore expect to be thrown back increasingly on its own resources, the most valuable of which are its land and its hardworking people. Unless some alternative valuable export commodity is found to replace its labour (which is unlikely unless oil is discovered), Yemenis may be faced with a great reduction in the material standards they have recently acquired, and may have to try to subsist once again, as they did for centuries, on the land. Sadly, in many areas this will no longer be possible as the fields and terraces have been destroyed by the elements and the communities which tended them have been depleted. In qat-producing areas, however, it will be seen that the crop has performed a kind of holding operation — it has kept alive the agricultural potential and kept the people on the land, tied socially and economically to their small rural communities. In a sense the revenues from qat which flow into areas such as al-Jabal, and thence into the surrounding regions, are equivalent in their effects to the agricultural subsidies which many Third World governments make to rural districts to keep agriculture viable, and to prevent the rural-urban population drift which is familiar throughout the developing world.

## Acknowledgements

The fieldwork on which this chapter is based was conducted on behalf of the Trustees of the British Museum, to whom I am grateful for special leave of absence. The periods spent in Razih were March to October 1977 and October 1979 to June 1980. Further information was provided by Ahmad Muhammad Jibran when he visited London from Razih in 1981; I should like to thank him for all his help both here and in al-Jabal. My gratitude to Ahmad and to all the other Jabalis who helped me will be expressed more fully and effectively when the main results of my research are published. My thanks also go to Dr Cynthia Myntti for her help in the field in 1977, and to Dr J. S. Birks for his painstaking and helpful comments on the first draft of this chapter, although he bears no responsibility for any remaining deficiencies.

## Notes

1. Tomas Gerholm, *Market, Mosque and Mafraj* (University of Stockholm, Stockholm, 1977), p. 56.

# 7 FISCAL AND BUDGETARY POLICIES IN THE YEMEN ARAB REPUBLIC

Abdulaziz Y. Saqqaf

## Introduction

On Thursday 26 September 1962 the Yemen Arab Republic (YAR) was born. The infant republic inherited none of the modern institutions and practices that other countries have long possessed. This was especially true of the financial and economic sectors. There was no Central Bank, no national currency,[1] no formal state budget, no public investments, no modern tax system, and so on. The subsistence agricultural economy was based on barter relations; whatever government bureaucracy had existed was primitive and inept; and the whole country revolved around one man — the Imam.

For the last 20 years the country has been struggling to catch up with the twentieth century. The dramatic growth in the modern sectors has forced the traditional sector to shrink to roughly a third of GNP; growing money incomes have led to a thorough monetisation of the economy; a modern government with the necessary administrative and financial institutions is in place; and, within the public sector, proper revenue and expenditure practices have become the order of the day. Today, public investments[2] are the driving force of the country's development programmes.

This chapter attempts to analyse the evolution of the government financial sector, in terms of institutions as well as annual budgetary figures. From those figures, we shall draw information on the volume of the domestic financial resource-base available to the government, the degree of dependence on foreign financing, and how the government has been financing its budgetary deficits. This in turn sheds light on the government's growing local and foreign debt. In a concluding section we look into possible future directions of Yemeni fiscal policies.

**Financial Institution-Building**

In October 1962, just a month after the September revolution, the
Yemen Bank for Reconstruction and Development (YBRD) was
established, with 51 per cent of the shares held by the government.
Until 1971 the YBRD was to remain the only bank of any kind in the
entire country. Thus, for exactly ten years, it functioned as the
government's central bank and as the public's commercial and
savings bank, as well as an investment bank. Another important
financial institution, the Yemen Currency Board (YCB), was set up
by the end of 1962. The responsibility of the YCB was to issue a
national currency. By July 1963 Bank Misr (Bank of Egypt), acting
on behalf of the YCB, had minted some 20–30 million republican
silver thalers. Of these, 8,375,000 thalers were placed in circulation
in Yemen during 1963/64.[3]

The first Yemeni paper currency was put into circulation on 8
February 1964: again, it was the YCB in collaboration with Bank
Misr which was responsible. In the initial issuance, between 1.2 and
1.5 million one-rial notes were distributed.[4] By mid-1964 a total of
6,970,000 rials in one, five and ten-rial denominations had been
issued. The paper rials were 100 per cent covered in gold, silver and
hard currencies, and they were, by law, interchangeable with the
Maria Theresa and republican silver thalers.

In 1964/65 the government issued its first budget. However, this
and the subsequent budgets were prepared at the end of the relevant
fiscal years, and they did not include large segments of public expenditures and revenues.[5] By 1968 the government gave up issuing even
those budgets because of the intensity of the civil war and the disrup-
tions caused by the sudden withdrawal of Egyptian budgetary,
military and other support. The remainder of the 1960s were very
difficult years. The financial crisis, reflected in the dramatic fall
in the value of the rial,[6] and the chronic shortage of money in the
government were best described by Robert Burrowes:

> The soaring rate of inflation, the collapse of the rial, and the
> growing deficits in the government budget and balance of pay-
> ments were only the most dramatic of the many economic and
> financial problems which the YAR faced during the early years of
> the Al-Iryani era (1967–74) . . .
>     The immediacy of these problems and the expediency they
> required is captured in the words of a prominent minister at the

time: 'About the only thing we could afford was paper, so we had money printed just as fast as we could.'[7]

The financial disarray was such that the Ministry of Treasury was literally shut down during the al-Kurshumi government in 1969. This state of affairs was not to give way to a structured form of government until peace was achieved in 1970. In mid-December 1969 the country applied for membership of the World Bank, the IDA, the IMF and the IFC; its acceptance was announced in Washington in May 1970. In 1970 an eight-man World Bank/Kuwait Fund delegation visited Yemen to evaluate its socio-economic needs, and advise the government on the best course to follow. The delegation urged the government to establish the following institutions:

(1) a central bank;
(2) a central planning organisation;
(3) an office for the budget, as a first step towards modernising the ailing Ministry of Treasury.

On 10 August 1971 legislation authorising the creation of the Central Bank of Yemen was passed. A month later, a number of foreign banks opened branches in Yemen.[8] The existing Technical Office was, in early 1972, transformed into the Central Planning Organisation. Finally, the Central Budget Bureau was established in 1972, and by 1974 it was joined to the Ministry of Treasury to create the Ministry of Finance. By all measures the fiscal year 1973/74 must be considered the base or departure-year for purposes of comparison. The government had its first real and modern budget in that year. The year 1973/74 was also the base-year for the first effort at planning the development of the country — the Three-Year Development Programme.

**Budgetary Policies**

*Expenditure Policies*

From the early days of the revolution, the government decided to take the measures necessary to bring about rapid socio-economic changes in the country. Every year, the government's fiscal policy report reiterates this obligation. As a result, an increasing portion of total government expenditures has been used to finance new investments. Table 7.1 indicates the percentage share of capital investments in the budget.

Table 7.1:    YAR Budget: Percentage of Capital Costs

| Fiscal year | Share of capital expenditure in budget % |
|---|---|
| 1970/71 | 2 |
| 1973/74 | 5 |
| 1974/75 | 16 |
| 1975/76 | 26 |
| 1976/77 | 30 |
| 1977/78 | 39 |
| 1978/79 | 53 |
| 1979/80 | 44 |
| 1981 | 47 |
| 1982 | 47 |
| 1983 | 41 |

Source: Ministry of Finance, (San'a'); various publications on the budget and final accounts.

The steady rise in the share of capital expenditures reflects the country's full thrust towards development. The conspicuous retreat in their share over the last few years indicates that society has accumulated large capital assets which require larger and larger recurrent costs to operate and maintain them.[9] The volume of capital expenditure will probably stabilise around its present level of some 3–4 billion rials (YR) annually. Similarly, total government expenditures will not increase greatly in real terms over the next few years and may actually fall. For the first time in many years, the authorised budgetary expenditures in 1983 were not, in real terms, higher than those in 1982. The figure for 1984 may actually show a decline even in current prices. Table 7.2 traces the growth of total expenditures over the last few years in current and constant prices.

Table 7.2:    YAR: Growth of Government Expenditures (in million YR)

| Fiscal year | Current prices | 1971/72 prices |
|---|---|---|
| 1971/72 | 227.8 | 227.8 |
| 1972/73 | 272.2 | 246.0 |
| 1973/74 | 339.6 | 254.2 |
| 1974/75 | 555.1 | 326.5 |
| 1975/76 | 800.6 | 421.4 |
| 1976/77 | 1,275.7 | 490.6 |
| 1977/78 | 2,166.6 | 677.1 |
| 1978/79 | 3,930.4 | 1,091.8 |
| 1979/80 | 4,513.1 | 1,049.6 |
| 1981 | 6,156.7 | 1,368.2 |

| 1982 | 8,474.8 | 1,765.6 |
| 1983 | 8,953.5 | 1,790.7 |

Sources: Ministry of Finance, *The Government Budget* and *Final Accounts Statistics* (San'a').
Central Bank of Yemen *Annual Reports* (San'a').
Abdulaziz Saqqaf, *Theories in Public Finance and the Fiscal System of the YAR* (al-Madani Press, Cairo, 1983), p 103.

According to the Minister of Finance, total government expenditures will stabilise at their present level. This is already evident from the tightening of allocations and appropriations, and the closer check on expenditures. The reasons for the slow-down of government expenditures are numerous. First, the domestic revenue base has not grown at the expected pace; second, many foreign sources of grants and soft loans have dried up or at least been drastically reduced;[10] and, third, the government is interested in curbing price-rises in the economy. While tightening total outlays, the government is restructuring its expenditures. The services and the productive

Figure 7.1:   YAR: Government Expenditures by Sectors

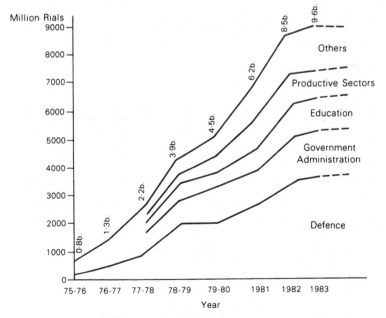

Sources: Ministry of Finance, *The Government Budget* and *Final Accounts Statistics* (San'a').

sectors (agriculture, industry, mining, and so on) have been receiving larger shares of the total budgetary pie. Figure 7.1 traces the budgetary allocations of the major sectors of government activities.

The tightening of government expenditures was especially aimed at recurrent costs, while considerable flexibility was practised in financing development projects. The philosophy behind this attitude was that development projects contribute towards capital accumulation, thereby helping to expand the productive base of the economy. Unfortunately for Yemen, however, such crucial items as maintenance costs, education and health costs are categorised as recurrent costs. Thus, the existing expenditure policies discriminate against them with the result that, although the country is rapidly accumulating capital assets, these are either badly under-utilised or suffer from accelerated depreciation.[11] At this stage, the present value of the marginal product of an extra rial spent in improving use of, or rather maintenance of, existing capital assets is definitely higher than the average present value of the marginal product of an extra rial spent on new investments. Therefore, the tightening of government expenditures should be based on the return per rial of expenditure rather than on the category of expenditures. This may mean that the rate of new project implementation must be reduced, and more allocations must be made for crucial recurrent costs.

*Revenue Policies*

The growth of YAR government revenue has been phenomenal. It rose from YR 79.4 million in 1970/71 to an expected yield of YR 5,460.3 million in 1983, thereby giving a compounded annual growth rate of nearly 40 per cent.[12] Table 7.3 indicates the dramatic growth of government revenues in current and constant prices.

Table 7.3:   YAR: Growth of Government Revenues (in million YR)

| Fiscal year | Current prices | 1971/72 prices |
|---|---|---|
| 1971/72 | 151.2 | 151.2 |
| 1972/73 | 199.0 | 179.8 |
| 1973/74 | 276.9 | 207.3 |
| 1974/75 | 406.6 | 239.2 |
| 1975/76 | 633.5 | 333.4 |
| 1976/77 | 1,312.2 | 504.6 |
| 1977/78 | 1,972.8 | 616.5 |
| 1978/79 | 2,867.8 | 796.6 |
| 1979/80 | 2,830.7 | 658.3 |

| 1981 | 3,443.9 | 765.3 |
| 1982 | 5,281.6 | 1,058.3 |
| 1983 | 5,460.3 | 1,092.1 |

Sources: Ministry of Finance, *The Government Budget* and *Final Accounts Statistics* (San'a').
Central Bank of Yemen, *Annual Reports* (San'a').
Saqqaf, *Theories in Public Finance*, p. 151.

Like other developing countries, the YAR gets most of its revenue from taxes on international trade, primarily customs duty on imports. Of total revenue, taxes make up 75 per cent while the balance comes from profits from government assets and investments, and from proceeds of government services. Direct taxes, especially taxes on industrial and commercial profits, although rising, continue to be marginal. The total tax revenue, excluding customs duty, is expected to exceed the YR 1 billion mark in 1984. Nevertheless, the tax capacity is estimated at well over YR 3 billion.[13] Figure 7.2 provides a break-down of the major sources of government revenue.

Figure 7.2:   YAR: Government Revenue by Sectors

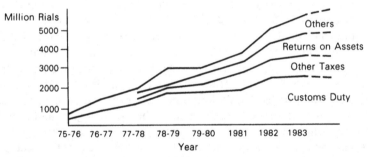

Sources: Ministry of Finance, *The Government Budget* and *Final Accounts Statistics* (San'a').

Any kind of revenue policy in Yemen will have to deal with the prospects of a falling revenue, especially from customs duty. First, the increasing industrialisation will mean more import substitution, thereby reducing government revenue from imports while, of course, increasing revenue from other forms of taxes. Second, the massive transfer of money income from Yemeni workers abroad to their families in Yemen has stabilised, and may have actually declined. It should be noted that such a transfer of income was responsible for triggering high consumption levels which were satisfied through larger and larger import volumes. Now that remittances have stabilised, however, financing those imports has become problematic. Thus the rate of growth of customs revenue has been falling, as observed in Table 7.4.

Table 7.4:    YAR: Rate of Growth of Customs Revenue

| Fiscal year | Annual growth rate of revenue (%) |
|---|---|
| 1976/77 | 235 |
| 1977/78 | 40 |
| 1979/80 | 16 |
| 1981 | 2 |

Source: Ali Sabunah, 'The Future of Customs Revenue in Light of the Economic Changes' in Abdulaziz Saqqaf (ed.), *The Means of Mobilizing Domestic Financial Resources in the YAR* (San'a' University, Dec. 1982), p. 2.

The major potential source of government revenue open to the Yemeni government at this stage is direct taxes. As it is, the government need not expand the tax base by legislating new taxes, it merely needs to have better collection methods. According to the chairman of the Tax Authority, only 37.6 per cent of the total tax dues in 1982 were collected.[14] By the end of 1982 only 192,117 persons and companies had paid their taxes to the Tax Authority, while 234,933 persons and companies in the urban centres had failed to pay.[15] In addition, the backlog of tax arrears has reached staggering levels. In its revenue policy, therefore, the government is best advised to refrain from further legislation of new taxes, and to concentrate on improved collection of existing taxes. The psychological and social perceptions of citizens will create major problems in the future if the government continues to legislate taxes which it cannot collect or enforce. It is better to enforce the existing tax laws in the country cautiously and gradually.

**Financing the Budgetary Deficit**

Although the total deficit in the government budget has been rising over the last 20 years, current revenues have more than covered current costs since 1976. None the less, the rate of growth of the deficit has reached alarming magnitudes, as Table 7.5 indicates.

Table 7.5: YAR: Volume of Budgetary Deficit (in million YR, at current prices)

| | 1973/74 | 74/75 | 75/76 | 76/77 | 77/78 | 78/79 | 79/80 | 81 | 82 | 83 |
|---|---|---|---|---|---|---|---|---|---|---|
| Deficit | 62.7 | 148.5 | 167.1 | | 193.8 | 1,062.6 | 1,682.4 | 2,713 | 3,193 | 3,259 |
| Surplus | | | | 36.5 | | | | | | |

Source: Ministry of Finance, *The Government Budget* and *Final Accounts Statistics* (San'a').

The principal reason for the growth of the budgetary deficit is increased government capital expenditures represented by investments in infrastructure, services and development projects. The growth of the deficit has been phenomenal. As a percentage of GDP, the deficit rose from a mere 3.45 per cent in 1978 to 8.29 in 1979, 19.58 in 1980 and to over 30 in 1981.[16] None the less, according to the Minister of Finance, the government is not alarmed by the rising deficit since most of the borrowed funds are used to expand the productive base of the country.[17]

The budgetary deficit is financed by domestic as well as foreign sources. Internally, the government has been relying on the monetary authorities, especially the Central Bank of Yemen, as Table 7.6 indicates.

Table 7.6:   YAR: Domestic Sources of Deficit Financing (in YR, at current prices)

| Fiscal year | Loans by Central Bank to: | | Loans by other banks to: | |
|---|---|---|---|---|
| | Government | Parastatals | Government | Parastatals |
| 1975/76 | 139.9 | 27.8 | 12.4 | 65.6 |
| 1976/77 | 145.0 | 4.0 | 4.5 | 59.3 |
| 1977/78 | 217.4 | 140.0 | 4.5 | 73.8 |
| 1978/79 | 304.0 | 308.3 | – | 79.0 |
| 1979/80 | 2,035.9 | 556.8 | 4.1 | 134.9 |
| 1980/81 | 4,272.7 | 735.1 | 4.5 | 189.5 |
| 1981/82 | 5,120.2 | 882.9 | 4.5 | 197.9 |

Sources: Central Bank of Yemen, *Quarterly Reports* (San'a').
Yemen Arab Republic, Central Planning Organisation, *Statistical Year Book 1981* (San'a', 1982), 11th Year, Tables 6/8–8/8.

The government has also financed the deficit through currency issue. Between 1975/76 and mid-1983 the money supply increased five-fold — from YR 2,509 million to over YR 13,000 million.[18] Finally, the government is at present studying the feasibility of issuing bonds. Although it is not intended that these bonds will finance the budget deficit *per se*, since they will be earmarked to specific projects, they will none the less provide funds to cover existing and future government expenditures.

The government of the YAR receives foreign aid of roughly YR 1 billion a year to cover the budgetary deficit. This assistance comes from non-Arab as well as Arab countries, notably the Kingdom of Saudi Arabia. In addition, the government has contracted many loans to provide it with the money needed to cover the deficit, and in hard currencies. Figure 7.3 traces the cumulative debt of the Yemeni government over the last few years.

Figure 7.3: YAR: Government Debt Burden (including rial and foreign debt)

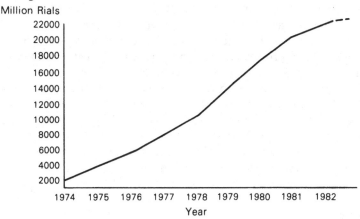

Sources: Ministry of Finance, *The Government Budget* and *Final Accounts Statistics* (San'a').

## Conclusion

In a broad perspective, the fiscal policy of the YAR government is aimed at achieving two objectives:

(1) to generate sufficient domestic resources which the government can use to continue the modernisation process in the country;
(2) to pursue a fiscal system which is conducive and contributive to the development process by limiting any excess fluctuations in the market forces, and by guiding investments, savings, consumption and production.

In general, the government has been fairly successful in achieving the first objective.[19] The achievement of the second objective, however, will require a more coherent fiscal policy. By limiting the growth of money supply, the government can help to curb inflation, and through the Investment Law it has been able to attract some new private investments. Nevertheless, there remain quite a few problems.

A phenomenal consumption spree, a negative government saving rate, and a rising import bill in the face of a falling hard-currency reserve situation are among the major problems.

Over the next decade, government domestic revenue must increase in real terms by at least 8–10 per cent annually if dependence on foreign financing is to be reduced. This can be done through more effective tax collection, an improvement in the tax system and more efficiency in the state-owned and mixed enterprises which will generate larger profits. At the same time, government expenditures must be reduced, even if that means reducing new investments, which must be based on priorities in the light of the opportunity costs and socio-economic returns on those investments. It should be understood that government borrowing will lead to larger future burdens. Therefore, borrowing cannot be part of an acceptable fiscal policy for the future. The proper strategy must include more rigid controls on government spending and better tax collection.

## Notes

1. Until 1964 Yemen used the specie system. Its currency was the Maria Theresa silver thaler minted in Europe.
2. The term 'public investment' is used here to mean government investments.
3. *USA Embassy Report: 1963* (US Embassy, Ta'izz, 1964), pp. 74–5.
4. Mohammed Said al-Attar, *The Economic and Social Backwardness of Yemen* (Algerian National Publications, Third World Series, Algiers, 1965), Arabic version, footnote p. 235.
5. World Bank, *The Economic Development of the YAR* (World Bank report EMA-25a, Washington DC, 16 Oct. 1970), p. 27.
6. From roughtly YR 1 = $1 in 1963 to YR 1 = $0.22 in 1969.
7. Robert Burrowes, 'State-Building in the YAR' (draft of a book, American University of Beirut, Jan. 1977), p. 11.
8. Habib Bank, the Arab Bank, the British Bank of the Middle East, United Bank Ltd, and so on.
9. Abdulaziz Saqqaf, 'Expenditure Policies and the Recurrent Cost Problem in the Yemeni Budget' in Abdulaziz Saqqaf (ed.), *The Means of Mobilizing Domestic Financial Resources in the YAR* (Proceedings of San'a' University Symposium, 12–14 Dec. 1982), pp. 5–6.
10. The glut in the oil market and the fall in oil prices have reduced the revenue of the neighbouring Arab oil countries which are the major source of aid and loans to Yemen. The Iran-Iraq War has also diverted assistance away from Yemen.
11. Saqqaf, 'Expenditure Policies', p. 1.
12. Abdulaziz Saqqaf, *Theories in Public Finance and the Fiscal System of the YAR* (al-Madani Press, Cairo, 1983), p. 154.
13. Abdul-Rahman al-Kuhaly, 'The Tax Capacity in the YAR' in Saqqaf (ed.), *Mobilizing Domestic Financial Resources*, p. 12.
14. Ibid., p. 12.
15. Ibid., p. 15.

16. Mohammed al-A'dhi, 'The Evolution of Government Revenue in the YAR' in Saqqaf (ed.), *Mobilizing Domestic Financial Resources*, pp. 23–4.

17. International Monetary Fund, *Government Finance Statistics Yearbook: 1982* (IMF, Washington DC, 1982), vol. VI, p. 53.

18. Central Bank of Yemen, *Annual Report 1981* (San'a').

19. International Monetary Fund, *Mobilization of Domestic Financial Resources in YAR* (IMF, Washington DC, 1982), p. 72.

# 8 THE DEVELOPMENT OF THE BANKING SECTOR IN THE YEMEN ARAB REPUBLIC

Taher A. Rajab

## Background

The beginnings of a modern banking system can be traced to the establishment of the Yemen Bank for Reconstruction and Development (YBRD) in October 1962, just one month after the September revolution. Before that there was no National Bank, no national currency, no Central Bank and so on. There had been two previous attempts at establishing banking services. The first, by Banque de l'Indochine in 1953, was short-lived and it closed down its only branch in Hodaida a year later. The second attempt was in 1959, when the Saudi National Commercial Bank of Jeddah opened a branch in Hodaida and representative offices in San'a' and Ta'izz. The subsistence-based Yemeni economy was demonetised, using silver as a means of exchange and payment. The silver specie system was based on Maria Theresa thalers minted in Europe. The country's foreign transactions were handled primarily through the branches of foreign banks and money-changers in the British Crown Colony of Aden.

In October 1962 the government of the Yemen Arab Republic (YAR) immediately embarked on the creation of a modern banking system. The Saudi National Commercial Bank was nationalised, and the Yemen Bank was formed with a 51 per cent government equity participation. In addition, the government created the Yemen Currency Board which was responsible for the issue of the national currency. Thus, in July 1963, a Yemeni silver rial was minted in Egypt, and some 20,000,000 rials (YR) were placed in circulation. By 8 February 1964 some 1,500,000 one-rial Yemeni paper currency notes were in circulation. By mid-1964 nearly YR 7,000,000 of paper currency in one-, five- and ten-rial denominations were in circulation. The paper rials were 100 per cent covered in gold, silver and hard currencies.

**Banking in the 1960s**

The Yemen Bank was established by government decree, with the purpose of introducing commercial banking services in the country and helping to finance development projects. It immediately established branches in the three major cities. Before 1962 almost all the trade between Yemen and the outside world was financed by foreign banks established in Aden. Thus the country's foreign trade was dictated by the terms and conditions of those banks. Even Maria Theresa thalers, which served as the Yemeni currency, were bought and sold at Aden Market according to the rates decided by banks and money-changers at Aden, based on the international price of silver. From the beginning, the Yemen Bank, being the only bank in the country, took over the government's accounts, channelled its foreign loans and aid, and financed its expenditures. Thus the Yemen Bank practically took on the activities of a Central Bank as well as a development and commercial bank.

Commercial banking activities in 1960s were the responsibility of the Yemen Bank. During this period, it established a modern banking system in the country by opening current accounts, deposit accounts and saving accounts to the public. It also established business contacts with foreign banks in the United States, Europe and Japan. Through these foreign correspondent banks it become possible for the Yemen Bank to open letters of credit, and thus finance the country's imports and exports. For the first time in the history of what was now the YAR, internal and external trade was being financed directly by a national bank. As a result, the Yemen Bank began gradually to replace the foreign banks in Aden, and freed the economy from dependence on them.

In the same period the Yemen Bank took on the role of a development bank, by establishing different companies, with equity participation by the government and the private sector. For example, the Petroleum Company, the Foreign Trade Company, the Drug Company, the Tobacco and Matches Company and the National Electricity Company were all established during this period. The Yemen Bank, as well as being a promoter and major shareholder in these companies, was also their banker and financier. These activities helped to develop commerce and business in the public and private sectors of the economy, to widen contacts with the international market and to enlarge the scope of internal and external trade. Private citizens also benefited by taking personal loans from the

Yemen Bank to build houses for their own use or for leasing to others. Thus the bank contributed much to solving the housing problem for the waves of emigrants who came to the big cities from abroad and from the countryside. It also provided jobs for thousands of employees. The 1960s ended with the Yemen Bank as the only bank in the country to provide all banking services and finance to the government, the mixed and the private sectors.

**The Period of Peace and New Banks**

The beginning of the 1970s introduced a new stage in the development of banking in the country. This period was marked by internal and external peace for the YAR after the end of the civil war. Peace and stability made it possible for the government to begin thinking of the development of the national economy. In the field of banking, there were two main developments. First, the establishment of the Central Bank of Yemen; and second, permission for foreign banks to operate in the country.

Between 1962 and 1971 the role of the Central Bank was partly carried out by the Yemen Currency Board and partly by the YBRD. In the first week of July 1971 the Central Bank Law was passed by Parliament and on 27 July the Central Bank began its activities. The responsibilities of the Currency Board (the issuing of banknotes and the administration of the government's gold reserves and foreign currency accounts) were transferred to the Central Bank. At the same time all local accounts, loans and aid to the government, which had previously been held by the Yemen Bank, were transferred to the Central Bank. Thus the Central Bank became the government's banker. One of the first objectives of the Central Bank was to fix the rate of exchange of the Yemeni rial against the US dollar. Before the end of 1971 the rate was fixed at YR 5 per dollar and later in 1972 it was fixed at YR 4.5 per dollar. The Central Bank became the controller of all banking activities in the country and the activities of all commercial banks came under its supervision and regulations. Accordingly, all commercial banks opened accounts and deposited their legal and commercial reserves with the Central Bank. Table 8.1 shows the development of the profit and loss account of the Central Bank, taken from its different balance sheets.

Table 8.1:    YAR: Central Bank: Profit and Loss, 1972–80 (in YR)

|  | 30 June 1972 | 30 June 1975 | 30 June 1980 |
|---|---|---|---|
| Income from foreign assets | 10,255,026 | 58,359,656 | 619,803,002 |
| Income from various operations | 3,702,696 | 3,603,241 | 58,984,952 |
| Total income | 13,702,722 | 61,962,897 | 678,787,954 |
| Net profit | 9,836,810 | 37,500,000 | 425,000,000 |

Source: Central Bank of Yemen, various publications (San'a').

The second main development in the field of banking during this period was the government's open-door policy. This meant that the government adopted liberal free-trade and economic policies and, to gain the confidence of the outside world, it permitted foreign banks to operate inside the country. Among the foreign banks permitted to operate in 1971 and 1972 were the Arab Bank, the British Bank of the Middle East, Banque de l'Indochine, Habib Bank, United Bank and, later in 1975, the Bank of Credit and Commerce International and the First National City Bank. By mid-1972 the activities of all commercial banks had increased. For example, total loans increased sharply from YR 86.8 million at 30 June 1971 to YR 115.6 million one year later. During the same period, private-sector deposits increased to YR 9.2 million and public-sector deposits to YR 14.9 million. By mid-1975 the commercial banks were continuing to expand their activities, especially loans to all sectors which reached YR 142.2 million, while total deposits reached YR 155.1 million. Five years later, in mid-1980, total loans by commercial banks to all sectors had reached YR 370.6 million, and deposits with them had grown to YR 1,107.7 million.

The Yemen Bank, for the first time since it was established in 1962, found itself facing strong competition. The coming of foreign banks helped in two main developments. First, the country began to gain the confidence of the outside world, and many foreign companies started to establish business relations with local merchants, some helping to finance local projects for the private sector. Second, strong competition by the foreign banks forced the Yemen Bank to improve its services and to reach out to the different areas of the country. To meet the new challenge, the Yemen Bank opened new branches in the cities and the countryside, and, for the first time in the country's history, the inhabitants of the rural areas were able to use banking services and facilities.

**The Growth of the Banking Sector**

Since 1970 many international organisations have helped the YAR government to plan the development of the country. Thus, for the first time in the country's history, the government introduced the Three-Year Development Programme in 1973/74 and the First Five-Year Development Plan in 1977. In the field of banking, the government began to introduce specialised banks to serve the different sectors of the economy, such as agriculture, industry and housing. First, the Agricultural Credit Bank was established in 1975 with a capital of YR 100 million, paid up totally by the government. For the first time in Yemeni history, farmers found a financial institution to give them direct loans to develop their farms. In the past, farmers had had to ask wealthy landlords to provide them with loans at high rates and with difficult conditions: now the Agricultural Credit Bank has begun to give soft loans to farmers for all kinds of farming projects. It has therefore become cheaper and easier for the farmer to obtain a loan to develop his farm or agricultural project, and banking services have thus reached out to the rural areas of the country through the Agricultural Credit Bank.

A year later, in 1976, the Industrial Bank of Yemen was established by the government with the purpose of financing and developing industrial projects in the country. It was with the birth of this bank that an industrial class began to appear and to establish its identity separately from the traditional merchant-class. Another development in banking services and activities was introduced in a law establishing the Housing Credit Bank. This bank not only gave private loans to individual citizens to build their own homes, but also built blocks of houses which it then sold to individuals. The first project of this type has already been finished. Everybody in San'a' can today feel the impact of this bank on the level of house rents.

During the 1970s, when business and trade were expanding, the YBRD encouraged the establishment of joint banks, such as the Yemen-Kuwait Bank and the Yemen International Bank. The equities of these two banks were shared by the YBRD, local businessmen and foreign participants, such as Kuwaitis, Saudis and the Bank of America. The purpose of these two banks was to promote international banking and foreign investment.

## Conclusion

Within the last 20 years banking activities in the YAR have developed from very low levels to a modern banking system providing all kinds of services. During this period, international banking relations through both local and foreign banks have been developed. The YAR today has worldwide connections through correspondents all over the world. The import and export trade, as well as development projects, are now financed either by local banks or through credit lines from international banks.

## General References

Central Bank of Yemen, *Quarterly Reports* (San'a').
____ *Annual Reports* (San'a').
Government of the Yemen Arab Republic, *Report on the 20th Anniversary of the September 1962 Revolution — the Banking Sector* (San'a', 1982).
Abdulaziz Saqqaf (ed.), *The Means of Mobilizing Domestic Financial Resources in the YAR* (Proceedings of San'a' University Symposium, 12–14 Dec. 1982).
Reports of the Yemen Bank for Reconstruction and Development (San'a').

# 9 CONSUMPTION IN THE YEMEN ARAB REPUBLIC

Nigel Harvey

By the end of May 1983 Yemen's total reserves had tumbled by about $1 billion in almost two years to reach $431 million. That would cover about 2.6 months' imports of foreign goods at 1982 levels. According to the Central Bank, Yemen spent more money on visible imports in 1982 than ever before. It bought goods worth $1.96 billion (61 times more than in 1969–79) or about 69 per cent of the entire GDP in 1981. Its exports in 1982 — the famous Mocha coffee, some cotton, animal hides and, above all, biscuits for Aden — totalled about $5 million.

Of course, Yemen's real export is an 'invisible' — its labour. And in 1982 remittances back home from the Yemeni workers held up well, despite fears of a downturn. Up to one million of them, mostly in Saudi Arabia, were largely responsible for 'private transfers' in 1982, worth about $1.18 billion, a small increase on 1981, but $300 million down on the 1977/78 peak. Even with these remittances, soft loans worth some $260 million and grants, Yemen recorded its largest balance of payments deficit to date at $349 million.

That deficit — highlighted by the new low level of import cover in reserve — is pressing restraint and change on the pattern of imports and consumption that has so altered Yemen in recent years. The deficit has deepened each year since a modest $2 million start in the fiscal year 1979/80. The preceding years were spent amassing reserves from the unspent remainder of remittances flooding the country. But Yemen soon learned how to spend, amid a growing orgy of conspicuous consumerism.

It is an article of faith of the Second Five-Year Development Plan (1982–86) that increased domestic goods production is now a matter of 'utmost urgency' to counter imports. In theory, the plan puts a 1 per cent a year ceiling on growth in imports of goods and services. The 7 per cent target growth-rate in the GDP would be achieved with more output from local farms and new factories, while the composition of imports would shift from consumer goods (51 per cent to 40 per cent in the plan) in favour of more intermediate and capital goods.

The plan suggests that with this strategy and structural change in the economy under way, the payments deficit would lessen, having bottomed out in 1982. The 1982 current account deficit was actually $67 million less than allowed for in the plan, but the capital account surplus was $407 million short, largely because of a shortfall in loans.

However, some aid shortfall was anticipated almost immediately as the plan was drawn up in 1981, when an aid target of $600 million a year appeared more realistic. Expectations were dropped in mid-1982 for $100 million a year from the Arab Development Decade funds which failed to materialise. And however much of the remainder will prove to be available in the medium term, up to $660 million — a year's aid — will have to be spent reconstructing the Dhamar region devastated by earthquakes in December 1982. Finance Minister Muhammad al-A'dhi has indicated that Yemen expects reconstruction aid on top of development support. But only about half the $100 million needed for the initial reconstruction phase due to start shortly has been committed.

Yemen's switch from surplus to deficit came as no surprise. In part it followed the conscious decision that money spent on development was better used than left in the bank. Al-A'dhi continues to argue this, adding that, 'If we have a good policy — this is the main asset.' In April 1982, as potential aid donors were leaving a San'a' conference to launch the new development plan, Prime Minister Abd al-Karim al-Iryani openly admitted the deficit financing: 'This plan will continue to make heavy demands on the balance of payments — one has to be realistic. But I believe that by the end of the plan, the trend will start reversing.'

As early as 1977 a World Bank team was warning that, because of the volatility of foreign remittances and foreign aid as the principal sources of revenue fuelling an upswing in imports, the reserves might crumble. 'Yemen's present comfortable reserve position may therefore be a passing phenomenon', they reported, 'and could be eroded quickly.'

With only 2.6 months of import cover left, that erosion has in theory already happened. In Yemen, however, few events are so concrete, and al-A'dhi for one is somewhat scornful of macro-economic statistics in isolation: 'People who work only from desks make a lot of mistakes.' For Saudi Arabia, even with its own potential $20 billion deficit in 1983, the $400 million-odd deficit that Yemen might face remains, in the estimation of one international financial official, 'peanuts'. A Yemeni official has more eloquently described it as the removal from a very well-provided Riyadh breakfast table of no more than a little pot of caviar. The conventional wisdom is that Saudi Arabia, joined by Kuwait and the Gulf states, would ultimately step in to halt a real fiscal, and thence possibly political, crisis in its highly populous southern neighbour. But Saudi Arabia could tamper, and has already in the past, tampered with aid flows. Even now speculation bubbles in San'a' because of an apparent postponement of the annual Saudi-Yemeni joint commission.

Those questions might best be left for comment by political observers, but Saudi Arabia — having enjoyed the fruits of its Yemeni guest workers — clearly bears some responsibility for the impact on Yemen of almost a decade of economic and social distortion. Yemen has been denuded of a good 35 per cent of its workforce and much of its opportunity in that time to create and build up its own domestic economy. Agricultural output — the economy's mainstay — stagnated during the latter half of the 1970s, in good measure because of the ironic shortage of labour. Valuable cropland was abandoned or turned over in increasing quantities to the lucrative narcotic leaf *qat*, which is easy to grow and found a ready market among the remittance-based newly rich. Food alone accounted for 36 per cent of Yemen's 1981 import bill and expensive new tastes have been acquired. French chickens are flooding Yemen, for example, and may prove cheaper than the indigenous poultry now being promoted.

On the terraces, over-sized new tractors have helped damage centuries of work while elsewhere vehicles, great symbols of the new consumer wealth, are clogging ill-suited towns and streets or decorating villages which still have no fresh water. The proliferation of colour television has a deeper purpose as further help towards welding a national consciousness; San'a' and Aden also compete for viewers. One of the better-known damaging aspects of the new consumerism was a growing trend towards use of bottled milk for babies to replace breast-feeding until an international outcry brought pressure to bear against it. Women (among the illiterate 96 per cent) were unaware of the instructions to sterilise with great care. In a totally different context, industry suffered from lack of available labour and high labour rates in Saudi Arabia have helped push up the prices of local products. It is feared, for example, that local cement may prove more costly than the imports it is meant to supplant.

Private consumers were not alone in the propensity to spend and consume invariably on imported goods. The government itself, long hampered by relative poverty and great difficulty in taxing the wealth around it, also learnt to spend beyond its means. The Central Bank reported its 1982 deficit at almost $900 million, almost 50 per cent of spending. San'a' has become increasingly aware of the need to eye the running costs of new projects closely, even if soft finance were readily available for their construction. Late in 1982 poor road maintenance and the continued closure of 68 new health centres and 196 schools throughout Yemen highlighted the government's financial problems.

The government has been moving to solve its traditional quandary of how to tap private funds for the public good. However, proposals to issue bonds to finance projects' local costs and soak up liquidity with the institutions continue to flounder against Islamic opposition in the People's Constituent Assembly. Earlier in 1983 new customs tariffs were imposed, leaving food and essentials as well as most capital goods untouched, but raising more tax on luxuries, especially cars. A 1 per cent tax is also levied on all imports, for Dhamar reconstruction. However, Yemen's central government continues to face problems with goods imported overland from Saudi Arabia, often on major highways, and with goods undeclared for tax purposes. The Economy Minister, Muhammad al-Shohati, has publicly estimated that smuggling adds at least another 20–25 per cent to imports by volume.

The government is also studying possible increases in electricity, health and other charges in the bid to raise revenues and discourage excessive imports. Cutbacks on planned projects have also been made and others discussed. 'We have no problem adapting to available resources,' Prime Minister al-Iryani has said, 'especially as we do not commit ourselves to projects without [soft] finance.' One year after the situation described at the beginning of this chapter, when reserves had first fallen below the symbolically significant level of three months' import cover, there was no doubt that much had been done — of necessity — to tackle the deficit.

Prime Minister Iryani and both his finance and economy ministers had been replaced later in 1983 by experienced and well-known former cabinet members, perhaps politically better able to impress the need for the import controls already begun in the autumn by the Iryani team. These controls included a ban on fruit and vegetable imports during local seasons, tight management of the issue of import licences and thus letters of credit to finance imports, and several devaluations of the rial after more than a decade of absolute rigidity against the US dollar. They presented a package that could in theory drastically cut 1984 imports to two-thirds of previous levels. However, the controls also inevitably proved a boon to smugglers carrying goods across the northern border and sneaking or under-declaring them past customs officials.

But Central Bank and IMF data suggested that some improvement had already begun in 1983. The overall payments deficit fell 40 per cent to about $200 million and the current account deficit fell 8 per cent to some $550 million. These improvements resulted in large measure from a $150 million fall in visible imports to $1,728 million — including a 16 per cent fall in government imports to $420 million. Remittances also improved slightly, as reflected in the $50 million increase of private transfers to $1,200 million. Outward transfers, partly remittances from resident foreigners like Egyptian teachers, halved to $135 million in 1983. However, official transfers — principally aid grants from foreign governments — also slumped to $160 million in 1983, less than half the flow in 1981. The inflow of borrowed aid was also down slightly to $215 million.

Overall, foreign reserves (minus gold) continued to fall in 1983 until an end-October trough of $329 million coinciding with the start of the government's crackdown on imports and spending. After that they rose slightly before dipping back by the end of April 1984 — despite government efforts to ban virtually all imports except essential foods and industrial inputs.

With its reserve cushion gone, Yemen was beginning to control the heady consumerism of the boom days. But hopes for a new boom now focused on Ma'rib and the promising strike there by the Hunt Oil Company.

# 10 SOCIAL AND ECONOMIC CHANGE IN THE RURAL DISTRIBUTION SYSTEM: WEEKLY MARKETS IN THE YEMEN ARAB REPUBLIC

Günther Schweizer

## Introduction

In the Yemen Arab Republic (YAR), which is a relatively small country, there are several hundred weekly markets.[1] As far back as 1772 Carsten Niebuhr, the famous pioneer of Western research on Yemen, said, 'One can, perhaps, not find any land where there are more markets than in Yemen.'[2] The network of these periodic markets was, and still is, the most important distribution system for the rural areas. The main point to be dealt with here is the influence of recent development processes on the social and economic structure of the traditional market system.[3]

## Characteristics of the Marketing System

There are at least 400 to 500 weekly markets in the YAR. Nowhere are the names, locations and days of those markets systematically recorded — either officially by an authority or unofficially in other sources. Figure 10.1, depicting the 325 weekly markets which the author has so far identified and located, is based on many hundreds of items of information.[4]

Some 50 markets (Figure 10.1) have been investigated more closely. The number of traders and the goods they offered were recorded at each of those weekly markets. Systematic enquiries were made not only of the persons responsible for the market (*shaikh al-suq, hakim al-suq*) but also of a representative selection of traders and craftsmen in the markets.

The size and importance of the weekly markets are very diverse. While only some 30–50 traders congregate at the smallest markets, in most markets this figure is in the hundreds and the largest markets are attended by more than 1,000 traders or craftsmen. Quite often the number of potential customers reaches several thousand in any

Figure 10.1:    YAR: Weekly Markets

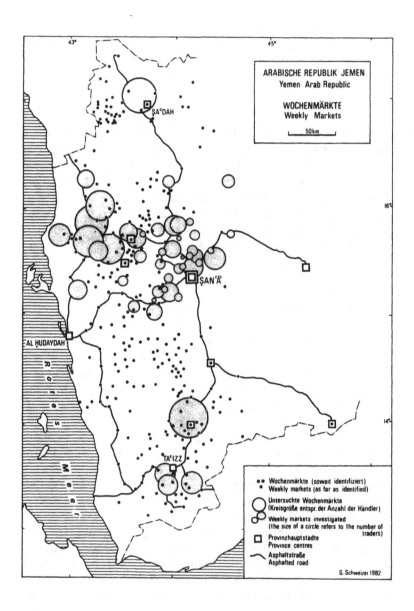

Source: G. Schweizer, 1982.

one market. The average number of traders is around 250 (excluding the livestock market and the *qat* trade).

The spatial distribution of the weekly markets is determined primarily by the distribution of the population and this in turn depends upon the agricultural potential. In places where, for example, isolated massifs such as Jabal Shahara, or largish irrigated oases such as lower Wadi Mawr, occur as enclaves suitable for agriculture and are more densely populated, the number of weekly markets increases. In contrast, in the east of the country, which has few settlements, there is only a small number of weekly markets although some oases, such as those of Ma'rib, should have a corresponding agricultural and population potential. Possibly it is the lack of protection and perhaps a greater reliance on long-distance trading which prevent the establishment of weekly markets in that region.

The network of weekly markets is, however, not only a spatial but also (because of the market-days spread over the week) a temporal or spatio-temporal system. Interestingly, the market system in Yemen has a different temporal pattern from that of other Islamic countries (Table 10.1). Of the 325 markets surveyed, 60 are held on Thursdays compared with only 38 on Fridays and Saturdays. This means that the network of central places — and in Yemen the weekly markets must be viewed as periodic central places — varies considerably in its density on the different days of the week, and the areas pertaining to the central places vary in extent.

Table 10.1: YAR: Temporal Distribution of Weekly Markets in Comparison with other Islamic Regions

| Market Day | Yemen Arab Republic[a] | Central Anatolia[b] | North-Eastern Anatolia[c] | Northern Syria[d] | Asir (Saudi Arabia)[e] |
|---|---|---|---|---|---|
| Fri. | 38 | 27 | 9 | 9 | 6 |
| Sat. | 38 | 16 | 11 | 6 | 13 |
| Sun. | 50 | 11 | 3 | 7 | 21 |
| Mon. | 42 | 17 | 11 | 6 | 25 |
| Tues. | 50 | 14 | 7 | 5 | 21 |
| Wed. | 47 | 14 | 9 | 3 | 12 |
| Thurs. | 60 | 16 | 9 | 7 | 22 |
| Total | 325 | 115 | 59 | 43 | 120 |

Sources: a. Investigations by G. Schweizer in 1981–83.
b. Beate Oettinger, 'Die Wochenmärkte und ihre Rotationen im westlichen Mittelanatolien', *Erdkunde* no. 30 (1976), pp. 19–24.

c. Wolfram Fischer, 'Periodische Märkte im Vorderen Orient, dargestellt an Beispielen aus Nordostanatolien (Türkei) und Nord-afghanistan', unpublished PhD thesis, University of Tübingen, 1982.
d. Mohamed Cheikh Dibes, *Die Wochenmärkte in Nordsyrien* (Mainzer Geographische Studien, 13, Mainz, 1978).
e. Kamal Abdulfattah, *Mountain Farmer and Fellah in Asir, South West Saudi Arabia* (Erlanger Geographische Arbeiten, Sonderband 12, Erlangen, 1981).

One special feature of Yemen's weekly markets is their location in relation to the settlements: only a few of the markets are attached to permanent settlements or even to small towns with a permanent *suq*. The great majority of them are merely open-air markets on sites which are virtually unvisited on other days of the week. The markets are held either in open fields or, in some cases, in a collection of small market-sheds which are not, however, used throughout the week. It is interesting to note that these sheds are the traders' private property while the land on which they stand is owned by other people and, as a result, rentals or market fees may be levied.

Even if the market is sited near a village, there is no functional connection between the settlement and the weekly market. A functional and spatial link between the weekly market and permanent settlement can be observed only in some small towns which also have a permanent suq as well as being the site of a weekly market. Sa'da, Khamir, Raida, Amran, al-Dahi and al-Udain are examples of such small towns. Yet even in these towns the traditional permanent business quarter, the suq, is almost deserted throughout the week because many shops remain closed on non-market-days. The permanent suq also comes to life only on the weekly market-days.[5] From this observation we can conclude that the small towns' permanent trading centres are really no more than an appendix to the weekly market.[6]

**Development Processes**

The main development processes affecting the weekly market system are summarised in Figure 10.2. The first chain of cause and effect dates back to the end of the 1960s, when the country developed links with the world market; imported goods became available and now determine the consumption behaviour of broad strata of the population. Yet this became possible only when private capital had been generated by migrant labour, which forms the root of a

Figure 10.2:   YAR: Recent Development Processes and their Influence on the Weekly Market System

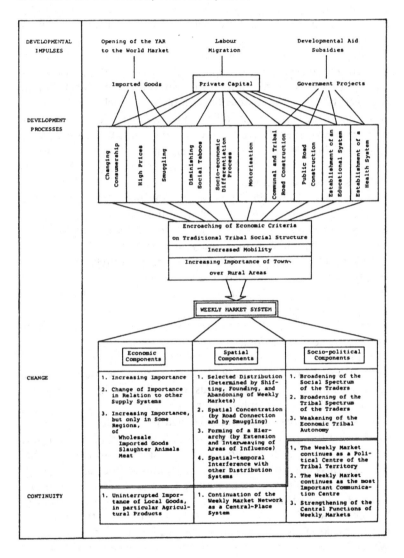

second chain of cause and effect. Finally, a third line begins with the government's projects based on development aid operations, especially the road-building programme. In combination with the capital obtained from abroad, the latter permits the general motorisation of passenger and goods transport.

It is not within the scope of this chapter to examine all the development processes listed in Figure 10.2. The smuggling factor (i.e. imports of goods from Saudi Arabia without paying duty) should, however, be briefly discussed. This smuggling, which involves solely goods imported from industrialised countries, is particularly active in the north and east of the country even though the routes used and the volume of the imports are greatly dependent upon the current political situation. Not only small items, such as chewing-gum, cigarettes and plastic toys, are imported, but also large quantities of imported foods (sugar, wheat and flour) or building materials (cement and structural steel); luxury goods, such as radios and television sets, and valuable capital goods, such as generators, motor vehicles, bulldozers and other building machinery, are also smuggled.

As a result of the large-scale smuggling, an entirely new type of weekly market has developed, the wholesale market for smuggled goods. As examples of these markets we can cite al-Matun in the Jawf, Suq al-Malahit on the north-west frontier, and Suq al-Talh north-west of Sa'da; 120 traders or carriers with heavily-laden large lorries were counted among the 1,100 or so sellers represented at Suq al-Talh. Apart from the urban centres of San'a', Hodaida and Ta'izz, these wholesale weekly markets are now the country's main centres for the distribution of goods from which many retailers from all parts of the country obtain their supplies.

An interesting feature from the social aspect is that smuggling and the trading linked with it are considered as a kind of 'honourable trade', not only for the Bedouin in the east, but also for the tribal farmers; this contrasts with the contemptuous attitude towards non-agricultural activities, such as trading and many crafts, an attitude embedded in the traditional system of values. This observation can be incorporated into a wider context, in other words, the encroachment of economic factors upon the traditional social structure. Whereas poverty and wealth were not previously important elements in assessing the social status of a person or family, they are now becoming increasingly significant. Social taboos are beginning to crumble, as, for example, those connected with under-privileged occupational groups such as butchers, potters, garlic- and other vegetable-growers — all of them occupational groups which play an important part at the weekly markets. Vegetable-growing has in fact experienced a considerable social revaluation — at least in some regions.

### The Impact of Development Processes upon the Weekly Market System

The development processes set out in Figure 10.2 have diverse effects upon the traditional weekly-market system. To classify these, we shall distinguish between the formal, economic, spatial and social components of the change.

The alteration of the buildings of the market-place or market settlement must be mentioned as the main formal aspect of the change. The old stone market-sheds which are typical of the weekly markets in the highlands and western mountain area are no longer big enough for the greater volume of goods offered by the individual traders. The same applies to the low sheds made of leaves or the simple shade-giving roofs of the Tihama markets. Whereas, a few years ago, the goods offered by a trader were limited to one donkey-load, nearly all the sellers now arrive by car or lorry with, in most cases, several traders combining to share the high transport costs.

The old market sheds are hardly used any more since they are too small for the greater volume of goods.[7] Nowadays the goods are set out in open spaces in or around the fringe of the complex of market sheds, or new market buildings are erected. Unlike the old open market sheds, these are lockable so that the goods can be stored. Needless to say, ownership or the tenancy of a permanent shop also increases the trader's willingness to attend every day, even if he has little prospect of selling any noteworthy quantities except on market-days. Consequently, in many weekly markets the trend in recent years has been towards permanent market settlements which have arisen from the market-places and comprise many, in some cases hundreds of, permanent shops and store-rooms. These are built from corrugated iron, cement bond-stones or even concrete.

As examples of this trend, we can cite the large markets of Suq al-Malahit (Nahiyat al-Zahir), Suq al-Khamis al-Haij (Nahiyat Abs) or Suq al-Muharraq (Nahiyat Khairan), all in the northern Tihama. Yet this trend can also be seen in the highlands; the markets of Suq al-Khamis al-Sarara (Iyal Yazid) or al-Rujum (west of al-Tawila) can serve as examples. One of the most interesting cases of this development of a market settlement is Bait Harash, 2 km east of Raida; since 1979 a large planned modern market settlement has quickly been built, containing not only many shops and storerooms but also a wide range of other central-place facilities, such as several filling-stations, a large education centre, a hospital and a mosque. It seems nothing short of paradoxical that this market or central place should be established only 2 km from the old centre and Tuesday market in Raida and — contrary to every economic and locational consideration — also as a Tuesday market. This paradox can be explained by the fact that the new market of Bait Harash has been founded by the Hashid tribal confederation to compete with the old market of Raida which is controlled by the Bakil. This also proves that the tribal influences still remain as strong as ever in the northern highlands of Yemen.

In the consideration of the economic components of the change, the first question regarding the evolution of the weekly markets is simply whether these are being weakened by the recent development processes or whether the traditional supply system can hold its own against those processes. Unfortunately, only a few comparative data[8] are available but they are sufficient to indicate the development of the weekly markets since the early 1970s, i.e. for the decade during which the greatest changes have so far occurred in Yemen's economic development. Table 10.2, in which all the available data are collated, shows that every one of the eleven weekly markets previously surveyed has increased in size; in other words, the number of traders attending the markets has risen. The growth-rates vary: for Suq Baw'an (Nahiyat Bani Matar) the rise is only 16, or 31 per cent in ten years, while for Suq al-Sabt al-Suwaiq (Nahiyat Ibb) it is well above 100 per cent in six or seven years;[9] other markets, such as al-Rawda near San'a', have experienced an even higher growth-rate.

Table 10.2:    YAR: Development of Selected Weekly Markets

| Weekly market | Market day | Number of traders[a] | | Growth rate (%) | Region |
|---|---|---|---|---|---|
| | | Period | 1970s | 1981/82 | |
| Suq Baw'an[a] | Thurs. | 1971–82 | 217 | 284 | + 31 |
| Suq Sahab[a] | Mon. | 1971–81 | 191 | 254 | + 33 |
| Suq al-Sarara[a] | Thurs. | 1971–81 | 96 | 152 | + 58 |
| Al-Rawda[a] | Sun. | 1971–81 | 44 | 241 | +448 |
| Suq al-Thuluth (Bani Hushaish)[a] | Tues. | 1971–81 | 114 | 431 | +278 |

North-central highlands

| | | | | | | |
|---|---|---|---|---|---|---|
| Al-Zahir[b] | Sun. | 1973–82 | 215 | 406 | + 88 | Tihama (Wadi Mawr) |
| Al-Mu'arras[b] | Sat. | 1973–82 | 300 | 736 | +154 | Tihama (Wadi Mawr) |
| Suq al-Khamis al-Haij[b] | Thurs. | 1975–81 | 350 | 838 | +139 | Tihama (Wadi Mawr) |
| Suq al-Dabab[c] | Sun. | 1972–82 | 205 | 310 | + 51 | Southern mountains |
| Suq al-Bi'rain[c] | Wed. | 1972–82 | 142 | 297 | +109 | Southern mountains |
| Suq al-Sabt al-Suwaiq[d] | Sat. | 1975–82 | 303 | 760 | +151 | Southern mountains |

Sources: a. Personal communication by Walter Dostal (Vienna).
b. Hermann A. Escher, *Wirtschafts- und sozialgeographische Untersuchungen in der Wadi Mawr Region (Arabische Republik Jemen)* (Beihefte zum Tübinger Atlas des Vorderen Orients, Reihe B. 23, Wiesbaden, 1976).
c. B. Mitchell and H. A. Escher, *Yemen Arab Republic Feeder Road Study. A Baseline Socio-economic Survey of the Taiz-Turbah Road Influence Area* (2 vols., The World Bank, Washington DC, 1978).
d. Horst Kopp, *Agrargeographie der Arabischen Republik Jemen* (Erlanger Geographische Arbeiten, Sonderband 11, Erlangen, 1981).
e. For 1981/82: investigations by G. Schweizer.

The thesis that the importance of the weekly-market system has been eroded as a result of recent development processes, as we would expect during the transition from a subsistence to a market economy, is therefore clearly refuted. When assessed in terms of the number of traders, the supply system operating through the weekly markets has become more important. At the present time it is impossible to say whether this absolute increase in importance is also a relative increase, in other words, in comparison with other supply systems. The situation seems to differ from region to region.

It would be interesting to continue or extend the comparison in Table 10.2 to cover the goods offered for sale. Unfortunately, there are hardly any comparative data concerning this aspect which could provide information on the development of those goods in either quantitative or qualitative terms. In this respect the principal question is the extent to which local products have so far been supplanted by imported goods. This comparison is possible only for Suq al-Sabt al-Suwaiq near Ibb, thanks to the functional map prepared by H. Kopp:[10] when assessed in terms of the number of traders, imported goods in 1975 accounted for 37 per cent of the total custom while in 1982 this fell to only 26 per cent, according to the author's survey of the market (see also Table 10.3). To some extent, however, Suq al-Sabt may be a special case since it is decidedly an agricultural market and the weekly market is also the largest livestock market in the entire country.

Table 10.3:　YAR: Types and Origin of Goods Offered in Selected Rural Weekly Markets

| Weekly market | Market day | Total no. of traders[a] | Percentage of traders by origin of goods offered[a] | | Number of Livestock | | Region |
|---|---|---|---|---|---|---|---|
| | | | Local | Imported | Cattle | Sheep Goats | |
| Al-Zahir | Sun. | 356 | 62 | 38 | — | 480 | Tihama |
| Al-Mu'arras | Sat. | .713 | 67 | 33 | 53 | 850 | Tihama |
| Al-Raigha | Mon. | 330 | 61 | 39 | — | 330 | Tihama |
| Suq al-Thuluth al-Badwi | Tues. | 565 | 63 | 37 | 83 | 900 | Wadis |
| Jum'at Sari' | Fri. | 72 | 54 | 46 | 3 | 47 | Wadis |
| Suq Sharas | Sun. | 224 | 62 | 38 | 137 | 109 | Wadis |
| Suq al-Dabab | Sun. | 285 | 68 | 32 | 138 | 561 | Southern region |
| Suq al-Bi'rain | Wed. | 202 | 72 | 28 | 53 | 279 | Southern region |
| Suq al-Sabt al-Suwaiq | Sat. | 655 | 74 | 26 | 698 | 1,345 | Southern region |
| Suq al-Sarara | Thurs. | 154 | 56 | 44 | — | — | North-central highlands |
| Suq Bait Na'am | Wed. | 94 | 71 | 29 | — | 20 | North-central highlands |
| Suq Sahab | Mon. | 254 | 62 | 38 | 10 | 30 | North-central highlands |
| Suq al-Khamis (Bani al-Harith) | Thurs. | 281 | 62 | 38 | 74 | 54 | North-central highlands |
| Suq Sha'b (Arhab) | Mon. | 105 | 69 | 31 | 7 | 30 | North-central highlands |
| Suq al-Thuluth (Bani Hushaish) | Tues. | 421 | 67 | 33 | 61 | 30 | Eastern region |
| Suq Barran (Nihm) | Sat. | 53 | 55 | 45 | — | 50 | Eastern region |
| Al-Matun (Al-Jawf) | Mon. | 123 | 42 | 58 | 16 | 128 | Eastern region |
| Turnover by trader and by market day (YR) | Min. | | 50 | 500 | | | |
| | Max. | | 3,000 | 30,000 | | | |

Note: a. Livestock trade and qat trade excluded.

The structure of the goods on offer in 17 weekly markets is classified in more detail in Table 10.3. People familiar with Yemen who can constantly see how the country is flooded with imported goods may at first be surprised that the proportion of those goods is not all that high. Only in a few markets does it rise to 40 per cent, at least when assessed in terms of the number of traders. Traders offering local goods form the majority in every market. These quantitative findings are, however, made less absolute by the fact that the number of traders is always taken as the basic unit of measurement. In no case should the findings be taken to represent the value of the goods or the sales of any specific sector (see Table 10.3). The maximum daily turnover of a trader in local fruit or vegetables is 150–300 rials (YR), while for a wholesaler of imported goods selling anything from wire-mesh fencing to cartons of cigarettes this turnover is at least ten and may even be a hundred times (YR 30,000) greater.

Viewed as a whole, therefore, the structure of the goods on offer in the weekly markets may be characterised as follows: first, local goods retain their importance; and, second, the significance of imported goods, when judged by the number of traders, seems surprisingly small but, when expressed in terms of turnover, may be enormous, at least in the north and east of the country (see Table 10.3, the last two regions), where almost all the imported goods on offer have been smuggled in.

In this chapter we can only briefly refer to other economic developments, such as the relation between the wholesale and retail sectors or the livestock and meat offered for sale (Figure 10.2). In this respect regional factors play an important part, as can easily be seen by examining the sample markets in the east of the country, shown in Table 10.3.

The spatial and social elements of the change and permanency of the weekly-market system will deliberately be examined together, since they are closely interrelated. This close connection between society and geographical areas results from the fact that, in their position as the principal groups generating action or interaction, the Yemeni tribes are defined mainly by their territory; in other words, the regional differences in the country are essentially determined by its division into tribal areas.

The previous example of the establishment of a new market at Bait Harash has already indicated the extent to which a weekly market is linked with the relevant tribe or — more frequently — with one of its sub-divisions. Dostal argues that the tribal weekly market is a means of ensuring the economic autonomy of a tribe.[11] In fact, every weekly market is under the absolute control of a tribal group, usually a division of the tribe. The main function of that group is to guarantee the market-peace by means of its political power. If, for example, the group is not strong enough to obtain expiation for a murder in the market by means of compensation or arbitration, the market is abolished. This is not just a theory of tribal law: during his fieldwork in 1981–83, the author was able to investigate four such cases around San'a' alone.

Although tribal disputes can lead to the closure of markets, they usually result in the weekly market being moved to the territory of another tribal group whose power is strong enough to ensure peace in the market. Economic considerations concerning the site play hardly any part in this process: in other words, the location of this 'central place', and thus the network of central places, is to a large extent determined by social or socio-political and not only by economic factors. The tribal assembly alone decides upon the closure and transfer of the weekly markets and the establishment of new markets. Needless to say, these decisions also take into account economic or transport factors within the latitude allowed by the tribal conditions. In recent years, in fact, some markets have been moved to sites of newly constructed highways[12] or new markets have been established there[13] and remote weekly markets have become less important,[14] but there are also examples where markets on sites with good economic and transport conditions have been closed or have declined.[15]

Taking a general view, it can be said that road-building and the resultant focusing of the flow of traffic have led to a selection and concentration of the network of weekly markets on sites with good communications (Figure 10.3), but these economic and transport influences may be supplanted by tribal factors. The latter consideration applies in particular to the smugglers' markets in the north of the country whose development depends not only upon the relations between the tribes but also upon the relations between a tribe and the central government and Saudi Arabia.

Figure 10.2 indicates a number of other spatial and socio-political components of the change for which empirical proof can be provided. They will be analysed elsewhere and supported by empirical findings. Although a number of changes have occurred and are still occurring in the weekly-market system in relation to the economic, spatial and social or tribal factors, elements of permanency can be found. It is surprising, but in fact typical of Yemen, that these elements are strongest in the socio-political area.

The weekly market continues to be the political centre of the tribe, the place where the assembly of all able-bodied men is held and where the decisions are taken which determine the tribe's destiny and its attitude towards the influences of the modern development processes.

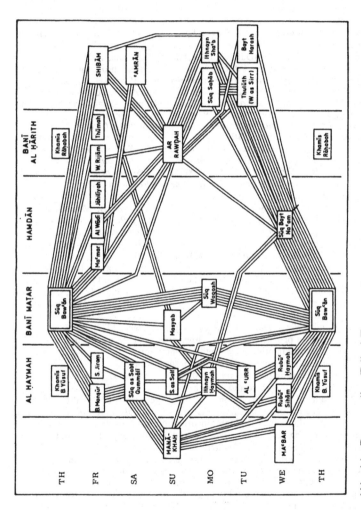

Figure 10.3: Weekly Routes (by Tribal Territories) of Selected Market Traders Interviewed in Suq Baw'an

## Notes

1. A summary of the literature on weekly markets can be found in R. J. Bromley, *Periodic Markets, Daily Markets and Fairs. A Bibliography* (Monash Publications in Geography 10, Melbourne, 1974), and *Periodic Markets, Daily Markets and Fairs. A Bibliography Supplement to 1979* (University College of Swansea, Centre for Development Studies, Monograph 5, 1979). A list of more recent works, especially for the Near East, is given in the bibliography of W. Fischer, 'Periodische Märkte im Vorderen Orient dargestellt an Beispielen aus Nordostanatolien (Türkei) und Nord-afghanistan', unpublished PhD thesis, University of Tübingen, 1982.
   The weekly markets of the YAR have not been systematically investigated but references to individual markets or regional networks of markets can be found in many works, such as: W. Dostal, 'Sozio-ökonomische Aspekte der Stammesdemo-kratie in Nordost-Jemen', *Sociologus*, no. 24 (1974), pp. 1–5, and *Der Markt von San'a'* (Austrian Academy, Vienna, 1979); H. Escher, *Wirtschafts- und sozial-geographische Untersuchungen in der Wadi Mawr Region (Arabische Republik Jemen)* (Beihefte zum Tübinger Atlas des Vorderen Orients, Reihe B. 23, Wiesbaden, 1976); E. Niewöhner-Eberhard, 'Täglicher suq und Wochenmarkt in Sa'dah, Jemen', *Erdkunde*, no. 30, (1976), pp. 24–7; H. Kopp, *Al Qasim. Wirtschafts- und sozialgeographische Strukturen und Entwicklungprozesse in einem Dorf des jemeni-tischen Hochlandes* (Beihefte zum Tübinger Atlas des Vorderen Orients, Reihe B. 31, Wiesbaden, 1977) and *Agrargeographie der Arabischen Republik Jemen* (Erlanger Geographische Arbeiten, Sonderband 11, Erlangen, 1981); B. Mitchell and H. Escher, *Yemen Arab Republic Feeder Road Study. A Baseline Socio-economic Survey of the Taiz-Turbah Road Influence Area* (The World Bank, Washington DC, 1978); and *Yemen Arab Republic Feeder Road Study. A 'during construction' Survey of the Taiz-Turbah Road Influence Area* (The World Bank, Washington DC, 1978; R. Wilson, 'Regular and Permanent Markets in the San'a' Region' in *Arabian Studies* V (University of Cambridge, Middle East Centre, 1979), pp. 189–91; S. Carapico and R. Tutwiler, *Yemeni Agriculture and Economic Change*, (American Institute for Yemeni Studies, San'a', 1981); R. B. Serjeant and R. Lewcock (eds.), *San'a'. An Arabian Islamic City* (World of Islam Festival Trust, London, 1983).

2. C. Niebuhr, *Beschreibung von Arabien* (Copenhagen, 1772), p. 28.

3. This is only a provisional report. Other aspects of the weekly markets in the YAR will be examined in other papers and a monograph.

4. Systematically interpreted for this list of markets are:
   1. The official maps 1:50,000, 1:250,000 and 1:500,000.
   2. The special literature and travel books.
   3. Results of an enquiry among students of geography at San'a' University.

In each of the regions visited, various sources were also questioned about the weekly markets in the vicinity. Valuable information was provided by various people familiar with Yemen, especially Gabriele and Horst Kopp, Edith and Werner Dubach, Gerd Puin and Matthias Weiter.

5. Niewöhner-Eberhard, 'Täglicher suq', also reports that even in Sa'da, the largest and by far the most important town in the north of the country, only about a quarter of the shops in the permanent suq are open on most weekdays (p. 25).

6. Even in the small-town centres where the number of itinerant traders at the weekly markets is small in comparison with the number of permanent shops — Kuhlan, for example — the shop-owners claim that the turnover is very slight on non-market-days, which means that almost the entire weekly turnover is obtained on the weekly market-day.

7. It is interesting to note that at least some of the old market sheds are still used almost exclusively by the traders in 'traditional goods', for example, those selling

coffee-beans and *qishr* (dried husks of the coffee-bean), *shamma* (finely ground tobacco-leaves used for chewing) and also meat.

8. Dostal, *Der Markt von San'a'*, and also information kindly provided by him in correspondence (13 Dec. 1982); Escher, *Wirtschafts*, p. 119; Mitchell and Escher, *A Baseline Socio-economic Survey*, vol. I, p. 159, and *A 'during construction' Survey*, p. 11; Kopp, *Agrargeographie*, pp. 168–9.

9. The livestock available in the market has in fact increased many times over in Suq al-Sabt al-Suwaiq (Nahiyat Ibb) — this could not be included in Table 10.2.

10. Kopp, *Agrargeographie*, p. 169.

11. Dostal, 'Sozio-ökonomische Aspekte.'

12. A typical example is the transfer of the central weekly market in Nihm from al-Madid to the new Ma'rib road where the new Suq Barran weekly market has grown up on the site of a former road-builders' camp.

13. One example for a new establishment is the Suq Wadi Rijam or Suq Hitarish Friday market on the Ma'rib road a few kilometres north-east of San'a'.

14. Examples: Suq Waqash in the region of the Bani Matar, Suq al-Qita' in Nahiyat al-Mahwit, Suq Jum'at Sari' in Nahiyat Bani Sa'd and Dhaifan in Nahiyat Raida.

15. Examples: Suq al-Thuluth (Bani Hushaish), Suq al-Wadi in Wadi Zahr north-west of San'a', al-Ma'mar between San'a' and Amran, Ma'bar between San'a' and Dhamar, and so on.

# 11 THE IMPACT OF EMIGRATION ON SOCIAL STRUCTURE IN THE YEMEN ARAB REPUBLIC

Ahmed al-Kasir

The phenomenon of emigration by Yemenis to seek work has acquired several very complicated dimensions because of its great impact on every aspect of Yemeni life. The rate of emigration has expanded tremendously over the last few years. Its effects have interacted greatly with the factors of development and change in Yemeni society. Indeed, emigration has become a dominant factor in the cultural, social and economic life of the country.

We are, of course, referring to the wave of contemporary emigration. Modern Yemeni emigration started as a result of such factors as the backwardness of the social division of labour, the absence of urban centres to provide employment and the non-availability of work opportunities in non-agricultural fields.[1] This means that emigration in Yemen has stemmed from factors which are different from those which motivated the modern European emigration movement. The large scale of European emigration overseas in the nineteenth and early twentieth centuries resulted from the export of commodities and capital, and colonisation. Since emigration in Yemen has resulted from the backwardness of the division of labour in the first place, the expansion of its scale in current circumstances has made it the one variable which tends to neutralise the other social variables and nullify their effect.

Development and growth are directly related to the emigration process. For example, the local financing of the Second Five-Year Development Plan (1982–86) depends totally on the remittances from expatriates. Estimates of this Plan indicate that 47.2 per cent of its requirements will be financed through 'national savings, including the remittances of the Yemeni expatriates'.[2] It is worth noting that the domestic saving rate was negative during the First Five-Year Plan (1977–81). This means that the domestic financing of the Second Plan depends totally on the remittances of expatriates. One of the paradoxes is that while emigration leads to the decline of production in Yemen in general, yet we look towards it in order to rebuild what it destroyed.[3]

This chapter will deal with the changes brought about by the emigration process in the structure of production, especially in agriculture. It will also treat the impact of these changes on social relations and on the social structure as a whole. In addition, the new economic activities which have appeared in the cities as a result of emigration will be analysed.

**The Impact of Emigration on Agricultural Production**

The first aspect to attract attention is the acute shortage in the agricultural labour force. This is due, of course, to the emigration of agricultural workers and farmers to petroleum-rich Arab countries. According to the Co-operative Population Census carried out in 1981, the total number of emigrants (long-term and short-term) reached 1,396,123.[4] At that time, the labour force in the whole country was only 1,201,699.[5] Since the majority of emigrants are labourers and farmers from rural areas, the impact on agriculture is immediately apparent.

The results of a survey of three Yemeni villages conducted by the author in 1982 indicate that the majority of those who had reached working age left their village and went abroad for employment. For example, the survey showed that the proportion of emigrants to the total adult male population in Amad village (Iyal Suraih district, San'a' province) is about 22 per cent. This percentage is higher in two other villages; it amounts to 66 per cent in Khozaiga and in Hawaisiya (the two villages are part of Maqbana in Ta'izz province).

The shortage of manpower in the agricultural field has led to a series of important and complicated developments which can be summarised as follows:

(1) a rise in the real wages of workers in the field of agriculture (allowing for other factors such as inflation) and a general real rise in the costs of production factors;
(2) a change in the structure of agricultural production;
(3) a decline in grain production;
(4) the abandonment of a proportion of the cultivated land;
(5) an inability of the income from many crops to cover production costs. Hence many farmers began to search for other means of earning their living. An active migration movement began from the countryside to the city; before that, the main current of

emigration from the countryside was towards employment abroad.

We shall deal in some detail with various of these developments in order to evaluate their impact on the social aspect of Yemeni life.

The shortage of agricultural manpower has led to the abandonment of part of the land. Although Yemen is favoured with a high ratio of land to man, extensive land areas have not yet been exploited. Moreover, emigration leads to a further decrease in the farmland already cultivated. 'The area known now to be suitable for cultivation is about 3.5 million hectares in addition to grazing land and marshes which cover 1.6 million hectares. But the land under cultivation is about one million hectares.'[6]

The natural result of leaving part of the land without cultivation is a decrease in the overall area of cultivated land, in grain production and in various other crops such as cotton. The data of the Second Five-Year Plan (1982–86) indicate that total grain production decreased by 14 per cent and cotton production by 63 per cent between 1975/76 and 1980/81.[7] The total production of maize, corn, barley, sorghum and millet was 940,000 t in 1975/76, but dropped to 808,000 t[8] in 1980/81. Table 11.1 compares the development of the area cultivated with corn, barley, maize, sorghum and millet between 1975/76 and 1979/80.

Table 11.1:    YAR: Areas under Grain Cultivation, 1975–80

| Year | Area ('000 ha) | Production ('000 t) |
|---|---|---|
| 1975/76 | 1,197 | 940 |
| 1976/77 | 924 | 760 |
| 1977/78 | 768 | 712 |
| 1978/79 | 826 | 778 |
| 1979/80 | 812 | 788 |

Source: Yemen Arab Republic, Central Planning Organisation (CPO), *Statistical Year Book 1981* (San'a', 1982).

The table shows that the area under grain cultivation in 1979/80 was only about 68 per cent of the area for 1975/76, and that grain production in 1979/80 was about 84 per cent of the 1975/76 figure. The area cultivated with some other crops had, in fact, increased during the same period. The increase in vegetable production was about 43 per cent; in potatoes 72 per cent, and in fruits 35 per cent. But these percentages give an inaccurate impression; a large part of the rise was caused by an increase in productivity, not of the land under cultivation. In actual fact, the increase in the cultivated area of these crops has been marginal and it reclaimed only a very small part of that which was abandoned by grain cultivators. The area under grain cultivation fell by 385,000 ha[9] between 1975/76 and 1979/80, as we have seen. But the increase in the areas for vegetables, potatoes and grapes during the same period was only 12,900 ha, in other words, only 3.35 per cent of the area abandoned by grain cultivators.

Table 11.2 illustrates the increases in more detail. The expansion (which is relatively limited) in growing crops such as vegetables reflects an important trend in Yemeni agriculture, which is towards growing crops of high cash value and quick returns. While part of the land, especially the marginal areas, were being abandoned, efforts were concentrated on the rich lands, which have access to water and whose owners invested in special machinery such as tractors. But this intensification in the exploitation of good land is only possible for farmers who have liquid assets available to them. Such farmers have begun to expand the growing of vegetables for marketing in nearby cities and they have given up growing grains.

Table 11.2: YAR: Areas of Selected Crops under Cultivation, 1975–80

| Year | Dry legumes Area ('000 ha) | Prod. ('000t) | Vegetables Area | Prod. | Potatoes Area | Prod. | Grapes Area | Prod. |
|---|---|---|---|---|---|---|---|---|
| 1975/76 | 76.0 | 76.0 | 20.0 | 183.0 | 6.8 | 76.0 | 8.8 | 42.0 |
| 1976/77 | 72.0 | 82.0 | 22.2 | 210.0 | 8.6 | 100.0 | 10.0 | 47.0 |
| 1977/78 | 76.0 | 77.0 | 23.6 | 226.0 | 9.3 | 107.0 | 10.2 | 45.0 |
| 1978/79 | 74.0 | 79.0 | 26.9 | 230.0 | 9.5 | 116.0 | 10.2 | 49.0 |
| 1979/80 | 72.0 | 80.0 | 26.4 | 254.0 | 10.6 | 127.0 | 11.5 | 55.0 |

Source: CPO, *Statistical Year Book 1981*.

A question arises here. What is the reason behind the tendency towards growing crops of high cash value while cotton-growing is neglected? The author believes that the answer is related to the shortage of agricultural workers and to high wages. Cotton-growing is labour-intensive; it has therefore decreased in spite of cotton's importance as a cash-crop and as a raw material necessary for the development of the textile industry.

**The Expansion in Qat-growing**

The current expansion in *qat*-growing reflects the tendency towards crops which are of high cash value and which are not labour-intensive. The expansion in growing qat therefore occurred at the expense of growing grains and cotton. In addition to the high profit realised from qat, it does not require intensive labour in comparison with some other crops, especially cotton. Moreover, the survey mentioned above concerning Amad village confirms this expansion in the cultivation of qat. This village had not grown qat ten years previously. There were no means of irrigation except rain-water and the water carried over long distances. Four years after qat-growing was started for the first time, three men who had returned from abroad began to grow qat and they were followed by three others in the same village. But the most important expansion in growing qat occurred in 1982; more than 20 new fields for qat appeared in the village. One of the factors helping that expansion was the digging of wells for drinking-water in the village in the second half of 1981. The qat cultivators began to buy the water and transport it to irrigate the qat fields.

Expansion in qat-growing can easily be seen throughout the country. As was mentioned in the draft of the Second Five-Year Plan, the spread of qat, because of the rising income realised by its growers, led to a decrease in the agricultural products available for local and external marketing.[10] This point should be emphasised. As the example of Amad village illustrates, the new qat fields occupied the areas that had been used for growing crops such as maize, barley, lentils and beans. World Bank experts emphasise that expansion in growing qat is at the cost of another crop, coffee. 'The second crop substitution has been extensive substitution of qat to replace another tree crop, coffee.'[11] We do not have accurate details concerning the areas in which qat is cultivated. We have only the results of the selective agricultural census made by the Ministry of Agriculture and Fisheries in the various provinces between the years 1977/78 and 1982/83. These results showed that the qat-cultivated areas in all provinces were 47,213 ha, or 4.56 per cent of the total area under cultivation.[12]

An important consequence of these developments can be seen in the country's increasing dependence on imports in order to satisfy its food needs. In 1980 the value of imported grain and grain products reached 176 per cent of the corresponding figure for 1975. The list of imports now includes maize, corn and barley. The value of imported maize in 1981 was more than four times the value imported in 1974, which was the first year in which Yemen began to import maize.[13]

The majority of those who practise agriculture cannot expand either vegetable-growing or qat-growing. They therefore face a serious problem; growing traditional crops, especially grains, is no longer profitable, for the price of the product does not cover the costs of growing. Hence, the relation between the landowner and the farmer began to change. Landowners began to agree that the farmers should get a large proportion of the crops.

The consequence of all the previous developments was that the inhabitants of the countryside could no longer depend on agriculture as the chief source of income. Emigration became the chief source of income to satisfy the needs of everyday life for large numbers of rural families. Here we witness an important process represented in the transformation of the countryside into a marginal productive source. This explains the appearance of an active internal migration movement, that is, migration from the countryside to the main cities, in addition to emigration abroad. This is prompted by the current process of modernisation.

Previously, the main current of emigration flowed directly from the countryside to outside the country. Then some of these emigrants returned to settle in the cities so that going abroad was a transitional stage between the Yemeni village and the Yemeni city. But today the process has been shortened; migrants move from the village directly to the city without passing through a foreign country. We should note, however, that the current growth of the main cities in the Yemen Arab Republic (YAR) is still due, to a certain extent, to those who return from emigration.

## New Economic Activities and the Change in Social Relations

Many of the productive projects established after the September revolution of 1962 have been connected with emigrants. We can look at some of those aspects of the new economic activities in which returning emigrants engaged and which were responsible for work opportunities. Emigrants established small-scale projects. For instance, we find that most of the small factories and workshops established in San'a' during the last five years have been set up by returned emigrants. It has also become clear that the majority of the workers in these establishments have acquired their crafts and skills during their work abroad. Moreover, the owners of these small establishments and the workers were all living in villages before emigration abroad. A survey of 105 project samples in San'a' indicated that 55 per cent of the new establishments that appeared in San'a' during the preceding five years were set up by returned emigrants. Many of these establishments are engaged in the fields of welding, carpentry, aluminium shaping and car-repairs.

Moreover, those returned emigrants contributed to the introduction of new crafts and industries that were not previously known in Yemen; for example, the manufacture of building-blocks of cement and sand. This new phenomenon will, of course, affect the traditional type of architecture in Yemen. Nowadays many small factories are making this kind of building-block in the various cities and towns. The spread of the phenomenon is attributed to the emigrants in the first place. This fact is amply demonstrated by the example of the inhabitants of Amad village who have returned from Saudi Arabia and established, by themselves, 25 factories of this kind in San'a'. Thus we find that emigration, which appeared as a result of the decline of handicrafts in Yemen, has now contributed to the appearance of new craft industries and economic activities. We should emphasise, however, that most of these establishments are, in fact, very small and employ only from one to five workers.

This kind of economic activity has several social consequences:

(1) It creates two types of population movement. The first is represented in migration from the village to the city. We have noticed that the majority of workers in the block factories belong to the same village as the factory-owner. This form of migration leads to the appearance of small slums within the city. All the workers in these factories live in huts inside the factory itself but they go to the village every Thursday to spend Friday with their families.

(2) The second type of population movement is represented by the process of social mobility. This process allows some agricultural workers to work in non-agricultural vocations. On the other hand, it gives other people the opportunity to escape from the pressure of the traditional class-stratification in the village especially if they belong to an inferior category such as the *nuqqas* — the barbers (*muzayyinun*) or the weavers (*sunna'*).

For instance, we find that among the owners of building-block factories mentioned before, some belong to the category of nuqqas. When those emigrants returned from abroad and invested their savings in such projects they began to get away from the traditional ladder of social hierarchy. Thus a person would acquire a new social status according to his economic position, and not according to his original category of barber or weaver. This form of social mobility acquires new social implications in the conditions prevalent in Yemen. There are still some bases for the occupational division of Yemeni society into lower and upper categories. But we find that the movement introduced by the phenomenon of emigration is now contributing to breaking down that old social system, although it has not yet led to its collapse.

The importance of this factor is that it enables the members of categories called nuqqas to occupy new positions in the process of production and eliminate the traditional status which put them on the lowest rung of the social ladder. Perhaps this explains why the percentage of emigrants from the members of the lowest categories is higher than that of the members of tribes. For instance, the proportion of emigrants to total adult male population of Amad village is 22 per cent, but we find that this proportion rises to 37.5 per cent among the muzayyinun and sunna' who live in the same village. The percentage among the members of the tribes in the village is only 18.6 per cent.

(3) The changes caused by emigration in the field of agricultural production also affect the members of the tribes. They now realise the importance of growing vegetables, for example. Growing different vegetables and marketing them is no longer an occupation of which to be ashamed.

(4) Among the several changes caused by emigration is that concerning half-breeds (*muwalladun*), that is, people who were born in foreign countries to a Yemeni father and a non-Yemeni mother. Their impact is quite evident in social life although their number is not large. Most of them live in the main cities, where they are far removed from the traditional social structure which relates an individual's social status strictly to his birth. They have therefore rebelled against the traditional social stratification.

The continuity of this stratification inevitably means assigning those people to the lower grades of the social hierarchy. But in reality the muwalladun do not form a class in their own right. Neither do they belong to one class in particular, but are scattered among different classes. Among them we find the worker, the craftsman, the merchant, the government official, the intellectual and the employer. The non-traditional nature of those people's behaviour increases their effective role in the process of social change.


**Conclusion**

Emigration has resulted in developments at the economic level, both in the countryside and the city, which have led to changes in the field of social relations. The following points are important:

(1) The change brought about by emigration does not constitute a radical shift in social relations, but we may assume that emigration facilitates the process of change in this field. It leads to a reduction in the sharp traditional division of Yemeni society in occupational categories. We have seen how emigration helped some people to escape from the semi-closed circle within which the nuqqas were imprisoned. Emigration is a factor that helps to break down the old social structure, while at the same time facilitating the creation of a new set of social relations. These new relations are in the stage of formation and are not yet fully crystallised, but emigration is helping to remove the overlap between occupational and class divisions.

(2) The changes which occurred in the field of production led to an increase in the number of participants in the market economy. This is confirmed by the fact that the inhabitants of the villages now buy more foodstuffs than they produce. Moreover, the costs of producing certain crops now exceed their actual market price. This situation had led to a general tendency to look for new sources of income outside agriculture, such as working abroad or migrating to Yemeni cities.

(3) Migration contributed to the separation of large numbers of the population from the land. But this separation did not lead to the appearance of a new specific production-relationship. Most of those who were separated from the land are not yet connected with a very important condition for the appearance of this new relationship, that is, productive capital. Some of those who left the land depend on working abroad as a source of income. Those people will continue to work abroad and visit their country

periodically. Others invest the money they have saved while working abroad in projects in the service field such as groceries, commercial stores and taxis. Still others invest their savings in building houses either for themselves or to rent to others. We now find that many members of the tribes have built houses to let in San'a'.

Only a few of those who left the land have gone into a new production-relationship. Examples are those who invest their savings in a productive project and those who exploit the technical skill they acquired during their stay abroad, and work in their own country for a wage.

This chapter has attempted to present indicators for the changes which, as a result of emigration, are taking place in the field of social relations and social structure in Yemeni society. It does not include a survey of the chief constituents of the present social structure in Yemen; this topic would require a comprehensive study which took into consideration all the social variables.

## Notes

1. See also A. al-Kasir, 'Factors of Yemeni Emigration', *Al-Yaman al-Jadid* (April 1982), San'a'.
2. Yemen Arab Republic, Central Planning Organisation (CPO), *The Second Five-Year Plan 1982–1986* (San'a', March 1982), p. 115: in Arabic.
3. Ibid., p. 31.
4. Yemen Arab Republic, Confederation of Yemeni Development Associations, *Preliminary Results for the Co-operative Population Census* (San'a', Feb. 1981), p. 3: in Arabic.
5. CPO, *Second Five-Year Plan*, p. 20.
6. Ibid., p. 42.
7. Ibid., p. 12.
8. Ibid., p. 34.
9. The details of the agricultural census in all provinces indicate that the abandoned area reached 224,570 ha, that is, 16.6 per cent of the total cultivated area for all crops. They also indicate that the area fallowed was 90,237 ha, or 6.7 per cent of the total cultivated area.
10. CPO *Second Five-Year Plan*, p. 10.
11. Ismail Seragedin *et al., Manpower and International Labour Migration in the Middle East and North Africa* (The World Bank, Washington DC, 1981), p. 172.
12. Yemen Arab Republic, Ministry of Agriculture and Fisheries, *The Summary of the Final Results of the Agricultural Census in the Provinces of the Republic* (San'a', April 1983), p. 49: in Arabic.
13. Yemen Arab Republic, Ministry of Agriculture and Fisheries, *Special Circular on Foreign Trade in Agricultural Materials and Agricultural Needs, 1971–1980* (San'a', Jan. 1982), pp. 9–12: in Arabic.

# 12 EMIGRANT REMITTANCES AND LOCAL DEVELOPMENT: CO-OPERATIVES IN THE YEMEN ARAB REPUBLIC

Jon C. Swanson

## Introduction

On 26 September 1982 the Yemen Arab Republic (YAR) celebrated the twentieth anniversary of its revolt against the Islamic theocracy that had been the centre-piece of Yemeni politics for almost a thousand years. Under the last dynasty of *imams*,[1] Yemen consciously pursued a policy of cultural isolation, until in the late 1950s Imam Ahmad made a few hesitant steps towards the modern world. The autocrat's reluctant flirtation with progress was not enough to satisfy his detractors, however, and his death was quickly followed by a radical challenge to the government of his son and successor.

The subsequent transition from religious oligarchy to military republic was not an easy one and civil war devoured most of the nation's energies in the seven years succeeding the Imam's overthrow. As a consequence, the republicans had to await the second decade of their revolution before turning their attention to the development priorities for which they had fought.

The 1970s were remarkable not only as a period of relative tranquillity, but also as the decade in which migration assumed a central role in the nation's economy. Migration was nothing new for Yemen.[2] In contrast to recent trends, however, early migration drew a relatively small number of people from a few villages and had minor consequences for the economy as a whole.

Ultimately responsible for the wave of emigration were rises in the world prices of oil, which, by the end of the October War of 1973, had left Saudi Arabia and its neighbours on the Gulf awash in petro-dollars. The YAR, which has no commercially exploitable oil resources, was not included directly in this bonanza, but it did benefit indirectly. As the Saudis, Kuwaitis and other nations in the Arabian Peninsula invested in massive housing projects and other construction schemes that created labour demands exceeding their domestic resources, Yemen was able to export its labour force at

132

premium prices. As a result, what had been a trickle of migration in the 1960s became a torrent in the 1970s, involving at least 500,000[3] people out of a population variously estimated at six to eight million. In contrast to earlier migrations, this exodus touched every village and hamlet in the country.

The immediate economic results were a severe reduction in the local labour force and a huge increase in the amount of cash flowing into the country. Thus, while most Third World nations were facing the future with a surplus of labour and a dearth of capital, Yemen's leaders found themselves in the uncommon position of promoting their country's development under conditions of labour shortage and cash surplus.

In the spring of 1974, when queues were forming at passport offices around the country, a change in government brought to power a young army officer named Ibrahim al-Hamdi. One of the programmes he chose to emphasise as a means of increasing support for the central government and building infrastructure in rural areas was the co-operative movement. Rural co-operatives had been a part of the nation's political landscape since the early days of the revolution and had enjoyed sporadic government support. A year prior to al-Hamdi's takeover they were brought under the umbrella of a newly formed national-level organisation, the Confederation of Yemeni Development Associations (CYDA). Subsequent actions by CYDA in 1974, 1975 and later, routinised the organisation, administration and financing of district-level Local Development Associations (LDAs), and created Co-ordinating Councils at the provincial level. The goals of the co-operatives were established as the provision of clean drinking-water, access roads and health care.[4]

Under the tutelage of the central government, the number of co-operatives grew rapidly. Although in 1973 there were only 28 co-operatives, most of which were located in the southern provinces, by 1980 there were over 200 scattered throughout the country. The importance of government initiatives was especially important in the formation of LDAs in the northern provinces. A survey of 25 of Hajja province's 33 co-operatives conducted by the author in 1980 revealed no LDAs pre-dating 1975.

This chapter examines one of these LDAs with special reference to its role in mobilising migrant resources for rural development. Based on eight months of fieldwork carried out in the district of Bani Awwam in Hajja province (November 1980-June 1981),[5] it will show that while the LDA has a creditable record of achievement, it has barely scratched the surface of tapping migrant remittances for developing rural infrastructure. There are three major reasons for its inefficacy in this regard:

(1) It is structurally incapable of directly accessing migrant wealth through taxation.
(2) It has exerted no special effort to excite the interest and participation of the migrant community.
(3) It has been unable to win the confidence of the district's population.

**Environment and Society**

Bani Awwam is located in Hajja governorate in the north-west corner of the YAR. It is a rugged mountainous district averaging 1,000–1,200 m in elevation. Temperatures are moderate, with summer maximums of 86°F and winter minimums of 43°F. Its eight sub-districts (*'izla*) receive 500–600 mm of rain annually which falls in two summer maximums, April–May and July–August.[6] It should also be noted that there is considerable variation from year to year and that, while rains are usual, they are by no means reliable.

Although the district's name, Bani Awwam, suggests the unity of a single tribe this is not the case. The district's population, like that of much of the mountainous periphery, developed from successive waves of migration from the eastern and central highland plateaus. Its population includes tribes from both the Hashid and Bakil tribal confederations and, far from being unified, is divided into a large number of competing factions.

**Economy**

Bani Awwam's economy, like that of most of Yemen, has undergone enormous changes in recent years. Among other things, cash has come to play a much more important role in the lives of most people. Increases in both its use and supply have raised consumption levels markedly. People who a few years ago illuminated their homes with kerosene now own electric generators, televisions and radios. These same families are now likely to supplement their traditional diet of sorghum, millet and milk products with Canadian wheat, Chilean apples and Philippine bananas.

This new affluence is not due to higher productivity, increased cash-cropping or improved prices for agricultural products. To the contrary, it belies a profound underdevelopment, indeed, regression in the traditional agricultural sector which has experienced a decline in the cash-cropping of coffee[7] and a generalised fall in the production of grains. Agriculture in Yemen in general, and Bani Awwam in particular, has increasingly been displaced by emigration as the primary cash source for most families. At the same time the export of labour has led to domestic labour shortages, higher wages and a tendency to relegate agriculture to a secondary or adjunct subsistence role.

Bani Awwam has only recently become a region of emigrants. A few people did leave for Ethiopia at the time of the Italian occupation, but this minor exodus had little impact on the local society and economy. Migration to Saudi Arabia has had more far-reaching consequences for the region. Although it began as early as the 1950s, intra-Peninsular migration did not become extensive until the 1970s. According to the 1981 census, 16 per cent (5,577) of the total population are external migrants. Of these, 96 per cent are reportedly males, most between the ages of 16 and 40. They account for 36 per cent of the total male population.[8]

Most of this migration is temporary; indeed, it cannot be permanent as it is next to impossible for a foreigner to obtain citizenship in the countries of the Gulf. Emigrant Yemenis thus form a transient population of guest workers who remain in the country strictly at the pleasure of the host governments. Most are lone males whose political allegiance follows the same direction as their family ties, towards Bani Awwam and their home village.

The migrant's commitment to family and homeland leads him to minimise expenditures abroad in order to maximise the savings he will take back to his village. Most returnees claim that their expenses are minimal. Food in Saudi Arabia is subsidised by the government and most migrants report that they can eat for $3–6[9] per day or even less if they prepare all of their own food themselves. By contrast, housing is expensive, costing $2,850–8,600 per year, but this is usually shared among 8–12 people so that the monthly rent for any one person is at most $143.

Most migrants take jobs in construction. An unusually large number of Bani Awwamis are employed as tile-layers; however, no job is taboo for a migrant working outside the country.

Their usual tenure in Saudi Arabia is at least six months, though some remain longer and stays of several years are not uncommon. Nevertheless, most migrants return annually, some to work in the fields but more to enjoy the fasting month of Ramadan. The flow of returnees peaks during the weeks preceding the fast, when several times daily the reports of rifles and fire-crackers mark the arrival of a migrant. Such homecomings are joyous, not only because they reunite families, but also because the migrant returns with gifts and cash, at once the fruits of his labour and the trophies of his loneliness.

Few migrants like to leave home and all complain that their life away from their families is hard. However, they return year after year, lured by the cash they are unable to earn in Bani Awwam. How much cash does the migrant repatriate? The amount, of course, varies with his employment. Day labourers and stevedores earn between $28 and $34 per day.[10] Skilled workers such as tile-layers may obtain a daily wage of $85 or more. Such workers are, however, hired by the job or by the day and may be employed only ten or twenty days out of a month. Some salaried workers from the district may work for as little as $285 per month, although this usually includes housing.

The more successful migrants are able to remit money regularly throughout the year, although all prefer to return home with the bulk of their savings intact, an amount which usually ranges between $1,400 and $5,700. With over 5,000 migrants working outside, this aggregates to a very substantial sum. Very little of his money, however, is used to finance development projects.

**Migrant Remittances and Development**

Because migrant remittances enter the economy privately in relatively small amounts, all emigrant societies have had problems harnessing them for infrastructure development and large-scale capital investment.[11] A multitude of techniques have been tried, although none has been very successful. In most cases they lead either to the development of black markets for goods and currency inside the country or they encourage people to hold and invest their money abroad. In either case, the money that does cross the border tends to be dissipated on consumer goods or marginally profitable investments such as shops and transport. Yemen has attempted to capture a portion of its migrants' remittances through increased duties on foreign imports. Unfortunately, its long borders with duty-free Saudi Arabia are virtually impossible to patrol, with the result that millions of dollars' worth of goods slip across the international frontier every month.

In as much as the LDA movement can offer tangible benefits at the local level, one would assume that it was in a stronger position to tap heretofore elusive migrant resources than the central government. The co-operative movement was initiated, however, to provide services and build political support in the relatively inaccessible rural areas. Its role in harnessing migrant capital was largely an afterthought. Thus, LDAs were provided with no statutory power to levy taxes nor was special emphasis placed on engaging migrants in the development process. As a consequence, many if not most of them have barely realised their potential for mobilising what is the largest single source of cash in rural Yemen.

Certainly this appears to be the case in Bani Awwam, where $480,000 was spent on infrastructure projects between 1978 and mid-1981. The direct contribution of Bani Awwam's 5,361 adult male migrants to these projects was, however, less than $16 per person. In order to appreciate why the LDA's record for tapping migrant income is so dismal, the history, organisation, financing and day-to-day operations of the LDA must be examined within the district's socio-political context.

**History**

The LDA in Bani Awwam was only slightly more than five years old at the time of this study. The first administration was elected in the autumn of 1975. At that time the area had no roads and virtually no schools or trained teachers. For all practical purposes, the Bani Awwam LDA was a government-sponsored democratic institution superimposed on a relatively remote and uneducated population with a strong sense of local autonomy at every level from the village to the district, a deep-seated suspicion of the central government and no prior experience with either democratic structures or development.

The first LDA (1975–78) tended to confirm local scepticism of the central power structure. Often faulted for its inactivity and corrupt leadership, it completed only two projects during its tenure and its treasurer resigned because of his dissatisfaction with its operations.

The dubious performance of the first LDA hardly created a sanguine atmosphere for its successor. Although the second co-operative completed eight water projects and over 150km of roads during its first two and a half years in office, it was unable to dispel the legacy of suspicion which it had inherited or achieve a broad base of public support. Contributing to this failure is an organisational structure which concentrates decision-making at the top and encourages little sustained grass-roots participation once the leadership is in place.

**Organisation and Leadership**

The formal structure of all LDAs is prescribed by CYDA, although it may vary somewhat in detail. Thus, the size of the current LDA General Assembly in Bani Awwam differs from that of its predecessor. Nevertheless, the same basic organisation is shared by all LDAs. It consists of two parts, the General Assembly and the Administrative Board. Members of the General Assembly are elected at the sub-district level. They in turn elect an Administrative Board consisting of four officers and three members at large. The officers constitute a chain of command headed by a president, general director, financial secretary and treasurer.

The General Assembly of the Bani Awwam LDA includes 33 members from eight sub-districts.[12] CYDA regulations provide for only one meeting of the General Assembly per year, hardly enough to promote broad-based participation and the free flow of information. According to informants, even this regulation has not been observed. In fact, the General Assembly met only once in two and a half years to elect LDA officers and draw up a plan for development in the district. Officers complain that it is difficult to assemble members because of transportation problems in the district, which as yet has a poorly developed road network. It is also true that the General Assembly has little real power. In spite of these factors and CYDA's requirement of only one meeting per year, more frequent conventions of the General Assembly would be a valuable means of encouraging increased public support and disseminating information. Barring regular meetings, General Assembly members could be systematically employed on an informal basis for these purposes. Unfortunately, neither of these courses has been followed.

Most of the power in the LDA is concentrated in the hands of the LDA officers. Officers are responsible for authorising projects, paying bills, lobbying the central government and generally over- seeing the development of the district. The signatures of all four are required for project authorisation and expenditures, and are usually obtained by the treasurer who often travels about the district in his role as director of religious foundations.

The Administrative Board includes an impressive array of promi- nent citizens from the area. However, co-ordinating their activities and maintaining communication with local citizens is hampered considerably by the fact that three of the four officers, and one of the three members at large, live or spend substantial amounts of time in the provincial or national capitals. Their presence near these power centres is not without its advantages in that it allows them to lobby for projects back home. Nevertheless, they remain only sporadically accessible. Furthermore, since the LDA has no perma- nent office in Bani Awwam and holds no regular meetings, the lines of communication between the Administrative Board, the General Assembly and the citizens are very weak. This lack of regular inter- course is a major factor sustaining the suspicion and mistrust that surround the LDA and its activities. Much of this dissatisfaction revolves around finances, for most people are convinced that the LDA is mishandling their money.

**LDA Finances**

Financing for the Bani Awwam LDA and its activities is derived from three sources: local taxes, CYDA support and citizen contri- butions. The principal source is *zakat*, a fixed tax of 10 per cent on agricultural production which is collected in the district and for- warded to the provincial capital. There funds are divided between the central government and the LDA, with the latter's share credited to the Co-operative Bank in Hajja City.[13] In 1980 these revenues totalled $187,000; however, the LDA does not receive this entire amount.[14]Subtracted immediately from these totals are the *'amalat*, stipends paid to the *shaikhs* and *'aqils*, respectively sub-district and village leaders. The remaining 85 per cent is divided between the government and the LDA according to a formula of 25 per cent for the government and 75 per cent for the LDA. Thus, the LDA share in 1980 was $119,000.

Not all of this money is available to the LDA for infrastructure projects. The four officers' salaries claim $8,000 and teachers' subsidies about $11,000. Official entertainment and miscellaneous expenditures of $5,000 and $10,000 must also be deducted, leaving about $83–93,000. In addition, the LDA receives approximately $22,000 from CYDA,[15] but this still means that it has only some $115,000 for projects to share among 34,000 people scattered through eight different sub-districts.

It is important to realise that all of these funds are collected by agents of the central government and redistributed to the LDA. The co-operative has no role in collecting taxes. Nor does it have the statutory power to increase its income by raising existing taxes or developing new revenue sources such as a tax on remitted income. Its ability to finance large-scale projects over a period of years through loans or bond issues is non-existent. Even its capacity to provide for the recurrent costs of maintaining and repairing existing infrastructure is severely curtailed. The LDA has no choice but to operate on a strictly pay-as-you-go basis. Moreover, its primary source of regular, reliable income is based on a declining sector of the economy which is taxed at a fixed rate.

The LDA's only other revenue comes from citizen contributions, which are collected by sub-district shaikhs and village 'aqils on a project-specific basis. The contributions amounted to 45 per cent of the $480,000 spent on projects between 1978 and mid-1981. It is only through such citizen donations that the LDA realises any direct benefits from migrant remittances. These are, however, minimal. If the total $220,000 in citizen contributions were divided equally among the district's 5,361 adult male migrants, the per migrant donation would amount to only about $16 per year. In fact, citizen contributions are not collected from migrants alone but are shared among all adult males so that the migrant's contribution is even less. The inability of the LDA effectively to increase its share of migrant wealth is a consequence of its failure to pursue migrant support actively, coupled with a general lack of confidence in the LDA.

## The LDA and the Emigrant Community

Although LDA officials complain of the failure of migrants to accept a greater share of the burden for local development, they seem oblivious of the need to take a more active role in soliciting migrant participation in LDA affairs. Nowhere is this more apparent than in the case of LDA elections. According to the rules of CYDA, local co-operative elections are held every three years from about November to December. Elections at the end of the calendar year do not, however, suit the migration pattern. The majority of migrants return home for the fasting month of Ramadan and this would be the ideal time to hold elections if the goal were to maximise migrant involvement.

Of course, the failure to co-ordinate elections with the migration pattern can be charged to CYDA. Nevertheless, even if elections are not held at Ramadan, the local LDA could hold meetings, disseminate information and invite migrant suggestions during this period. Similarly, migrants could be kept abreast of co-operative activities during the year if representatives were sent to Saudi Arabia. This is less of a logistical problem than one might imagine as Bani Awwamis tend to be concentrated in Jeddah and one or two other cities. Moreover, the Saudi Kingdom is only about a day's drive from the district. The LDA could also make use of the constant trickle of migrants, who come and go throughout the year, to transmit letters describing LDA activities. While not all of the district's migrants are literate, there are enough for information to be transmitted readily.

In fact none of these things are done. Indeed, the LDA's Administrative Board generally disregards the importance of informing people of its activities, explaining its problems and inviting the kind of broad-based participation necessary to win popular support. As a result, the LDA is the subject of constant rumour and the target of unending suspicion.

### Politics, Process, and Participation

Perhaps the most frequently heard comments on the LDA are, 'kulluhum lusus' (They are all thieves) and 'yakulu al-fulus' (They eat all of the money). Such sentiments are repeated by young and old alike. In the spring of 1981 this disaffection manifested itself in a direct challenge to the LDA leadership. A dissident faction led by a young army officer from the district confronted officers of the LDA at CYDA headquarters in San'a' and attempted to have them arrested for corruption. The LDA resisted and escaped. Later a commission was despatched from San'a' to investigate the allegations. The LDA was exonerated, but, predictably, the opposition claimed it was a whitewash.

For its part, the LDA Administrative Board has maintained that local shaikhs and 'aqils have frequently collected money for projects and then pocketed part of the money before turning it over to the LDA. In one such case, local leaders are said to have held back some $18,000 in citizen contributions for a road project. On the other hand, the LDA's detractors have charged that in this instance the LDA turned a blind eye to the impropriety in exchange for the shaikhs' silence with respect to the LDA's own malfeasance.

It is ultimately impossible to thread through such a maze of allegations and counter-allegations or to determine the extent to which such charges represent a power struggle between one faction and another. It is likely that the accusations are magnified out of all proportion. What is real, however, is that most people *believe* that their hard-earned money is being mismanaged, mishandled and misplaced, and that the LDA is responsible.

The suspicion and hostility exhibited towards the LDA are based on three factors:

(1) The LDA's identification with the central government, which has traditionally been viewed with scepticism by the rural population.
(2) Competition for scarce resources in a marginal environment, which fosters envy and rivalry at every level of rural society.
(3) The LDA's inexperience with the requirements of democratic forms.

Throughout Yemen's history there has been a constant struggle between state power and local autonomy. Until the revolution, the primary role of the central government was the maintenance of an orderly political environment in which to collect taxes. The provision of services and the improvement of material conditions in the countryside were not conspicuous features of the policy or ideology of the imamate. In these circumstances, it is not surprising that the rural population grew to resent the state and view it with suspicion. The residue of this mistrust persists today despite the republican government's concerted efforts to improve conditions in the rural areas. Thus, in so far as the impetus for the initiation of the LDA came from the central government, its legitimacy is held in doubt and its motives are open to question.

Attitudes towards the central government are only one of the problems faced by Bani Awwam's LDA. One of the less attractive characteristics of traditional agrarian societies is the jealousy which pervades human relationships. In Bani Awwam people often refer to the *hasad* (envy) of their fellow villagers, and questioning the motives and belittling the accomplishments of one's neighbours are common features of village life. George Foster[16] has explained this characteristic of peasant society in terms of what he calls the 'image of limited good', arguing that peasants tend to view the universe and its potential rewards as finite. Accordingly, the economic pie is perceived as fixed, and the success of one's neighbour can occur only at the expense of one's own well-being. While some cultural determinists have treated this attitude as an independent variable responsible at least in part for peasant conservatism and under-development, others have argued more convincingly that the 'image of limited good' represents a realistic perception of environments which do in fact have limited resources.

Yemen has both a marginal environment and a limited resource base. Competition for land and water has marked every level of the society from the family to the tribe, the sub-region and the region. An LDA in such an environment is faced with the difficult task of moderating between the demands of the various sub-regions under its aegis. Recently, for example, American engineers designed a water project which will serve two of Bani Awwam's sub-districts. Its source is a perennial stream bounded on the south by a third sub-district. Before any work had been initiated on the project save for the preliminary design and cost estimate, the shaikh of the third sub-district had accused the LDA president of attempting to steal his water and had vowed ominously that he would not permit this to occur.

A more dramatic example of such intra-regional conflict occurred early in the spring of 1981. This incident resulted when tribesmen from an adjacent sub-district, acting with the owner's permission, attempted to transfer a tractor from the road project on which it was working to a new project site in their area where it had been pre-viously obligated. Such a move would have caused the suspension of work on the first road, which had already been slowed by granite formations along the projected route. Residents to be served by the first project refused to allow the tractor to be shifted and, brandish-ing arms, threatened bloodshed if the tractor were moved. Negotia-tions failed and the situation was resolved only when some eleven policemen were brought from the provincial capital to remove the machine forcibly.

It has been argued that the egalitarian tribal structure of rural Yemen and its tradition of local autonomy have pre-adapted the society for a democratic local organisation like that of the LDA. There are, however, fundamental differences in both the structure and function of the two socio-political forms. First, while tribes have an ideology of egalitarianism, in reality political and economic power are usually concentrated in the hands of a hereditary elite. Though leaders must be and generally are responsive to their constituents, there is no systematic means of regularly changing them. By contrast, equality is a formal element of the LDA in that each member has an equal vote and there exists an orderly mechanism for changing the leadership on a regular basis. Second, membership in the tribe is a birthright, whereas membership in the LDA is voluntary. Legitimacy is, therefore, an intrinsic characteristic of the tribe but must be acquired by the LDA. Third, the function of the tribe has been to protect existing resources, assure access to the means of production and maintain the *status quo*. The role of the LDA, on the other hand, has been to develop resources and provide services. Its activities are, therefore, often a threat to the established economic and social order. Fourth, although both the LDA and the tribe are territorial, there is no necessary correlation between the two. The LDA, operating at the district level, frequently finds itself caught in the middle of the conflicting interests of competing tribes. In the circumstances, the tribe is as often the nemesis of the LDA as the foundation of its success.

As a voluntary democratic organisation, the LDA is unique to the political experience of rural Yemen. Its officers, lacking experience with the dynamics of such organisations, have been more concerned with building projects than building legitimacy. To the extent that the LDA can rely on funds collected and disbursed by the central government, its incentive to increase public involvement is diminished.

In order to improve its effectiveness in providing services and building infrastructure, however, the LDA must increase its revenues. Given the deterioration of the agricultural sector, the obvious source of new income is migrant remittances. The LDA's capacity for tapping these funds is directly proportional to its ability and willingness to invite the participation, not only of migrants, but of the entire community. Only in this way can a broad base of support be developed which cuts across tribal loyalties and transcends traditional rivalries.

## Conclusion

Although Bani Awwam has a respectable record of achievement, its potential for exploiting migrant resources has not been realised. Experience with other LDAs in Hajja and Hodaida provinces suggests that it is by no means unusual in this regard. Indeed, the author is familiar with only one LDA which actively pursues migrant support for local development projects. In this case, the LDA president makes periodic journeys to Saudi Arabia to solicit such support.

The LDAs' obliviousness of their emigrant communities suggests that CYDA should develop a coherent emigrant policy. The umbrella organisation must provide the LDAs with both the tools and the direction necessary for involving migrants in the development process. Their inability to do so is a reflection of the Yemeni government's own ambivalence towards the LDA movement.

Yemen's history has been a tug-of-war betwen state power and local autonomy, with the result that the centre mistrusts the periphery almost as much as the periphery suspects the centre. The LDAs are situated squarely in the middle, representing the state to the villager and the tribesman to the state. Not until this ambiguity is resolved will the LDAs realise their full potential.

## Notes

1. The imams were at once the religious heads of the Zaidi sect of Islam and the secular leaders of Yemen.

2. Most of this early migration was directed to Aden, nearby Djibouti or overseas. Vietnam, Madagascar, the East Indies, East Africa, Europe, and the United States all have or have had Yemeni migrant communities. For a more complete review of the history of Yemeni migration, see: J. C. Swanson, *Emigration and Economic Development: the Case of the Yemen Arab Republic* (Westview Press, Boulder, Colo., 1979), ch. IV.

3. This is a very conservative estimate. The 1981 census suggests a total emigrant population of 1,394,778. Confederation of Yemeni Development Associations, *Summary, Final Results of the Cooperative Population Census*, (Central Planning Organisation, San'a', 1981) p. 9.

4. A. El Muayyad, *Al-Ta'awun: Cooperative Movement in Yemen, Its Beginning and Development* (Confederation of Yemeni Development Associations, San'a',) pp. 3–28.

5. Thanks are due to the United States Agency for International Development and Cornell University for their support of this research.

6. Japan International Co-operations Agency (JICA), *Report on Master Plan*

*Study for Hajjah Province Integrated Rural Development in the Yemen Arab Republic* (JICA, Tokyo, 1980), pp. 2–15.

7. Contrary to the popular stereotype, coffee has been replaced by sorghum and millet and not *qat*, the popular stimulant.

8. These census figures were obtained directly from the Financial Secretary of the Bani Awwam LDA shortly after the completion of the CYDA-sponsored census of 1981.

9. All figures cited in this paper are in US dollars converted at the pre-1983 rate of approximately YR 4.5 to US$1.

10. Although Yemeni workers are unique in being able to enter Saudi Arabia without a labour contract, their employment situation there has been adversely affected by a general slowing of the Saudi economy, together with competition from East Asian workers. As a result, day labourers find fewer opportunities for work and wages have declined. The magnitude of this decline appears to be about 10 per cent for casual labourers and as much as 50 per cent for some salaried workers such as drivers.

11. A review of the effects of emigration on sending societies may be found in J. C. Swanson, 'The Consequences of Emigration for Economic Development: A Review of the Literature', *Papers in Anthropology*, no. 20 (1979), ch. 1.

12. Seats are not apportioned equally among the sub-districts. Nor, for that matter, are they distributed according to population although there is a vague correlation. In fact, there is no logical system constituted because this is the number the various sub-districts chose to elect. Each representative is entitled, however, to a full vote in the subsequent election of the Administrative Board. Apparently this somewhat novel electoral system did not result in controversy since the officers were all elected by fairly wide margins.

13. This system has been changed recently so that LDA shares are now transferred directly to CYDA and disbursed to the LDAs by the central agency.

14. This represented a $20,000 increase over 1979. However, the rise was due primarily to artificial inflation of the cash values of crops, the production of which actually remained the same or declined slightly from the previous year.

15. CYDA's revenues come from a variety of levies on commercial vehicles, cinema, airline and bus tickets, and customs duties. They thus indirectly tax migrant remittances, albeit to a limited extent.

16. George Foster, 'Peasant Society and the Image of Limited Good' in Jack Potter and May Diaz (eds.), *Peasant Society: a Reader* (Little-Brown, Boston, 1967), pp. 300–23.

# 13 LABOUR EMIGRATION AND INTERNAL MIGRATION IN THE YEMEN ARAB REPUBLIC — THE URBAN BUILDING SECTOR

Günter Meyer

## Modern History of Labour Migration in North Yemen

In the densely populated highland areas of Yemen, labour migration has a long tradition reaching back to pre-Islamic times. The modern period of North Yemeni migration evolved during the second half of the nineteenth century, when an increasing number of mainly young men of rural origin moved into the British Crown Colony of Aden in search of work. Many of them became seamen and reached as far as India, Vietnam, or Indonesia, the United States, France or the United Kingdom, where some settled in the ports or industrial cities. Others tried to find work as merchants in East Africa, especially in Ethiopia and Sudan. They often married native women and stayed there permanently, or they returned to their home villages after having spent a period of up to several decades abroad.[1]

This type of long-term emigration has decreased considerably since the 1962 revolution and even more after the end of the civil war in 1970. A strong return flow of North Yemenis, who had been working in Aden and Ethiopia, set in and brought the figure of approximately 330,000 long-term emigrants in 1970 down to about 200,0000 in 1980.[2]

At the same time, however, a rapidly growing number of short-term emigrants moved to Saudi Arabia. The mid-1970s, in particular, are characterised by a dramatic increase of this type of labour emigration. Attracted by high wages in the neighbouring country, about half a million North Yemenis were working in Saudi Arabia in 1980.[3]

## General Effects of Temporary Labour Emigration

There are numerous scientific investigations into the economic and social impact of such large-scale labour emigration processes in different parts of the world. Most of these studies come to the conclusion that the migration of foreign workers, although improving the standard of living of the families of the migrants concerned, frequently proves negative for the labour-sending countries in its overall economic effects, especially in the long run.[4] Among other things it has been repeatedly shown that:

(1) vocational expertise and skills acquired in highly industrialised states are not easily applied in the underdeveloped home countries of the foreign workers;
(2) the repatriated earnings tend to be spent not on productive investments but predominantly on consumption.

Effects such as these have also been observed in the Yemen Arab Republic (YAR). The increasing labour emigration to the oil-producing states of the Arabian Peninsula did lead to a vigorous influx of capital to North Yemen; during the 1970s, however, there was a simultaneous rise in the inflation rate to 30–50 per cent a year, and imports — particularly consumer goods — increased fifteen-fold during the period 1973–78, so that from 1978/79 onwards private cash transfers were no longer able to make up for the continually increasing deficits in the trade balance.[5]

In contrast to the predominantly negative experiences which have generally been the outcome of investigations into re-migration with regard to the know-how acquired abroad and the utilisation of remittances made by foreign workers, R. P. Shaw advanced the thesis that, in the above-mentioned context, the construction sector in the Arab world in particular ought to assume a key role for a positive economic development in labour-sending countries. To substantiate his idea, Shaw argued that the building sector is a leading employer of migrants in both international and internal Arab labour markets. Thus unskilled workers from poorer countries can get an on-the-job training in the oil-rich states and can, by their return, contribute invaluable skills to the development of their home countries, which have embarked on ambitious construction-development programmes.[6]

## Employment in the Building Sector and Migration in the YAR

Anyone who tries to compare Shaw's general thesis with the present situation in the YAR will easily find numerous facts to support the view mentioned above. In 1980/81, for example, about one-third of the country's gross investment was spent on construction and dwellings.[7] At the same time, approximately half of the total industrial workforce was involved in the building sector (manufacturing of building materials, metal fabrication, wood-processing industry, and so on).[8] In addition, trade involving building materials and fittings plays a considerable role in the tertiary sector of the Yemeni economy — as may readily be observed when strolling through urban business streets.

The general thesis on the relationship between labour migration and the construction industry in the Arab world permits a number of consequential conclusions to be drawn in regard to the Yemeni labour market and the associated migration processes. It must be assumed that a considerable proportion of the return migrants, who had been working in the building sector of Saudi Arabia, will not permanently return to their former rural settlement but will rather decide to move to one of the rapidly expanding cities where building construction is booming. There the return migrants can expect a much better chance both to apply their new skills and to invest their savings productively by setting up firms involved in the building sector. This coincidentally will lead to the creation of further new jobs in the cities and an increasing demand for labour. In the YAR, however, where in 1975 still no more than 11 per cent of the population lived in urban settlements with more than 2,000 inhabitants,[9] an additional demand for workers in the cities can only be met by a further increase in rural-urban migration, or by labour immigration from countries with lower income levels.[10]

## Empirical Surveys and the Data Base

The theoretical exposition presented above is examined by questioning employees in the urban building sector about their migration behaviour and their socio-economic circumstances in order to find out more about the pattern of both temporary labour emigration and internal migration.[11] In 17 urban centres, among them the six

largest cities of the YAR, employees in the following branches of the
building sector were included in the survey:

(1) Firms specialising in the production of building materials,
    including firms producing concrete building-blocks and floor
    tiles as well as brickyards.
(2) Handiwork and assembly firms, manufacturing prefabricated
    components such as:
    — timber doors and window-frames;
    — iron gates, window grilles and water tanks;
    — stucco windows with tinted glass; and
    — aluminium doors and window-frames.
(3) Retail and wholesale firms dealing in plumbing and building
    materials.

Building firms in the narrower sense have not been included.
Apart from a few Yemeni and foreign construction firms, which are
chiefly concerned with large projects, the majority of new building
work is carried out either by the owner himself with additional
hiring of building trade artisans, or under the supervision of
builders who do not employ a regular labour force but pass on *ad
hoc* orders to self-employed specialists whenever the need arises.
The artisans and entrepreneurs of this sort in the building trade,
mostly without official registration, elusive in the main, escape even
a near-complete survey owing to their activities on continually
changing building sites. On the other hand, the locations of firms
included in the survey, which rely on their accessibility to customers,
are relatively easily pinpointed in the course of a systematic, and in
part repeated, combing of all the streets in an urban centre.

During two field enquiries, carried out in autumn 1982 and in
spring 1983, a total of 7,149 employees in about 2,700 firms belonging to the urban building sector were questioned by the author. So
far the complete results from the first period of survey in San'a' are
available, while only some selected data have been evaluated from
the second field enquiry. On the basis of these data materials, this
chapter will attempt to examine different features of the Yemeni
migration system and the impact of labour migration upon economic and social development in the urban settlements of the YAR.

**Previous Migration Experiences of Employees in the Urban
Building Sector**

If one asks workers from the construction industry in any North
Yemeni town about their place of birth, one will find that only very
few of them are of urban origin. Among the 7,149 persons questioned in the context of this investigation, native inhabitants of the
respective towns were in the minority and totalled no more than 10
per cent of the workers, while the overwhelming majority consisted
of rural-urban migrants. At the time, however, when these people
decided to move from their village to a town, many of them had
already worked abroad. As is shown by Figure 13.1, about 30 per
cent of the employees had previously joined the flow of temporary
labour emigrants before they took up their present activity in one of
the 17 investigated urban settlements.

As far as the direction of the emigration flow is concerned, the
different sectors of the circles in Figure 13.1 clearly indicate that
migration to the oil-producing states of the Arabian Peninsula pre-
dominates. The earliest cases of temporary employment in Saudi
Arabia, which are included in the terms of the investigation in
San'a', go back to the mid-1950s, whereas the peak occurred in the
period 1975–78. The total length of stay in Saudi Arabia, which is
often made up of several single journeys, usually extends over a
period of four to ten years, and in exceptional cases of even up to 20
years. An increasing frequency in the number of trips to the neighbouring country is accompanied by a decrease in the length of time
spent abroad: this ranges from an average of three years and nine
months on the occasion of the first journey to 18 months during the
fourth work period in Saudi Arabia.

Whilst many of the workers from the Hujariya, which is situated
south of Ta'izz, had previously worked in Aden, others — especially from the districts of Rida' and Dhamar — had initially been
employed in Ethiopia or in Sudan, or in other overseas states. As
mentioned above, these countries have a considerably longer tradition as a target of Yemenis seeking work than do the oil-producing
states of the Arabian Peninsula. The oldest former emigrant in
San'a' returned from Ethiopia, for example, was registered as
having already arrived in Addis Ababa during the First World War.
He had worked there as a trader, as did many other Yemenis. Early
in the 1970s he, too, had joined the crowd of those who, after
decades spent in African states, were then returning home, hoping

Figure 13.1:    Previous Migration by Employees in the Building
Sector of 17 Urban Settlements In the YAR

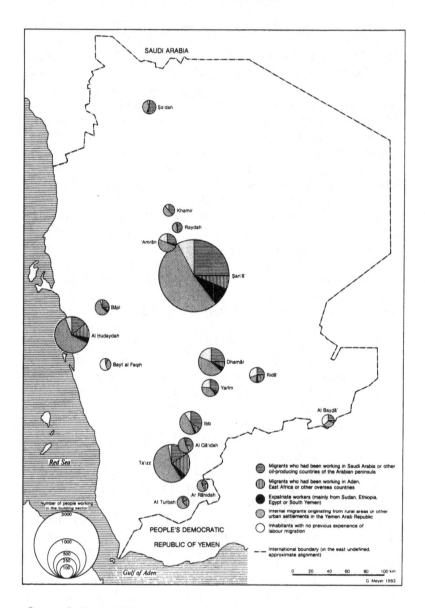

Source: G. Meyer, 1983.

for a considerable improvement in the economic starting-position so far as the investing of their capital accumulated abroad was concerned, once the 1962 revolution had done away with the rule of the Imam and the civil war had come to an end.

### Spatial Aspects of Rural-urban Migration

The catchment areas of urban centres correlate strongly to the size of the respective settlements. This general rule can also be applied to the spatial system of internal migration in the YAR. Whereas the vast majority of rural-urban migrants in small towns with less than 5,000 inhabitants (Turba, Raida) originate from rural settlements within a distance of up to 10 km from the urban centre, the radius of the main migration into large towns with 30,000 to 40,000 inhabitants (Ibb or Dhamar) is extended to about 30 km. Much wider are the catchment areas of the three major cities Ta'izz (about 116,000 inhabitants in 1981[12]), Hodaida (126,000) and San'a' (279,000). As Figure 13.2 indicates, the rural-urban migrants who work in the building sector of the capital originate mainly from the central and southern highlands. There are almost no migrants from the northern and eastern parts of the country. This may be explained by the fact that in those areas the influence of the central government is still small, thus permitting the tribes to preserve to a large extent their autonomy and their traditional system of social values, according to which life in a Yemeni town is regarded as inferior in comparison with life in a tribal settlement.

The Tihama is another region which is strongly under-represented among the migrants working in the building industry of the capital. Those few employees from the western lowlands who were questioned in the context of the survey had come to San'a' only on a seasonal basis, to work there for a period of some weeks in firms producing concrete building-blocks. It seems that the social barriers between the ethnically and religiously different population groups of the central highlands and the Tihama are very strong, so that only relatively few people from the western lowlands have settled in San'a', while the number of people who have moved down from the central highlands to live permanently in Hodaida is also very small. There is one extremely mobile group of people in the YAR who seem to care neither about social barriers nor about the distance factor in connection with their decision to move to different urban centres.

Figure 13.2:    Internal Migration to the Three Major Cities of the YAR by Employees in the Building Sector

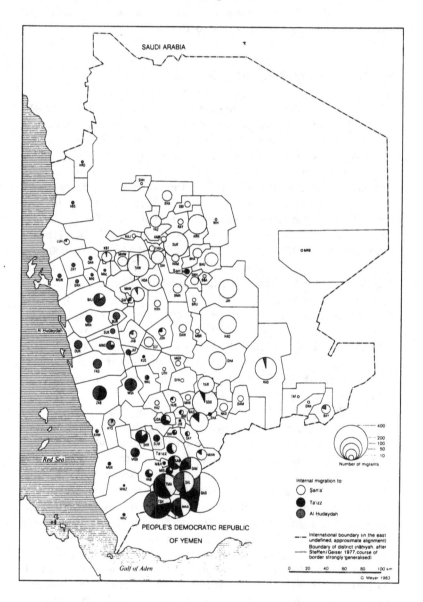

Source: G. Meyer, 1983.

They originate from the Hujariya and are probably to be found in almost every urban settlement of the YAR.[13] In the course of the survey, a surprisingly high number of migrants from the Hujariya were questioned not only in the three major cities (Figure 13.2) but also in small and remote towns such as Khamir and Sa'da.

## Migration Pattern of Employees in the Building Sector in San'a'

In order to facilitate a more discriminatory approach to the migration behaviour, those employed in the building sector of San'a' were divided as follows: first, proprietors of firms, members of the family or close relations of the proprietors; second, other labour from the place of origin of the proprietors; and, third, other employees with no close connection with their employers. The migration patterns of these four groups are represented in Figure 13.3. The diagram shows that only a small proportion of all the firms' managers registered in San'a' in autumn 1982 were born in the capital, whilst the overwhelming majority had moved in from the villages. Approximately two-thirds of the managers of firms had previously been employed abroad; some did not move straight to San'a' after their return, but worked in other Yemeni towns such as Ta'izz or Hodaida before deciding to migrate to the capital.

Having set up business in San'a', many of the proprietors preferred to employ members of their family or close relatives, most of whom came direct from the villages. Only very few had returned from abroad. The same applies to the remaining employees from the home villages of the proprietors, many of whom constitute seasonal labour; they continue to cultivate their fields in the home village, coming to work on building sites in San'a' only during those months when the fields require little attention. A group of this kind can also be discerned among the other employees. In addition, there is a considerable number of employees from countries with lower wage levels, especially from Sudan.

Individual branches of the building sector characteristically diverge from the general pattern of firms presented here. This can be illustrated by the following example of two selected groups of firms and their employees. Nearly all proprietors of 120 firms producing concrete building-blocks in San'a' are of rural origin and have previously worked in Saudi Arabia. They employ relatively few members of their own families or closer relatives but numerous seasonal

Figure 13.3:  Migration Pattern of Employees Registered in the Building Sector in San'a'

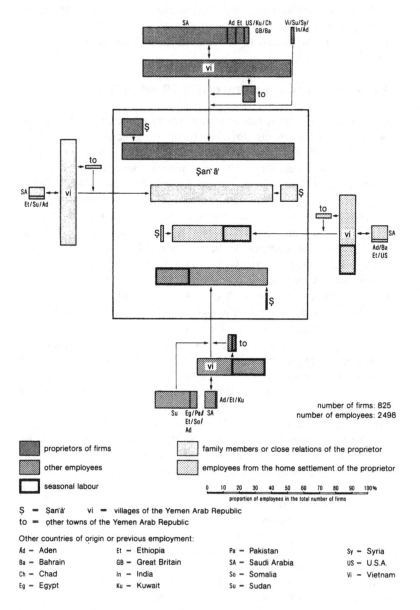

number of firms: 825
number of employees: 2498

proprietors of firms

other employees

seasonal labour

family members or close relations of the proprietor

employees from the home settlement of the proprietor

0  10  20  30  40  50  60  70  80  90  100%
proportion of employees in the total number of firms

Ş = Şan'ā'    vi = villages of the Yemen Arab Republic
to = other towns of the Yemen Arab Republic

Other countries of origin or previous employment:

| | | | |
|---|---|---|---|
| Ad – Aden | Et – Ethiopia | Pa – Pakistan | Sy – Syria |
| Ba – Bahrain | GB – Great Britain | SA – Saudi Arabia | US – U.S.A. |
| Ch – Chad | In – India | So – Somalia | Vi – Vietnam |
| Eg – Egypt | Ku – Kuwait | Su – Sudan | |

workers from their home villages and other villages, as well as a remarkably large number (about 150) of Sudanese workers. This is evidently a very recent development, for all the Sudanese questioned at these production plants had come to the YAR for the first time in the summer of 1982. Among them was a group of six young teachers who proudly declared that they earned as much as piece-workers making concrete blocks in San'a' in four days as they could in one month as teachers in Sudan.

Somewhat different are the composition and migration pattern of the employees who work in firms manufacturing wooden doors and window-frames in San'a'. As this kind of craftsmanship has a long tradition in Yemen, it is obvious that labour emigration is of relatively minor significance in that branch. But even here, approximately every third proprietor of a firm has previously worked abroad, usually in Saudi Arabia and sometimes in Aden. Characteristic of the employment structure of these firms is the relatively high proportion of family members or close relatives of the proprietor. If there is no son or younger brother to help in the workshop, heads of firms are commonly prepared to take a younger nephew of about ten years of age, or other boys from their village. Many of these boys attend school in the mornings and work for their bed and board in the joinery during the afternoons and evenings. This pattern is typical for other branches, too, and is an important feature for the understanding of the general system of rural-urban migration in the YAR.

### Relevance of Temporary Labour Emigration for the Acquisition of Vocational Expertise and Capital

Taking up the introductory theoretical exposition again about the key role of the building sector in the economic development of the labour-sending countries, we must also investigate where the owners of the firms under consideration have acquired their vocational expertise and the capital to set up their enterprises. Figure 13.4 answers this question as regards the proprietors of firms operating in the building sector of San'a'. As expected, the oil-producing states quite clearly dominate in the acquisition of vocational knowledge and even more so in their role as sources of capital. In this respect, the influence of Saudi Arabia is not only extremely strong among the owners of firms producing concrete blocks but also among the welders manufacturing iron gates and among the proprietors of small industrial establishments assembling aluminium doors — all of them branches which were unknown in Yemen until recently.

**Figure 13.4: Acquisition of Expertise and Capital Needed for Setting up Business by Proprietors Operating in the San'a' Building Sector**

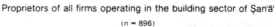

Proprietors of all firms operating in the building sector of Şan'ā'

(n = 896)

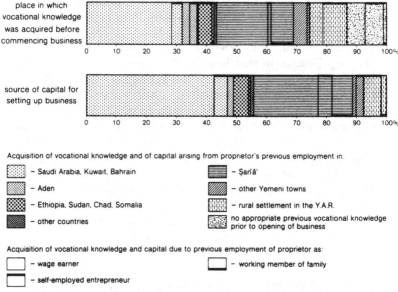

On the other hand, temporary labour migration to Saudi Arabia has been of only minor importance, or of hardly any relevance at all, as a source of skill and capital for the owners of firms belonging to traditional branches of the building sector such as brickyards and workshops for stucco windows or for timber doors. Most of the proprietors of these groups of firms have acquired the necessary know-how in San'a', predominantly as wage-earners, but to a small extent as self-employed entrepreneurs or as working members of the family in their fathers' businesses.

A small number of managers gained their vocational expertise in other Yemeni towns or in their home villages. However, there are also a few entrepreneurs who had no specialist vocational knowledge when setting up business, having previously worked in other branches of employment. This group is highly over-represented among the owners of retail and wholesale firms dealing in plumbing and building materials. Among them are numerous people who deployed the capital acquired abroad in some other capacity in order to establish a business in San'a', and many farmers, who, having become rich by growing *qat* or grapes, invested their money in the commerce of the capital.

## Evolution of a Local Migration System: a Case Study from the Hujariya

In order to illustrate the development of a migration system concerning migrants from the same area of origin, the migration history of 417 employees who worked in the urban building sector and came from the rural district of Aruq in the Hujariya was examined in detail. Aruq is situated some 5–10 km south-west of al-Rahida and can be characterised as a rugged mountainous area with scattered, small-size settlements. Figures 13.4 and 13.5 indicate that many migrants from Aruq had been abroad before they moved to one of the urban centres in the YAR. The earliest migration flow began after the Second World War and was directed to Aden, Ethiopia, Sudan and Djibouti, where nearly all migrants dealt in groceries or clothing, with the exception of a small number who worked as carpenters in Aden. After the 1962 revolution they gradually started to return to the YAR. The majority of the group of migrants who came back from Aden and East Africa during the 1960s settled in Ta'izz and Hodaida and opened wholesale and retail firms dealing in building materials. Those migrants who arrived from Ethiopia during the 1970s did the same, but most of them chose San'a' as their place of residence.

Another group of migrants went to Saudi Arabia after 1955. At the beginning a small number of them learned how to work as welders, manufacturing iron gates, window grilles and water-tanks — an occupation previously unknown in Yemen. After these early migrants had succeeded in establishing themselves in this trade in Saudi Arabia, relatives and other inhabitants of Aruq followed them and — often with the support of their precursors — moved into the same area of work. This type of 'chain migration' applies not only to labour emigration, but also generally to rural-urban migration in the YAR.

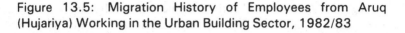

Figure 13.5: Migration History of Employees from Aruq (Hujariya) Working in the Urban Building Sector, 1982/83

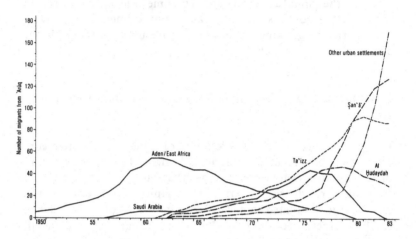

When in the early 1970s the first return migrants from Saudi Arabia set up firms for manufacturing iron gates in the three major cities they, too, attracted young migrants from Aruq and provided them with jobs in their new workshops. After some years as wage-earners, many of these internal migrants had acquired sufficient experience in welding and had saved enough money to set up firms of their own. This pattern was repeated by other return migrants. Thus the number of welding establishments in the three major cities grew tremendously and led to a considerable over-capacity — all the more so since the rapid increase in the number of firms has since 1978 in no way been matched by the rise in building activities.

The result of this development is clearly indicated by Figures 13.5 and 13.6: the number of migrants from Aruq has decreased in Hodaida since 1979 and in Ta'izz since 1981. Even the influx of migrants into San'a' has recently slowed down. In the meantime a continuously increasing number of migrants fom Aruq, who had been wage-earners in the three major cities, have moved into smaller towns and have opened new welding firms of their own. This led to the next flow of rural-urban migrants from Aruq to the respective small towns. Similar instances of this latest trend of internal migration towards small and medium-sized urban settlements have also been observed among the employees in other branches of the building industry.

Figure 13.6:   Direction of the Flow of Migrants from Aruq and their Occupation, 1982/83

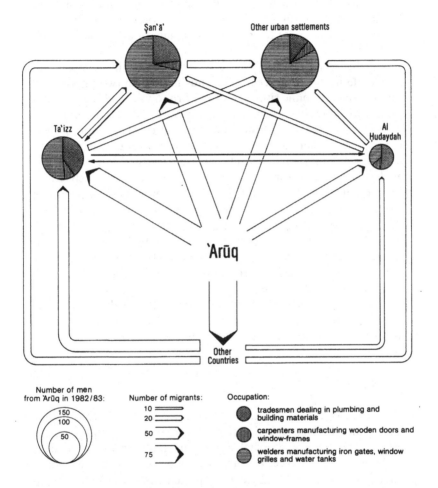

**Integration of Rural Migrants in Urban Centres**

It is characteristic of employees in the urban building sector that the overwhelming majority of wage-earners from rural origins live alone or together with male relatives in town, while the other members of their family stay in their rural settlements. Among the owners of firms, the proportion of those who did not take their families with them to town is smaller but still considerable. This is clearly indicated by the following example from San'a'. From among 774 proprietors of firms who came from rural settlements, nearly 40 per cent lived without their family in the capital. Most were living at their place of work — in a separate part of their shop, in a small hut on the site of their production plant or in a corner of their workshop.

Whether or not, and at what time, the other family members will also settle in the urban centre depends mainly on two interrelated factors: the economic situation of the firm-owner and the duration of his work in the town. As the economic situation of return migrants who saved a considerable amount of money during their period of work abroad is, in most cases, much better than the starting-position of internal migrants coming directly from a village, it is evident that many former labour emigrants can relatively easily afford to live with their family in a rented flat or their own house in town. For an internal migrant without previous experience in labour emigration, however, it is in general much more difficult and it takes more time to acquire enough capital to rent or build a house in town where he can live together with his family. This is demonstrated by Figure 13.7 which shows, for example, that among a group of migrants who had worked in San'a' for a period of four to six years, the vast majority of the return migrants were residing with their families in the capital whereas most of the internal migrants were still dwelling without their families in San'a'.

### Conclusion

The results of the investigation show very clearly the extraordinary importance of labour emigration and internal migration for the current economic and social development of the urban centres. Although the employees of only one sector of the urban economy have been examined, it is to be expected that most of the basic migration patterns presented in this study are exactly the same for the vast majority of the urban population in the YAR. Knowledge of migration processes of this kind is by no means of purely academic interest. It is also of considerable significance for national development planning — especially at the present time, when the exodus of population from rural areas to the few rapidly expanding cities is still at a relatively early stage. It is not yet too late to prevent the uncontrolled acceleration of this process by taking appropriate

Figure 13.7:   Housing Situation and Duration of Work in San'a' for
Two Groups of Firm-owners with Different Migration Experiences

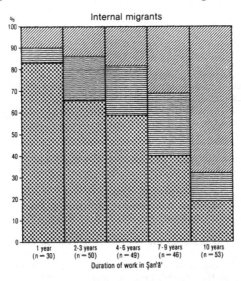

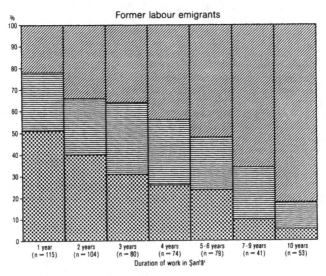

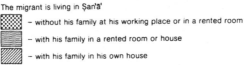

The migrant is living in Ṣan'a'

- without his family at his working place or in a rented room

- with his family in a rented room or house

- with his family in his own house

governmental measures for the development of the rural areas and small towns.


## Notes

1. For an account of the history of Yemeni migration, see J. C. Swanson, *Emigration and Economic Development: the Case of the Yemen Arab Republic* (Westview Press, Boulder, Colo., 1979), pp. 47–55.

2. Estimates from H. Steffen, 'Arbeitsemigration aus der Arabischen Republik Jemen in die Erdölförderstaaten der Arabischen Halbinsel', *Geographica Helvetica* (1981), pp. 73–82.

3. Ibid., p. 75.

4. See J. C. Swanson, 'The Consequences of Emigration for Economic Development: A Review of the Literature', *Papers in Anthropology*, no. 20 (1979), pp. 39–56.

5. Steffen, 'Arbeitsemigration', pp. 78–80.

6. R. P. Shaw, 'Migration and Employment in the Arab World: Construction as a Key Policy Variable', *International Labour Review*, no. 118 (Sept.–Oct. 1979), pp. 589–605.

7. Yemen Arab Republic, Central Planning Organisation, *Statistical Year Book 1981*, (San'a', 1982), p. 344.

8. Yemen Arab Republic, Central Planning Organisation, *Preliminary Results of the Industrial Survey 1980* (San'a', 1981): in Arabic.

9. See H. Steffen *et al.*, *Final Report on the Airphoto Interpretation Project of the Swiss Technical Co-Operation Service Bern*, (Zurich, April 1978) p. I/150.

10. Instances of such a kind of 'replacement migration' have already been reported from Jordan during the 1970s; see J. S. Birks and C. A. Sinclair, *International Migration and Development in the Arab Region* (International Labour Office, Geneva, 1980), pp. 86–7.

11. The author's investigations were carried out in the context of an interdisciplinary research project on Yemen, under the overall direction of Professor Horst Kopp of the Department of Geography, Tübingen University, and with the financial assistance of the Volkswagen Foundation. The total results of the survey will be published in: G. Meyer, *Arbeitsemigration, Binnenwanderung und Wirtschaftsentwicklung in der Arabischen Republik Jemen untersucht am Beispiel des städtischen Bausektors* (Jemen-Studien Bd. 2, Wiesbaden, 1984).

12. Figures according to Confederation of Yemeni Development Associations, *Population Census 1981, Final Results* (San'a', 1982).

13. The extremely high rate of mobility among pupils from the Hujariya has been stressed by Steffen *et al.*, *Final Report*, p. I/117.

# 14 CHANGING ATTITUDES TOWARDS HEALTH: SOME OBSERVATIONS FROM THE HUJARIYA

Cynthia Myntti

When anthropologists and medical specialists talk about health, what they are most often referring to, in fact, is its opposite, illness. They focus their attention on ways people use to rid themselves of illness through cures or what might more appropriately be called 'sickness care'. Surprisingly little attention is given to health, what it means to people and what they do to promote and protect it.

The definition of health is so imbedded in local culture that it is often difficult for people to articulate what it means. If, for example, one were to ask Yemeni villagers to define health, they might answer: 'Health is a state in which the body works normally' or 'Health is the absence of illness.' Yet if one observes how people live in rural Yemen, it is evident that health has clear determinants which are socially and culturally defined and is a state of being which is actively sought through numerous daily practices. Indeed, Yemen has a rich tradition of what might be called 'preventive medicine'.

This chapter will examine local practices which promote health. It is based on two years of anthropological fieldwork (1977–78) in a village near Turba, in the Hujariya district of Ta'izz province. It will attempt to show that preventive medicine is not a new concept in Yemen, but rather one that is fundamental to the traditional life-style. Aspects of traditional health care will be described, with attention drawn to ways in which both practices and attitudes are changing. The chapter will conclude with suggestions as to how the Yemeni government might build on traditional notions of preventive medicine.

In Yemen the traditional rules for a healthy existence derive from a variety of sources: classical Arabic medicine, based heavily on Greek humoral pathology; medical prescriptions found in the *hadith*; use of medicinal herbs and physical manipulation based on centuries of experience and interaction with the local ecology; and fears of a lively and particularly malevolent spirit world. Together these provide the aetiological and curative repertoires which guide local health practices. Based on these sources, the most important prescriptions for the promotion of health can be summarised into four general categories:

(1) the balanced diet;
(2) the routine purge;
(3) protection against external elements;
(4) female reproductive health.


**The Balanced Diet**

In the community studied, one hears with surprising frequency comments such as: 'Strange, we work less now than in the past but our bodies ache more' or 'In the past we used to be much healthier than now because we ate foods like sorghum porridge (*'asid*). Now we are eating modern foods like white bread and macaroni. This is why we are always ill.' Clearly, an important link has always been perceived between diet and health.

Villagers categorise foods according to a simplified humoral classification: The ideal diet balances food qualities so that no one item is in excess; it also defines which foods are appropriate, depending on the season, condition and age of the person. Priority is given to strengthening foods, those considered as having a heating effect on the body and as stimulating body activity. These are called variously hot, heavy or dense, and include meats and meat broths, fenugreek sauce (*hulba*), eggs, sorghum porridge and breads. However, if taken in excess, they cause diarrhoea. Thus mothers with infants will usually avoid such foods for fear of stimulating body activity and possibly causing diarrhoea in their babies.

Foods termed cold and light in local classification, by contrast, are viewed as depressing body activity and are especially good in hot weather or for weaning infants. Among these are included: wheat-breads, rice, macaroni, potatoes and biscuits. Too many cold foods, however, cause the digestive system to clog up and cause constipation, a condition which leads to body aches, headaches and weakness.

The theory underlying conceptions of the balanced diet is that bodily health (i.e. body-strength and growth) depends on an internal balance which is based on a properly functioning digestive system. Digestion is the key, for it is through digestion that the body acquires its necessary nourishment. A related folk theory concerning digestion is the importance of purgatives.

## The Routine Purge

In local thought there is a clear relationship between purity and health, and this is no more clearly stated than in the prescription for routine purges. No matter how careful a person is in following a proper diet, impurities accumulate in the digestive system. Thus to ensure proper functioning of the digestion, impurities must be cleansed routinely from the system. Local substances such as senna leaves, castor beans, resin from the aloe plant and imported laxatives are used.

Purgatives are used as preventive medicine and are also important ritually. For example, one must be pure to make the pilgrimage. One aspect of the proper pre-pilgrimage condition is visceral purity, accomplished through the use of senna (*shurbat sana makki*). Trips to traditional healers are usually preceded by a purge, to clean the 'heart'. Moreover, the Ramadan fast is often likened to a purge, for it also is seen as an internal cleanser and is very beneficial for the health.

## Protection Against External Elements

The health of man is influenced, often negatively, by his environment. In the natural environment of Yemen, the sun and hot winds are much-feared threats to the health. For example, additional layers of clothing, particularly on the head, and herbal sunblocks for the skin protect the body from the harmful heating effects of the sun. The sun is said to 'dry the brains' and 'take blood from the face'. Environmental harm is manifested by symptoms such as fevers, headaches, insomnia and diarrhoea. In the village population, those thought particularly vulnerable to the drying and heating effects of the sun and winds are mothers in the post-partum period and newborn infants. Thus one reason for keeping mother and baby in cool dark rooms for 40 days after birth is to avoid the perceived drying and heating effects of the environment.

Just as threats to health are thought to exist in the harsh natural environment, so too are threats perceived in the social environment.

Envy and greed are seen to be the impetus behind forms of black magic (*sihr*) and the evil eye (*'ain*) which can strike to make a person ill. Preventive actions are many and usually involve the use of a spiritual veil (*hijab*) or amulet, as protection. One may deliberately avoid drawing attention to desired goods by hiding them. For example, women in the Hujariya always wear a black overdress to cover their best clothes and gold from public view. Healthy babies may be made less enviable by being kept dirty. In addition, commonly used amulets include medals or small containers with verses of the Qur'an, salt and other substances worn sewn into a cloth, or the decoration of one's house with the pungent plant rue (*sadhab*).

### Female Reproductive Health

Ethnographic data from the Hujariya suggest that the foundation of female health is reproductive health. Among women this means the necessity of regular and adequate expulsion of menstrual blood and vaginal fluids, particularly following childbirth. These substances are highly polluting, although the processes of expulsion in themselves are viewed as cleansing. Women encourage the expulsion of these substances in a variety of ways, including special massages and herbal infusions. Should female sexual substances build up, the body becomes dense (*thakhin*) and full of pain. In fact, density due to inadequate expulsion of menstrual blood is a common complaint of women at the time of menopause.

Not only must females encourage the adequate expulsion of sexual fluids, but they must perform carefully prescribed ablutions after being in the polluted state. Inadequate purification is viewed as a hazard to health; if a woman does not wash properly, her uterus can become 'locked' and she is rendered sterile. During the author's period of research in the village, all cases of sterility encountered were attributed to improper purification.

In a society where barren women lack marital security (for they are easily divorced) or are pitied for having no loyal support in old age, the social importance of fertility cannot be overestimated. Fertility is fundamental to the definition of female health. For example, following a difficult childbirth in the village, the following practices were observed:

(1) a special infusion of cinnamon, jujube fruit, thyme and sugar

(*qahwat al-wilada*) was served to the new mother to encourage
the expulsion of the pollutants;

(2) the woman's underclothes were fumigated with incense so as to
tighten the vagina and avoid infection;

(3) a specialist was brought in to massage the uterus back into its
proper place;

(4) the new mother was fed chicken soup and raisins to encourage
blood production to regain her strength; and

(5) the room was decorated with rue to prevent spiritual harm to
mother and baby.

These practices were described as 'insurance for fertility'.

In sum, health has traditionally been maintained within the con-
fines of the household, and actively promoted in everyday living. To
be sure, medical specialists have always existed in most rural Yemeni
communities but the essence of health has been the personal life-
style, not treatment by specialists. Moreover, the knowledge of how
to achieve health has not been the monopoly of formally trained
healers but is held by ordinary people. Women, in particular, have
been active promoters of the health of their kin through attention to
diet, purifications and protection from the environment.

## Health: Recent Changes

The basic determinants of health as locally defined — growth,
strength and fertility — are as important in today's definition as
they have always been, ways of achieving this state are beginning to
change. Two major forces are effecting this change. The first is the
expansion of modern medical services. The second is the accelerated
integration of Yemen into the world economic order of the last
decade through labour migration, the inflow of remittances and an
increase in imported consumer goods.

The provision of modern medical care by the state bureaucracy
has begun, in effect, to diminish personal responsibility for health.
Medical care has become the domain of specialised persons in
government establishments or entrepreneurial self-styled healers
such as pharmacists and doctors. Both operate within the framework of modern Western medicine, possess esoteric healing knowledge and are sought out mainly for cures. Moreover, their curative
technologies have become identified as progressive and desirable.

The expansion of government and entrepreneurial sickness care has coincided in recent years with a new-style consumerism and, in some senses, the resort to modern medical care can be understood in the same light. Yemenis now consume imported packaged drugs or expensive medical services just as they consume imported foods or buy a television or other prestige commodity.

The most striking consequence of the new bureaucratic and socio-economic realities in Yemen is a shift in attitudes, with a trend away from active self-reliance in health to the passive purchasing of health. In other words, people increasingly *buy* health in the form of tablets or injections rather than *live* health. In addition, many of the prescriptions for healthy living held by ordinary people in the past are losing their specific applicability as life-styles change. In particular, the notions of a balanced diet and internal purity are being abandoned by the young and urban-oriented generation. New foods are not being fitted into the old categories. These trends are particularly clear in the Hujariya, a comparatively modern and wealthy district, where changes in the diet are significant (the foods now most commonly consumed there are rice, tinned mackerel, macaroni, potatoes and white bread). One also notices among the youth that less importance is given to threats from the environment.

Of all the traditional health-promoting behaviour outlined above, seemingly the most enduring is that related to female reproductive health. Personal responsibility for health promotion remains high and, even in cases where village women seek the services of modern medical specialists, they are supplemented simultaneously with the traditional fertility-promoting practices.

Yemen is clearly at a crossroads in the provision of health care for its citizens. Will it choose the route which so many nations — developed and developing alike — have taken and medicalise health? That is, will responsibility for health be taken away from the people and put into the hands of doctors? This would be a mistake in Yemen, where a constructive preventive philosophy is still implicit in the lives of ordinary people. Indeed, contrary to the opinions of many medical experts, all that is traditional is not harmful.

The argument proffered here is not that all aspects of traditional health care are beneficial or that they should be promoted. What is being advocated is, simply, a recognition that prevention is not a new concept in Yemen; health-planners should take advantage of this attitude. An assessment of traditional practices should be made; health-care providers could then encourage those which are beneficial, ignore those which are neutral and change those which are harmful.

The communication of modern health messages would be much more efficient if put in terms that ordinary people understand and if it were directed to address their concerns. Villagers already see the connections between diet and health, personal hygiene and health, and even the environment and health. Health education could modernise the content of messages while using the traditional framework for their arguments.

The following areas merit encouragement and expansion: a strengthening diet for lactating mothers; the importance of a balanced diet (in the modern scientific sense) for body maintenance and growth; how to avoid harm from the natural environment (contagious respiratory diseases like TB due to poor ventilation; waterborne diseases like diarrhoea and bilharzia from polluted water); and the importance of personal hygiene, extended to household tasks like food preparation.

Uses of the purge or amulets which are neither harmful nor helpful could be ignored. Still other practices need changing. For example, children are fed 'cold' foods during weaning to avoid diarrhoea and suffer from malnutrition as a result. They are kept away from exposure to the sun, also to avoid diarrhoea, and, as a result, commonly develop rickets. Mothers could be taught instead that their children suffer from intestinal disorders because the water they drink is impure and full of microbes from an unsanitary natural environment. Similarly it could be argued that 'heating' foods and exposure to sunshine are necessary to strengthen infants.

The challenges are great, but the opportunities are many. The constructive, traditional philosophy of self-reliance and personal responsibility for the promotion of health is present in Yemen. The modern medical establishment would do well to build on it, not encourage the Yemeni people to lose it.

# 15 ASPECTS OF EDUCATION IN THE YEMEN ARAB REPUBLIC[1]

Peter Clark

## Introduction

Until the 1962 revolution, modern public education was limited in both quality and quantity. Some educational institutions were founded during the second Ottoman occupation, including a teacher-training college and a technical school.[2] These were discontinued by Imam Yahya. At the time of the revolution there were four government secondary schools providing an Islamic education with some modern refinements. The pupils were largely sons of prominent Yemenis whose neutrality was secured by taking their sons as hostages.[3]. Standards were not internationally acceptable, as those who went on to further education in Egypt and elsewhere discovered.[4] In the 1940s and 1950s some schools were established by private initiative. Many Yemenis migrated to Aden and those with appropriate residential qualifications attended Aden government schools. Others went to schools set up by wealthy Yemenis in Aden.[5]

The formal public education system improved greatly after the revolution and especially after the end of the civil war in 1970. The school system was brought into line with that of Egypt — six years of primary, three years of intermediate (in Yemen called preparatory) and three years of secondary schooling. During the civil war, the Republic received much assistance from Egypt and Egyptians have formed the bulk of the corps of teachers. The curriculum has been based on Egyptian models. Both quantitatively and proportionately the Egyptian contribution has increased although decision-making has remained in Yemeni hands.

## Schools

During the last 20 years the number of pupils enrolled in primary schools has increased over tenfold, from 61,335 in 1962/63 to

172

705,061 in 1982/83.[6] In 1971/72 enrolment was 12 per cent of children of primary-school age, whereas in 1981/82 the proportion was 48.7 per cent. There is a high drop-out rate: in 1967/68 it was estimated to be 63 per cent, while, at the time of writing, it is down to 25 per cent. This is partly because only one in four primary schools can offer facilities for all six grades.

Enrolment at the preparatory-school stage is 7.2 per cent of children of that age group and at the secondary-school stage 2.5 per cent. The wastage rate is much less. Because enrolment at these two levels is so much lower than at primary level, the smaller number of schools (142 secondary schools in 1982/83) allows for adequate facilities; but the number of those successful in the school-leaving certificate is frequently higher than the intake of pupils two years earlier. This suggests repeaters and a determination on the part of pupils that, having come so far, they ought to have something to show for it.

The statistics show considerable variations of sex and region. Males have consistently been favoured in the provision of education but the progress of girls' education has been consistent and many teachers report greater motivation on the part of girls. Although the proportion of girls receiving school education must be one of the lowest in the world, in Yemen it has been the area of fastest growth with the most profound social implications. In 1982/83 girls formed 15.7 per cent of pupils in primary schools, 14.2 per cent of pupils in preparatory schools and 15.7 per cent in secondary schools. Thus, in spite of pressures on adolescent girls to leave school and get married, and in spite of conservative views about girls having a public career, the proportion of girls advancing through the system is maintained.

The province of Ta'izz has almost half of the country's intermediate and secondary schools. This province contains the Hujariya area which, for a century and more, through migration to Aden and thence to Europe, Britain and the United States, has been exposed to the stimulus and competition of foreign influences. People of this province have had to rely on their native wits, supplemented by expertise and qualifications, rather than on connections (although they also help) or the management of inherited wealth or occupations. Many of the schools of Ta'izz province are full and operate a shift system to meet the demands of the community. By contrast, schools in Mahwit and Sa'da provinces are often under-subscribed.

**Further and Higher Education**

Other institutions of secondary education exist alongside the secondary schools. Primary-school teachers and intermediate-school teachers are trained in teacher-training institutes, of which there were 38 in 1982/83 with 2,807 students. The Faculty of Education at the University of San'a' trains secondary-school teachers. Other vocational secondary schools have been established although they have, in the eyes of students and parents, lower status than the 'academic' secondary schools. In 1969/70 one commercial secondary school was founded; in 1982/83 there were six with 556 students. One technical secondary school was founded in 1970/71; in 1982/83 there were four with 544 students. Industrial and agricultural secondary schools were founded in 1979/80. In 1982/83 there were two of the former with 596 students and two of the latter with 200 students.

The University of San'a' was founded in 1970. There are currently five Faculties — Arts, Science, Commerce, Law and Education. In 1981/82 there were 6,634 students registered for degrees but this is higher than the number actually studying. There are plans for the establishment in the next three years of new Faculties of Medicine, Agriculture and Engineering. Most of the teaching staff are Egyptian but Yemenis occupy the senior positions: Rector, Vice-Rector, Deans and Deputy Deans. Other further education is provided by training institutions attached to Ministries (such as the Health Manpower Training Institute) and public corporations. Teachers are generally from outside Yemen.

**Administration**

Yemen has a weak governmental infrastructure with limited fiscal resources. Because of the need to create a system, capital costs are continuous and hence unit costs are high. Unlike Lebanon, with which it has many other features in common, Yemen has no flourishing private educational sector. The country relies heavily on support from outside. The Second Five-Year Development Plan (1982/83–1986/87) expects to finance its 2,300 million rial (YR) programme with 68 per cent funding from outside.[7]

Many of the expatriate Arab teachers are financed from oil-rich states with a small contribution from Yemen. (Some of the teachers of English, similarly financed, come from Pakistan.) This is seen as a form of aid to poorer Arab countries, for the salaries they receive in Yemen are far higher than what they would earn in their own countries. The Yemeni contribution is below that of a salary for a Yemeni teacher. Hence there is a financial disincentive to the displacement of foreign teachers by nationals. In 1982/83 there were 1,935 Yemenis and 11,279 expatriates teaching at primary schools. At preparatory and secondary schools there were 309 Yemenis and 3,487 expatriates. The number of foreign teachers increases each year, but does not keep pace with the increase in pupils. There is usually a 30 per cent increase in primary-school enrolment each year and the teacher/pupil ratio in primary schools has worsened from 1:43 in 1978/79 to 1:53 in 1982/83. The University and teacher-training institutes are producing only a trickle of graduates and the system will continue to rely heavily on foreign teachers.

**Special Features**

A number of special features affect the working of the system. Government policy is to make education free and available to all; it is not, however, compulsory. The momentum for the establishment of schools may come from private initiative. The demand has to be met and imposes strains on the Ministry of Education's endeavours to budget and to plan. The Ministry is a massive spender of public funds. Demands on public money steadily increase and far outstrip provision made by taxation and customs dues, the two main sources of government revenue.

Decision-makers in the Ministry, the provinces and in the schools are inadequately trained. Many able individuals have been placed in senior posts at a young age because they are qualified Yemenis. But they lack (as they are the first to acknowledge) the experience or the training to distinguish the wood of policy and planning from the trees of administrative survival work. Decision-making is referred upwards and this aggravates the situation. The system, like many others, is not geared to coping with rapid change.

Some of the dynamism of the country's education comes from Aden. For a generation before 1962 Yemenis migrated to the modern city of Aden, where a secular pattern of education, based on European and Indian models, had been built up.[8] Well-educated Adenis became fluent in English. Aden Colony in the 1950s was small enough for controlled educational planning and experimentation. Since the establishment of the People's Democratic Republic of Yemen (PDRY), many of this generation of Anglophone Adenis have migrated to the Yemen Arab Republic (YAR) and have had a distinct impact on the social, commercial and intellectual life of the country. They have a strong influence in the University and their terms of reference are international.

This touches on one of the most striking features of the educational system. Most of the structure of modern secular education is derived from outside the country: syllabus, teachers, the design of schools, much of the funding. Schooling can be an alienating process from the day the rural child goes to his village primary school and has to adjust to the strange accent and values of a Cairene teacher to the day he or she graduates from the University of San'a' in cap and gown derived from medieval Europe. During much of his school and university career the student will have read foreign books and been taught by foreign teachers.

Meanwhile a current of traditional Yemeni education persists.[9] A traditional elitist and male culture and scholarship — poetry, history, religious studies — continues, only incidentally affected by the educational revolution of the last 20 years. The Qur'anic schools have lost their monopoly but mosque education is vigorous and helps to form the minds and faith of many young people today as it has done for centuries.[10] The links between the two systems are forged by headmasters, always Yemeni and frequently pillars of the local community in a traditional way — *qadis* or merchants or leaders of prayer in the mosque. Their presence legitimises the strange features of the modern educational revolution.

## Conclusion

In one generation enormous progress has been made and the map of education has changed totally. The range of choices people have in controlling their own destinies has extended dramatically. An infrastructure for social and economic development has been built up to provide a body of well-trained men and women with the capacity to exploit the resources of the country and make it into a viable, prosperous modern state. The Second-Five-Year Plan is only consolidating this infrastructure. The plan aims to expand teacher-training, to diversify further and higher education, to develop adult literacy and basic skills, to build up the University and to establish a College of Islamic Studies. But the course of the next few years has been set by the unprecedented transformation of the last twenty.

## Notes

1. An earlier version of this chapter, entitled 'Education Programmes in the Yemen', was submitted to the American Institute for Yemeni Studies (AIYS) for the AIYS Social and Institutional Profile of Yemen. Much of the chapter is the fruit of discussions over the last three years with Yemeni and foreign educationalists. I wish to acknowledge debts to Abdu Rabbu al-Jarrada, Professor Muhammad Abdu Ghanim, Yahya al-Nunu, Abdul Fattah Jamal Muhammad, Abdul Basit Babikr, George Kassis, Ahmed Ghalib, Brian Clissold, Tim Butler and Chris Ramsden. I alone may be held responsible for errors and opinions.

2. R. B. Serjeant, 'The Post-Medieval and Modern History of San'a' and the Yemen, ca. 953-1382/1515-1962' in R. B. Serjeant and Ronald Lewcock (eds.) *San'a', An Arabian Islamic City* (World of Islam Festival Trust, London, 1983), p. 98.

3. Ibid., p 100.

4. Mohammed Ahmad Zabarah, *Yemen, Traditionalism vs Modernity* (Praeger, New York, 1982), p. 16.

5. L. Douglas, 'The Free Yemeni Movement', unpublished PhD thesis, University of London, 1983.

6. Ministry of Education, *Khittat wa Ihtiyajat Tanmiyat al-Ta'lim li Am 1982/1983* (San'a', 1983).

7. The World Bank, *Yemen Arab Republic. Fifth Education Project. Staff Appraisal Report* (Washington DC, 1983), para. 1.29.

8. See R. J. Gavin, *Aden Under British Rule 1839-1967* (C. Hurst, London, 1975), pp. 324-5; Sultan Naji, 'Al-Halatan al-Ta'limiya wa'l-Thaqafiya fi Adan khilal Fatrat Tab'iyatiha li'l-Hind' in *Al-Iklil* (Ministry of Information and Culture, San'a'), Year 2, no. 1 (1982), pp. 96-132.

9. For which, see R. B. Serjeant, 'The Mosques of San'a' — The Yemeni Islamic Setting' in Serjeant and Lewcock, *San'a'*, p. 316.

10. Documented by Isma'il Ali al-Akwa, *Al-Madaris al-Islamiya fi'l-Yaman* (University of San'a' Publications, San'a', 1980), *passim*.

# 16 THE DEVELOPMENT OF PRIMARY EDUCATION AND ITS PROBLEMS IN THE YEMEN ARAB REPUBLIC

Horia Mohammad al-Iryani

The Yemen Arab Republic (YAR) is one of the least developed countries in the world. This is the direct result of a long period of tyrannical Imamic rule which was further exacerbated by the succeeding civil war.

During the period of stability which started in 1970, the people began to wake from their deep sleep to face the dreadful challenge of poverty, ignorance and disease and to search for the most effective means of developing the country. Of this triple challenge, which aspect is the most dangerous and which one leads to the others? Does poverty lead to ignorance? Or does ignorance bring disease? And so on. As it was difficult to answer these questions, war was declared on all three in a complementary effort. But this attack on three fronts overstretched the country's resources and the question was again posed — which evil should be combated first? The final realisation was that ignorance brings poverty, and ignorance breeds disease. It deprives the individual of a basic human quality or right, namely the right to think. God said in the Qur'an, 'Of themselves, they have to think.' Ignorance leads to poverty; the ignorant person does not have the intellectual ability to raise his standard of living. Ignorance is the root of disease, because the ignorant person does not understand hygiene, sanitation, nutrition, and so on, which protect him against disease. Thus the old trio could be rewritten as: ignorance, ignorance, ignorance. Therefore, the attention paid to education increased day by day and education began to spread beyond the big cities into the countryside and the remote areas.

Education is crucial for the building of a modern Yemen. In this chapter, we shall study the educational structure in Yemen and search for the best methods to improve it. We shall concentrate on education at the primary stage, as it is the foundation of the educational structure; if this foundation weakens, the entire structure of education would collapse.

**A Short Description of Education in the YAR**

In order to give a brief survey of education in Yemen, we must consider two main historical periods: before and after the revolution of 1962.

*Before the Revolution*

This was the period of religious education which was distinguished by the spread of elementary schools, of one room each, on whose floors the pupils sat. The children were taught by a religious man known as 'master' or *shaikh*. The master's duty was to teach the children reading, writing, basic arithmetic and recitation of the Qur'an. The pupil who succeeded in reciting the whole of the Qur'an was given a big party at the school; he would walk at the head of the school parade, bearing on his chest a wooden board on which his name was written. The pupils walking behind him would sing religious songs and hymns. Sweets were later distributed among the children. If the child who completed the Qur'an was a girl, she would be dressed in a white robe with a crown on her head as if she were a bride. A woman experienced in such occasions would repeat some prayers and religious songs. At the end of the ceremony, the boy or girl was considered to have finished his or her education, even if the child had not spent more than one year in the school. After finishing reading the whole of the Qur'an, the boy would spend his time in his father's agricultural or commercial work or some other craft. As for the girl, she would prepare herself to become a good housewife in the future. Soon afterwards, the child would lose the ability to read even the simple words he had learnt at the small school, and so gradually would become illiterate.

The majority of the children from these elementary schools were illiterate. A very few of them would continue their studies in the principles of religion and Islamic law (*shari'a*); such studies were taught by experts in the field. The student who finished his studies in this field, or at least reached a reasonable level of knowledge, became a *qadi* or judge. The common custom at that time was that whoever became a judge usually belonged to a family of a high social standing whose men were members of the same profession. A judge was not necessarily a government official; he might practise his profession privately. For instance, he might settle disputes and spread justice by applying Islamic law in the village or the area in which he lived. He would charge the disputing parties certain sums of money for his income.

This kind of education classified the people of the country into two main groups: the class of judges, and the class of the farmers and the handicraft-workers.

## After the Revolution

This stage began with the September revolution of 1962 and it was marked by changing religious education to normal secular education. The number of schools increased every year. During this stage, education became more than the teaching of reading, writing, simple mathematics and some of the principles of religion. It became a means to improve people's lives. Education spread to cover every area in the country and it was no longer limited to a certain class. Free education gave people from all classes the chance to educate their children. The small elementary schools of the past decreased in number year after year, as they became replaced by primary, preparatory and secondary schools, and so on. In 1970 San'a' University was established and today plans are being made to start post-graduate studies in the University.

## Aspects of Development in Primary Education

Education in general, and primary education in particular, developed greatly after the September revolution. This development took several forms:

### Increase in Numbers of Pupils

The rapid increase in the numbers of boys and girls enrolling in primary schools is a remarkable phenomenon. While the number of pupils at the general primary stage in the school year 1962/63 (the year of the revolution) was 61,335, it rose to 705,062 in 1982/83, an elevenfold increase. Table 16.1 gives the annual statistics of pupils in the primary stage for the years 1962/63 to 1982/83, with the percentage annual variations in growth rate. It is noticeable that there was an increase in all years after 1968/69, with the exception of 1976/77. There are two main reasons for the erratic rate of growth: (a) inaccuracy in the statistics for the different years; and (b) leakage of pupils during this stage.

Table 16.1:    YAR: Pupils in Primary Schools, 1962–83

| Year | Number of pupils | Annual growth rate % |
|------|------------------|----------------------|
| 1962/63 | 61,335 | — |
| 1963/64 | 62,023 | 1.1 |
| 1964/65 | 66,961 | 8.0 |
| 1965/66 | 69,139 | 3.3 |
| 1966/67 | 63,366 | - 8.3 |
| 1967/68 | 66,830 | 5.5 |
| 1968/69 | 66,468 | - 0.5 |
| 1969/70 | 72,107 | 8.5 |
| 1970/71 | 88,217 | 22.3 |
| 1971/72 | 118,868 | 34.7 |
| 1972/73 | 153,807 | 29.4 |
| 1973/74 | 179,079 | 16.4 |
| 1974/75 | 232,784 | 30.0 |
| 1975/76 | 252,726 | 8.6 |
| 1976/77 | 220,159 | -12.9 |
| 1977/78 | 251,876 | 14.4 |
| 1978/79 | 251,967 | 0.04 |
| 1979/80 | 335,249 | 33.1 |
| 1980/81 | 414,273 | 23.6 |
| 1981/82 | 589,186 | 42.2 |
| 1982/83 | 705,062 | 19.7 |

Sources: Ministry of Education, *Education in Twenty Years* (San'a', 1982); and author's survey.

Table 16.2 gives the numbers of pupils distributed according to their grades and shows the variations very clearly.

Table 16.2:    YAR: Pupils in Primary Schools by Grades, 1970–82

| Year | Grade One | Grade Two | Grade Three | Grade Four | Grade Five | Grade Six |
|------|-----------|-----------|-------------|------------|------------|-----------|
| 1970/71 | 34,560 | 21,971 | 14,649 | 8,613 | 4,927 | 3,497 |
| 1971/72 | 50,261 | 30,026 | 18,739 | 10,579 | 6,048 | 4,212 |
| 1972/73 | 65,211 | 38,730 | 24,345 | 13,042 | 7,907 | 5,572 |
| 1973/74 | 71,321 | 43,222 | 29,769 | 16,888 | 10,402 | 7,578 |
| 1974/75 | 96,512 | 56,402 | 36,184 | 20,971 | 13,041 | 9,674 |
| 1975/76 | 105,896 | 58,932 | 39,120 | 23,399 | 14,070 | 10,699 |
| 1976/77 | 86,433 | 47,971 | 35,292 | 23,426 | 15,235 | 11,772 |
| 1977/78 | 91,804 | 57,784 | 41,729 | 28,081 | 18,884 | 13,704 |
| 1978/79 | 97,288 | 58,847 | 40,837 | 25,596 | 16,014 | 13,385 |
| 1979/80 | 145,215 | 70,491 | 49,640 | 33,279 | 20,138 | 16,486 |
| 1980/81 | 36,431 | 96,381 | 65,232 | 43,796 | 27,640 | 20,863 |
| 1981/82 | 129,845 | 87,887 | 58,499 | 37,682 | 26,417 | 26,417 |

Source: Ministry of Education, *Educational Statistics: 1979/80* (San'a', 1981).

The cause of variation is the high drop-out rate. A pupil may finish Grade One, for instance, and then he skips a year or two. This is true of all grades at this stage, especially as education is not compulsory. Thus the number of pupils who continue their studies until the end of the primary stage is much lower than the number of those who join Grade One. During the six primary years, 34,560 pupils who joined Grade One in the school year 1970/71, for example, were expected to reach Grade Six in the year 1975/76. In 1975/76, however, there were only 10,699 pupils in Grade Six; the balance of 23,861, or 69 per cent, were either drop-outs or repeaters. This process of leakage leads to instability in the number of pupils at the primary level, so that preparing a plan for the future is almost impossible. It is possible to determine the number of school-age children from the general population statistics. A hypothetical number of pupils who will enrol at school can also be established, but it is not easy to forecast the number of those who will continue their studies to the end of the primary stage.

## Improvements in Teaching Methods

Teaching methods in education have developed greatly since the revolution. In the past, the teacher used to read aloud and the pupils would repeat after him several times until they had learned the text by heart (the pupil was expected to make certain rhythmical movements with his body during the lesson to prove that he was paying attention). Nowadays the teacher discusses the lesson with his pupils; the pupils derive the content of the lesson from the discussion. The educational process has changed from mere delivery and prompting into give-and-take. As for teaching aids, in the past there was no more than an oblong piece of wood with one white side, called the 'board', on which the pupils wrote with sharpened pens made of a certain kind of plant and dipped in ink. After listening to the shaikh, the pupil would use the board to write down what he had heard. Nowadays this board has been replaced by a blackboard or glue-board and other educational aids such as wall posters, audio-visual aids, and so on.

## Development of the Curriculum

After the September revolution and the expansion of education, modern curricula were introduced in primary schools. Prescribed subjects at this stage became varied and numerous. They were no longer limited to the elements of reading, arithmetic and reciting the

Qur'an. New subjects were taught. In addition, the quality of the subjects was improved through the introduction of certain modifications aimed at expanding the scope of knowledge. In religion the pupil now studies *fiqh, hadith*, the Prophet's biography and God, while his past study in this course was no more than reciting the Qur'an.

## Expansion in School Building

The standardised school buildings of six class-rooms which were built after the September revolution have replaced the old elementary, 'small' schools of one room. Modern hygienic buildings replaced the old unhygienic ones. Table 16.3 shows the expansion in school building since the revolution, with an increase in primary schools and the gradual disappearance of the small elementary ones. As can be seen, the annual increase in school building since 1969/70 has been phenomenal, reaching its climax in 1979/80, when 832 new schools were built. This is the strongest possible evidence for the spread of education all over Yemen.

Table 16.3: YAR: Primary-school Building Programme, 1962–83

| Year | Schools | Class-rooms | Small schools | Pupils | Pupil/ school | Pupils/ grade |
|------|---------|-------------|---------------|--------|---------------|---------------|
| 1962/63 | 12 | 108 | 919 | 61,335 | 5,111 | 568 |
| 1963/64 | 18 | 125 | 877 | 62,023 | 3,445 | 574 |
| 1964/65 | 25 | 334 | 909 | 66,961 | 2,678 | 206 |
| 1965/66 | 28 | 266 | 969 | 69,139 | 2,469 | 274 |
| 1966/67 | 38 | 404 | 670 | 63,366 | 1,667 | 166 |
| 1967/68 | 39 | 420 | 710 | 66,830 | 1,713 | 171 |
| 1968/69 | 37 | 410 | 707 | 66,468 | 1,796 | 163 |
| 1969/70 | 52 | 475 | 648 | 72,107 | 1,386 | 154 |
| 1970/71 | 821 | 1,780 | | 88,217 | 107 | 53 |
| 1971/72 | 1,238 | 3,104 | | 118,868 | 96 | 48 |
| 1972/73 | 1,442 | 3,137 | | 153,807 | 106 | 53 |
| 1973/74 | 1,551 | 5,100 | | 179,079 | 114 | 38 |
| 1974/75 | 1,952 | 6,825 | | 232,784 | 119 | 39 |
| 1975/76 | 2,137 | 7,484 | | 252,726 | 118 | 39 |
| 1976/77 | 1,537 | 6,198 | | 220,159 | 143 | 35 |
| 1977/78 | 1,604 | 7,052 | | 251,876 | 158 | 39 |
| 1978/79 | 1,711 | 7,275 | | 251,967 | 147 | 36 |
| 1979/80 | 2,543 | 9,650 | | 335,249 | 131 | 43 |
| 1980/81 | 2,985 | 12,205 | | 414,273 | 138 | 34 |
| 1981/82 | 3,748 | 16,530 | | 589,186 | 157 | 39 |
| 1982/83 | 4,359 | 20,939 | | 705,062 | 161 | 40 |

Sources: Ministry of Education, *Education in Twenty Years* and author's survey.

**Problems of Primary Education**

The rapid development in primary education and the tremendous increase in the number of pupils joining schools have led to several problems which still face the country. The most important are outlined below.

*Shortcomings in Curricula*

Since curricula form the corner-stone of any education system, their shortcomings represent the most serious problem. We will discuss them under two main headings:

(1) *Shortcomings in Content.*   The prescribed school-books for primary education are prepared by other Arabs and not by Yemeni writers; as a result, the content of such books does not reflect the pupils' background. In some cases the content is so isolated from the pupils' environment and daily life that it holds no sense for them. In preparing these books the writers, who do not live in a Yemeni setting or with the Yemeni child and fail to understand his nature, simply assume his acceptance and understanding of the content. Secondly, the curricula of primary education do not allow for non-classroom activities, especially in the early grades. The curriculum is the school-book alone; this means that all efforts concentrate on building the pupil's mind without any consideration for other aspects of growth such as the physical and emotional. Such aspects are not only equal in importance to mental growth, but are also closely related to it.

(2) *Shortcomings of Exposition in Text-books.*   School text-books at the primary stage suffer from bad exposition and implementation. The books do not consider the mental age of the pupil when introducing the content; some have badly arranged subject matter. Examples of this are:

(a)The reading texts of Grade One: in this grade the child studies two reading books (each book is 100 pages long).
(b)*Mathematics for Grade One*: subjects in this book begin with writing and reading numerals before moving on to multiplication tables, as well as a little modern mathematics.
(c)*The Book of Social and Physical Environment*: no one can deny that this book contains topics which are very useful for the

child, but their exposition and implementation ignore the important fact that the child at this early age can hardly read long sentences or paragraphs of more than one sentence, which in any case fail to attract and hold his attention. On the contrary, the child may neglect the book. It is therefore true that, even if the content of a book is poor, its standard can be raised through good exposition and implementation.

### Differences in Pupils' Ages

One of the phenomena prevalent in primary education is that of the age differences between pupils in the same grade. A child of four, for instance, may sit next to a boy of twelve and this situation is harmful for both. It also poses a problem for the teacher, because each age requires a different approach. Moreover, the subject matter taught may be higher than the level of the younger pupil, or lower than that of the older one. This may lead to the pupil's loss of interest or, at the very minimum, to a poor standard of education.

### Frequent Absence

The phenomenon of frequent absence reflects a serious problem in the structure of primary education. The child who is absent for three successive months and then resumes his studies alongside pupils whose attendance has been constant will undoubtedly feel estranged to some extent. His educational level will certainly deteriorate even if he was among the most brilliant pupils before his absence. Apart from the serious consequences for his educational level, there will be a negative influence on his psychological state. Schools are unable to control pupils' absences because the educational law contains no provision to handle the problem. It is supposed to be settled between the school and the parents in a way that will help the child.

### Inadequate Classroom Accommodation

In spite of the large number of schools built every year, they are still unable to satisfy all the growing needs of education. The numbers of pupils are increasing more rapidly than the numbers of schools, as Table 16.3 shows. It also shows that the number of pupils per class has improved: the number since 1970/71 ranges between a maximum of 53 and a minimum of 34, which is reasonable. Unfortunately, there is considerable disparity in the distribution of pupils and pupil/class ratios in the different governorates of the republic. Even within the same governorate there are major differences. Taking the

San'a' governorate as an example, the number of pupils in the San'a' area is 32,692 and schools number 41; in al-Ashmur there are 935 pupils and 6 schools; in Khawlan, 6,381 pupils and 84 schools. In San'a' the average number of pupils per class is 61; in Khawlan it is 25. Even within the same school, pupil concentrations vary in different grades. Table 16.4 illustrates the distribution of pupils in different classes of the same schools.

Table 16.4: YAR: Number of Pupils per Class in Different Grades

| Grade One | Grade Two | Grade Three | Grade Four | Grade Five | Grade Six |
|---|---|---|---|---|---|
| 68.4 | 66.1 | 55.1 | 54.5 | 52.6 | 52.6 |

Source: Author's survey of 41 samples in San'a'.

If we study the relationship between the space of the classroom in primary schools and the number of pupils, we find a disturbing situation. The typical classroom in the standardised primary school is 20 sq. m and is designed to accommodate 35 pupils. In some schools, certain classes may contain more than 100 pupils; this means that the space designed for one pupil is occupied by nearly three. Bearing in mind how important it is for each pupil to have enough space for his or her movement, we can see clearly how unhealthy such a situation is.

For a clear perspective of the size of this problem in the next few years it must be remembered that education, as yet, is not compulsory in the YAR. It should also be remembered that less than 29 per cent of school-age children go to school, and that there is a high drop-out rate during, the six years of primary education. In spite of these factors, Yemeni schools are overcrowded. What would happen if primary education became compulsory, or if all children of school age went to school? And what would happen if all pupils remained at school? Would ten children be put in the space of one child? And what sort of educational results would those children achieve? If the logical solution is to build more schools, the present number of schools needs to be increased tenfold. One standardised primary school of six classrooms would cost about 700,000 rials (YR). It is easy to see the financial burden the country would have to bear because of the continuous need for schools, and the phenomenal rise in foreign teachers who already make up over 80 per cent of the teaching staff in the country. It is evident, therefore, that there can be no easy solution to this problem.

## The Need for Qualified Yemeni Teachers

The shortage of qualified Yemeni teachers is one of the most serious problems facing primary education, and one of the reasons for its deterioration. Indeed, there is a shortage of all kinds of Yemeni teachers. Table 16.5 shows the number of teachers (both Yemenis and non-Yemenis) at the primary stage over ten years, and highlights the continuous decrease in the number of Yemeni teachers and the great increase in the number of non-Yemeni teachers.

Table 16.5: YAR: Numbers of Primary-school Teachers, 1970–82

| Year | Number of teachers | | Total | Non-Yemeni teachers as percentage of total |
|------|---------|-------------|-------|---|
| | Yemenis | Non-Yemenis | | |
| 1970/71 | 1,726 | 54 | 1,780 | 3.0 |
| 1971/72 | 3,046 | 47 | 3,093 | 1.5 |
| 1972/73 | 4,053 | 200 | 4,253 | 4.7 |
| 1973/74 | 4,651 | 274 | 4,925 | 5.6 |
| 1974/75 | 5,552 | 221 | 5,773 | 3.8 |
| 1975/76 | 6,209 | 314 | 6,523 | 4.8 |
| 1976/77 | 6,651 | 333 | 6,984 | 4.8 |
| 1977/78 | 5,967 | 1,011 | 6,978 | 14.5 |
| 1978/79 | 3,785 | 2,085 | 5,870 | 35.5 |
| 1979/80 | 2,656 | 4,111 | 6,767 | 60.0 |
| 1980/81 | 2,496 | 7,330 | 9,826 | 74.6 |
| 1981/82[a] | 2,450 | 16,650 | 19,100 | 87.2 |

Note: a. Estimated.
Sources: Ministry of Education, *Educational Statistics: 1978–82* (San'a); and author's survey.

The continuous decrease in the number of the Yemeni teachers is related to one or all of the following causes:

(1) The decrease in the number of students joining the teacher-training institutes and the Faculty of Education at San'a' University. These represent the only sources for supplying teachers at the primary stage.
(2) The continuous leakage of teachers to other professions.
(3) The inaccuracy of the annual statistics concerning the number of teachers.

The statistics show a continuous rise in the number of the students at the teacher-training institutes, especially during the years 1979/80 to 1982/83. However, the students who graduate from these institutes do not always join the teaching profession, and this seems to explain the fall in the number of Yemeni teachers in spite of the rising number of trainee teachers. Another group of graduates may continue their studies at university, so this group will not be available for teaching in the primary schools. Once they graduate, they will teach in the preparatory or secondary stages. In addition, many female graduates marry and stop working so as to give all their time to home affairs. Thus the final number of Yemeni teachers in the field is much smaller than the number of enrolments.

It must be remembered that the scarcity of Yemeni teachers in the field means an increasing dependence on non-Yemenis. Depending on non-Yemeni teachers is, in fact, a serious problem which is easy to underestimate at this stage. If the question is considered objectively, and if the government tries to plan realistically for the future and to link its planning with the political and economic policies of the country, it will be clear that the YAR cannot depend to the present extent on non-Yemeni teachers, since they are beyond the government's control. Some day, for whatever reason, the foreign teachers may stop coming and education would come to a standstill. Moreover, there are negative educational side-effects resulting from this dependence on non-Yemeni teachers. The child in the primary stage moves directly from his home to school, from his parents and siblings to a strange world of unknown people. It is not difficult to imagine the situation when the child finds those strangers talking in a dialect with which he is unfamiliar, and observes certain habits and manners that are entirely different from his own. Thus, because of his bewilderment, the child may become disoriented and so the school fails in one of its most important roles, the educational one. One should not over-generalise on this basis, but it is nevertheless important to recruit Yemeni teachers in order to keep the balance in the psychological and emotional growth of the pupils at this stage of education.

**Suggestions and Solutions**

Primary education is in a very bad state and is in urgent need of improvement. The following suggestions are put forward for discussion:

(1) More attention should be given to school activities as an essential part of the school curriculum because they are important in promoting the pupils' skills and potential.

(2) The prescribed primary-level text-books should be written by people with a deep understanding of the educational aspects of the pupils' growth.

(3) Pupils of differing ages should no longer be put in the same grade. Pupils of the same age should be put in one grade, within their range of abilities.

(4) Laws to control pupils' attendance should be enacted; however, such laws should be put into practice cautiously.

(5) Yemeni teachers should be encouraged to remain in the field of teaching, and made to realise their value by stressing their role in building the society.

(6) The standard of the teacher-training institutes should be improved. The level of the students in these institutes is reflected in the level of education as a whole.

(7) Guess-work should not be accepted when drawing up educational statistics. Accuracy should be more highly valued.

(8) Attention should be given to in-service training courses in the field of making and using teaching aids for primary-school teachers. Consideration should be given to the use of such aids in the class-room in evaluating teachers.


**Conclusion**

This chapter has attempted a rapid survey of primary education during the last 20 years or so. There may be shortcomings in the treatment of some aspects, or over-concentration on others. But according to the common saying, 'The journey of one thousand miles begins with one step,' and this short study may be considered as the first step on such a journey. More should be written in this field and all concerned should persist in their efforts to improve the situation. Yemenis are proud of the spread of education in their country, regardless of the problems from which it suffers, and in spite of some shortcomings in the educational levels of the pupils. In conclusion, it is hoped that the Ministry of Education will make a comprehensive and objective study of primary education, on the basis of its being the most important of the various educational levels.

# 17 LOW ENROLMENT OF STUDENTS AT THE FACULTY OF EDUCATION AND ITS EFFECTS ON THE SECOND FIVE-YEAR PLAN

Mohamed A. Alkhader

One could say that education in the Yemen Arab Republic (YAR) prior to 1962 was a privilege for the 'chosen few'. Even so, the standard was very low compared to that of neighbouring countries. Reading, writing and the knowledge of some arithmetic were enough basics for a person to master in order to secure a job as a clerk in the Imam's quasi-government.

After the 1962 revolution, North Yemen faced an extremely difficult task, not only in the educational field but in all sectors of life. The whole infrastructure of society had to change and improve: the basic needs of modern life were not available. This revolution was not against illiteracy alone, but against all facets of backwardness.

Prior to the revolution, there were only twelve primary and two intermediate schools, and scattered religious schools called *kuttabs*; higher education was non-existent in North Yemen. Since the revolution, the North Yemen government, with assistance from some Arab and a few other foreign countries, has made tremendous efforts to expand its educational system. A large number of public, elementary (primary), preparatory (intermediate) and secondary schools was built during this period. In addition, religious, teacher-training, vocational and commercial schools and agricultural institutes were built by the government. The establishment of San'a' University was the highest educational accomplishment. The number of teachers, mainly expatriate, was greatly increased and the curricula were modernised. These developments have led to great improvements in both the quality and quantity of the educational services provided for the students. These accomplishments are highly valued by every citizen in the YAR, especially in that during this same period the country was engulfed in a bitter and destructive civil war which lasted for eight long years (1962–70).

Since the early days of the revolution, government leaders have held to the belief that the basic element for any future development plan for the country depends largely upon the availability of trained and educated native personnel. The shortage or absence of such human resources would, therefore, act as the most severe constraint on the implementation of any such plans. With more than 85 per cent of the population still illiterate, the need for educational development is as acute as ever. Thus, the Yemeni government established a policy which emphasised that education was the right of every citizen. It must be emphasised here that, since the revolution, access to all levels of education has been free for every Yemeni citizen.

After the many pre-revolutionary years of deprivation, the country witnessed a tremendous growth and expansion in all levels of education during the post-revolutionary period (Table 17.1). This, the fastest-growing educational trend in Yemen, is based on the fact that every parent who was not able to go to school in his childhood is insistent that his son or daughter does not suffer the same deprivation.

One can only praise the government's attempts to extend education to all urban and remote areas. Education and training are considered as major factors in the government's budget, reflecting its need and desire to build up reliable human and industrial resources. Unfortunately, North Yemen is presently experiencing a shortage of native teachers. This is a very serious problem indeed, not only from the educational point of view, but also as regards the social and developmental aspects.

Table 17.1: YAR: Student Enrolment in Primary, Intermediate and Secondary Schools, and Teacher-Training Institutes

| Academic year | Primary (elementary) | Intermediate (preparatory) | Secondary | TTIs |
|---|---|---|---|---|
| 1962/63 | 61,335 | 730 | — | — |
| 1963/64 | 62,023 | 1,032 | 84 | 55 |
| 1964/65 | 66,961 | 1,462 | 226 | 24 |
| 1965/66 | 69,139 | 1,426 | 433 | 90 |
| 1966/67 | 63,366 | 1,672 | 656 | 190 |
| 1967/68 | 66,830 | 2,007 | 711 | 215 |
| 1968/69 | 66,468 | 2,077 | 803 | 574 |
| 1969/70 | 72,107 | 3,118 | 939 | 432 |
| 1970/71 | 88,217 | 3,931 | 1,189 | 412 |
| 1971/72 | 118,868 | 5,768 | 1,496 | 618 |
| 1972/73 | 153,807 | 7,306 | 2,267 | 923 |
| 1973/74 | 179,079 | 9,362 | 3,098 | 1,357 |
| 1974/75 | 232,784 | 12,163 | 4,350 | 921 |
| 1975/76 | 252,726 | 15,619 | 6,050 | 1,306 |
| 1976/77 | 220,159 | 17,676 | 7,197 | 1,650 |

| | | | |
|---|---|---|---|
| 1977/78 | 251,876 | 21,263 | 7,973 | 1,617 |
| 1978/79 | 251,967 | 18,852 | 7,145 | 1,237 |
| 1979/80 | 335,249 | 20,764 | 8,229 | 1,515 |
| 1980/81 | 414,273 | 25,037 | 9,895 | 1,548 |
| 1981/82 | 589,186 | 32,243 | 10,297 | 1,902 |
| 1982/83 | 705,062 | 43,362 | 14,516 | 2,807 |
| Projected | | | | |
| 1985/86 | 806,528 | 60,868 | 18,979 | 4,839 |

Note: Annual series are not always comparable.
Source: Ministry of Education (San'a').

This chapter attempts to shed some light on the reasons for the scarcity of Yemeni teachers, in particular secondary-school teachers, resulting from the low enrolment of students at the Faculty of Education, San'a' University. It also attempts to analyse some of the constraints which reduce potential educational expansion and which, therefore, will have to be eased in order to maintain the momentum of educational development.

The unwillingness of people to become teachers is an international phenomenon, particularly in Third World countries. The effects of this resistance to joining the teaching profession on a country's economic and social development plans cannot be ignored. A country such as North Yemen, with limited resources, is in a critical situation because of the shortage of native teachers. The latest data (academic year 1982–83) show that only 19 per cent of the total number of primary-school teachers and 11 per cent of the total number of intermediate and secondary teachers are Yemenis (see Table 17.2). These alarming figures provide two difficult challenges to the existing educational establishment:

(1) to meet this urgent demand for trained Yemeni teachers at all levels; and
(2) to formulate the guidelines of a national educational policy.

Finally, even though the Faculty of Education has been in existence to train secondary-school teachers since 1970/71, the number enrolled in the Faculty as a proportion of all students has been decreasing alarmingly since 1973/74. The two principal factors which have influenced this decrease in student enrolment are as follows:

(1) *Social*: Although teachers are highly respected by many sectors of Yemeni society, they are still looked upon as of low social status. This situation has many adverse effects on teachers. Namely, this low status:

(a) reduces the teacher's interest in doing his job properly;
(b) diverts his energy outside the scope of education;
(c) potentially reduces what students might learn from him quantitatively and qualitatively; and
(d) causes him to lose self-confidence and, as a result, his creativity is affected.

(2) *Financial*: Teachers all over the world are among the lowest paid among individuals with a comparable education. In this regard, Yemeni teachers are no exception. Recent research carried out among students at San'a' University concerning their unwillingness to attend the Faculty of Education and become teachers

Table 17.2: YAR: Number of Teachers in Primary, Intermediate and Secondary Schools, and Teacher-Training Institutes

| Academic year | Primary (elementary) | Intermediate (preparatory) | Secondary | TTIs | Total |
|---|---|---|---|---|---|
| 1962/63 | 1,332 | 48 | — | — | 1,380 |
| 1963/64 | 1,278 | 68 | 5 | 2 | 1,353 |
| 1964/65 | 1,268 | 97 | 13 | 2 | 1,380 |
| 1965/66 | 1,238 | 95 | 25 | 5 | 1,363 |
| 1966/67 | 1,336 | 111 | 39 | 11 | 1,497 |
| 1967/68 | 1,499 | 113 | 42 | 11 | 1,685 |
| 1968/69 | 1,443 | 138 | 47 | 30 | 1,658 |
| 1969/70 | 1,449 | 207 | 55 | 20 | 1,731 |
| 1970/71 | 1,726 | 262 | 73 | 21 | 2,082 |
| 1971/72 | 3,146 | 293 | 113 | 36 | 3,588 |
| 1972/73 | 4,253 | 340 | 157 | 58 | 4,808 |
| 1973/74 | 5,547 | 596 | 206 | 123 | 6,472 |
| 1974/75 | 5,881 | 543 | 265 | 130 | 6,819 |
| 1975/76 | 7,807 | 1,003 | 347 | 211 | 9,368 |
| 1976/77 | 8,188 | 669 | 318 | 147 | 9,322 |
| 1977/78 | 6,968 | 685 | 476 | 106 | 8,235 |
| 1978/79 | 5,900 | 916 | 406 | 83 | 7,950 |
| 1979/80 | 6,767 | 1,061 | 481 | 149 | 8,458 |
| 1980/81 | 9,812 | 1,407 | 616 | 182 | 12,017 |
| 1981/82 | 11,894 | 1,849 | 708 | 249 | 14,700 |
| 1982/83 | 13,334 | 2,205 | 990 | 310 | 16,487 |
| Projected 1985/86 | 23,043 | 3,795 | 1,515 | 1,112 | 29,465 |

Source: Ministry of Education (San'a').

indicates that the major factor that influences their decision is the lack of financial incentives.

In this regard, teachers are discouraged by the low salaries that they receive compared to those paid to individuals working in the private sector. As a result, potential teachers seek higher salaries and better working conditions elsewhere.

Table 17.3:   YAR: Indicators for Higher Education

| Academic year | Total student enrolment in San'a' University | Student enrolment at Faculty of Education | | Graduates from Faculty of Education |
|---|---|---|---|---|
| | | (No.) | (%) | |
| 1970/71 | 64 | 11 | 17.2 | — |
| 1971/72 | 251 | — | 0.0 | — |
| 1972/73 | 434 | — | 0.0 | — |
| 1973/74 | 1,150 | 227 | 19.7 | — |
| 1974/75 | 1,856 | 242 | 13.0 | — |
| 1975/76 | 2,343 | 315 | 13.4 | — |
| 1976/77 | 3,143 | 344 | 10.9 | 157 |
| 1977/78 | 3,522 | 290 | 8.2 | 142 |
| 1978/79 | 3,305 | 220 | 6.7 | 123 |
| 1979/80 | 3,712 | 241 | 6.5 | 78 |
| 1980/81 | 4,519 | 472 | 10.4[a] | 66 |
| 1981/82 | 5,973 | 205 | 3.4 | 90 |
| 1982/83 | — | 282 | — | 123 |

Note:a. The increase in enrolment in this year was due to San'a' University's announcement of the establishment of the Faculty of Education in Ta'izz. The actual number enrolled in San'a' was less than 200.
Source: Ministry of Education (San'a').

It is worth mentioning here that, in spite of a recent 60 per cent salary increase, a teacher's income remains low compared to that of individuals with comparable education working in the private sector. This is clearly indicated by the number of teachers who change jobs, irrespective of their rank and tenure as teachers. Many never enter teaching, some resign and still others choose to enter administrative positions. For example, of the total number of graduates from the Faculty of Education up to 1980, less than 17 per cent are still teaching. The only way of curbing this educational brain-drain or wastage is for North Yemen somehow to provide its teachers with jobs that can match in attractiveness the higher-paying positions that are available to them elsewhere.

Among other factors which inhibited the enrolment of students at the Faculty of Education are the following:

(1) In spite of the fact that the Faculty of Education was the main reason behind the establishment of San'a' University, the truth is that it lost its identity as the 'mother college' in the early days of its foundation. Moreover, while other faculties grew in student enrolment and physical size, the Faculty of Education suffered in both respects. Even though the Faculty admitted its first eleven students in 1970/71, it was not until 1976/77 (three years later than expected) that the first group graduated.

(2) For many years, a general belief prevailed at San'a' University that the Faculty of Education was the college of the under-privileged and untalented. This belief prevailed until the end of 1980, when the Faculty was first given its own independent administration which was to bear full responsibility for its students. Since then, many reforms have been implemented, including improvements in the quality of students being admitted, the modernisation of curricula and improvements in the teaching methodology at the Faculty. As a result of these reforms the students have begun to feel satisfaction in belonging to a 'Faculty'.

(3) A former secondary-school building now serves as the Faculty of Education. This appears to have had an adverse psychological effect on students. They expect to see a more modern building than they are accustomed to see in their high schools. Other, neighbouring faculties, on the other hand, enjoy much more spacious and luxurious buildings.

(4) Teaching is a tough and demanding job as well as one of the least rewarding occupations. The amount of work demanded from a teacher besides teaching (26 lectures a week) constitutes a major disincentive for individuals joining this profession. For example, overcrowded classrooms, shortage of books and teaching-aids and involvement in other administrative and school activities create an additional burden on the teacher, causing a lowering of his morale.

(5) Finally, one of the major factors discouraging Yemenis from enrolling at the Faculty of Education is the long-standing government policy of guaranteeing employment to all academic graduates. This policy, which simply encourages massive bureaucratic expansion and the perpetuation of non-productive employment, should be altered to one which gives job priority to graduates from the Faculty of Education and other similar institutions.

Recently, a study was conducted with 300 present Faculty of Education students in order to obtain information about their commitment to teaching, to find out the likelihood of their continuing in the field of education, and to attempt to ascertain their perception of the social importance of their profession. Preliminary analyses of the data revealed the following:

(1) Many students (181 out of 300) have enrolled at the Faculty according to their own wishes and would like to be teachers. They are conscious of the high calling of their profession to educate future citizens.
(2) It was somewhat reassuring to find that 129 students consider teaching a respectable job and think the financial reward is reasonable.
(3) A large number of students (247) believe that society has ignored teachers, while others (250) believe that the extra work and low salaries are the main reasons for teaching being unattractive.
(4) A fair proportion of students (121) would like to work in other administrative jobs which are less demanding.
(5) 72 students enrolled at the Faculty simply because they were in need of financial support or because they were advised to do so by their parents.

It must be stressed that teaching is a hard job and the financial rewards are minimal. Taking this into account, along with the country's continuously rising need for secondary-school teachers, the author firmly believes that genuine steps must be taken to encourage Yemenis to become teachers. This would not only decrease the dependence on expatriate staff, but would be of particular significance in North Yemen, both socially and economically, since a policy of Yemenisation is logical and desirable. To that end the following suggestions to attract Yemeni students to the teaching profession would have to be implemented.

(1) The financial factor is the crux of the problem. Gone are the days when teachers were considered to be social reformers and spiritual leaders. Other professionals, such as surgeons and engineers, now occupy these positions. At the present time, teachers are attempting only to survive.
    The improvement of teachers' financial status could be accomplished through:

(a) increased salaries;

(b) the provision of an annual job allowance;

(c) improved benefits such as a housing allowance and generous social and medical allowances;

(d) benefits for teachers' dependants; and

(e) the implementation of a system of promotion and provision of salary incentives.

Other incentives provided for students at the Faculty, such as exemption from military service and the provision of financial support (accommodation, board and book-allowance) during the period of study, seem not to be attractive enough for the students to enrol and become teachers. This underlines the need for the policy to change in favour of an improvement in teachers' status after graduation. Some might say that the government is unable to offer high salaries to a large sector such as the teaching force. But it should also be remembered that the country spends vast sums of money on expatriate staff (see Table 17.4). Moreover, the country must never be caught out by a sudden shortage of expatriate staff.

Table 17.4: YAR: Expected Expenditure on Teachers (million YR)

| Academic year | Yemeni teachers | | Expatriate | | Total | Percentage of expatriate teachers paid by non-Yemeni sources |
|---|---|---|---|---|---|---|
| | Primary | Intermediate & Secondary | Primary | Intermediate & Secondary | | |
| 1982/83 | 60.7 | 13.4 | 496.1 | 95.3 | 744.3 | 78.8 |
| 1983/84 | 63.5 | 17.8 | 533.4 | 112.2 | 810.4 | 83.4 |
| 1984/85 | 66.3 | 22.5 | 694.3 | 129.8 | 998.3 | 83.4 |
| 1985/86 | 69.7 | 28.1 | 817.9 | 164.9 | 1,169.0 | 88.1 |
| 1986/87 | 73.6 | 34.0 | 905.8 | 197.9 | 1,299.4 | 88.1 |

Source: Ministry of Education (San'a').

(2) It is strongly recommended that a teachers' union be established. It should enter into meaningful forms of negotiation and cooperation with the government, not only with a proper concern for pay and conditions, but also to create a body of teachers, all of whom can serve North Yemen in the proper way.

(3) At the present time, teachers are not given the right kind of attention by the mass media. It is unfortunately true to say that
teachers are among the most neglected occupational groups of
society. The mass media should emphasise the importance of
education in North Yemen and introduce teachers as members
of a profession who perform a unique public service on the basis
of a code of ethics with little regard to their personal financial
gain.
(4) As mentioned above, the Faculty of Education in San'a' is the
only one in the country. Steps should be taken to set up other
Faculties of Education in Ta'izz and Hodaida in order to alle-
viate the shortage of teachers which prevails at all levels.

In its current five-year plan, the Faculty of Education intends to
initiate several academic programmes. For example, the General
Diploma programme (started 1983/84) is intended for those who
graduate from other faculties and wish to qualify to join the
teaching profession. The second programme, namely Special
Diploma in Education, is designed for Faculty of Education graduates. The fields of study in this diploma will be curriculum development, school administration and school supervision. It is hoped that
leaders will emerge from this programme and contribute to educational development in the YAR.

The third programme is for students at the Faculty of Education
who, at the end of two years, feel unable to continue any further.
They would be allowed to suspend their registration and would be
awarded a 'half-way' degree qualifying them to teach in intermediate schools. It would still be possible for them to continue to the
Bachelor of Science degree, when their situation permitted them to
rejoin the Faculty. The main goals of these programmes are to train
and keep all available local manpower in the teaching profession
and to produce the kinds and amounts of human resources required
for educational growth so that the country will, in fact, make good
use of these resources and be less dependent on expatriate personnel.

**Conclusion**

Yemen in the 1980s is experiencing a shortage of native teachers in
general, and secondary-school teachers in particular. This constitutes a major constraint on the economic and social development of

the YAR. The main problem is that the majority of teachers are leaving their jobs and another large group finds teaching a less attractive profession. This makes it difficult to meet the fast-growing domestic teacher plan.

The emphasis of this chapter has been focused on the main causes of Yemenis' unwillingness to enrol at the Faculty of Education and become teachers. Some suggestions on ways to ease this deficiency have been put forward. The large expatriate teaching staff (see Table 17.4) not only constitutes a heavy financial burden (estimated at 50 per cent of the Ministry of Education budget), but also makes the country vulnerable to any crisis in the future and slows down the process of Yemenisation as well. In the schools themselves, the continued coming-and-going of teachers results in a reduction in the quantity and quality of lessons and in constantly altered timetables.

Educational development in North Yemen is continuous and seems to grow in geometric progression. What now look like limited short-term anxieties could become major problems in a few years' time unless positive action to counter them can be built into the government's policies.

The country sets aside a considerable proportion of its resources (see Table 17.4) to provide an educational system to prepare its younger members for adult life. But with 5,000 schools, 800,000 students, 17,000 teachers (mainly expatriate) and only 300 teachers who graduate each year from the Faculty of Education and teacher-training institutes there is an enormous gap between the country's available manpower and its growing needs. Attempts to close this gap have been frustrated by the social and economic factors previously mentioned.

The world is full of elegant theoretical solutions which never seem to fit the particular problem under discussion. The hope for continued generous financial aid from Arab states or from oil finds in the YAR may be the only solution in the near future. Irrespective of this, it remains to be seen how well the government and the Ministry of Education respond to proposals for the improvement of the status of teachers in the country. There is no doubt that teachers, as well as everybody concerned, are likely to be greatly disappointed if these proposals are not carried out and their expectations are not met.

# 18 CULTURAL DEVELOPMENT IN THE PEOPLE'S DEMOCRATIC REPUBLIC OF YEMEN

Abdullah Ahmed Muheirez

The subject of culture and its development in the People's Democratic Republic of Yemen (PDRY) cannot, of course, be separated from that of Yemen as a whole. It is only in this century, and more precisely after the First World War, that different influences have affected both sections of Yemen, leading to the adoption of differing attitudes and the facing of differing challenges. The northern section was independent, closed to outside influences and deeply affected by sectarian and political strife, whereas the southern section was colonised and open to outside influences. The result was a widening gap in cultural and social attitudes between the two sectors. This chapter deals mainly with the development of culture in the South during and after the First World War until today.

## The Hinterland

### The Hadramawt

The southern section itself was also subject to various influences. The so-called Eastern Aden Protectorate, consisting of the Hadramawt, was drawn into British advisory relations in 1937 and, apart from coastal towns and Wadi Hadramawt itself, the rest was afflicted by tribal hostilities. A large percentage of the population migrated to Indonesia and East Africa. This migration has shaped the social and cultural texture of the Hadramawt, adding new blood to a stagnant social and economic situation. In Indonesia a new trend of both cultural and social life emerged: magazines and books were published, literary circles and cultural societies were born, and religious and political debates took place. All this was brought back to the Hadramawt and some even spread to the rest of the Arab world.

One of the products of this society was the famous poet and playwright Ali Ahmad Bakathir, who gained his reputation and indeed wrote all his work outside the Hadramawt. One of his most famous books is *Humam aw fi Bilad al-Ahkaf*; a description of life

200

in the Hadramawt in the 1930s, it could well be regarded as a historical document of social and cultural life at the time. In his preface
Bakathir has this to say:

> All of us know that in the Hadramawt there is a great deal of
> innovation in religion which should be forbidden and eradicated.
> In the Hadramawt there is ignorance that should be eliminated by
> the light of science. There is stagnation which should be ended. In
> the Hadramawt there are literary rights and privileges for the
> Alawis and others which should be terminated. There are also
> bad customs and habits to be corrected, chaos and highway rob-
> bery, bloodshed by the tribes which should be stopped.
> These things are seen by the eye, heard by the ear, touched by
> the hand and it is up to the Hadrami people to co-operate and
> seek reformation. It is not reasonable for any philanthropist who
> calls for action to be accused of hating the Alawis. The case is of a
> miserable land which should be saved and a sick people to be
> treated, and not a case of love and hate between factions of
> people.[1]

Bakathir is describing a movement that started outside the
Hadramawt and affected cultural thought and caused deep splits
there for a long time — the conflict between the Alawis and
Irshadis, which involved other learned people in Egypt and Syria.
This movement unfortunately caused a spirit of bitterness among
the Hadramis, but at the same time it created a rivalry which resulted
in the building of schools, philanthropic activities, and so on, and
discussions that have influenced social and cultural life in the
Hadramawt. The list of clubs and societies during this period is
impressive.[2] Some of the richer emigrants went back to the
Hadramawt, built large palaces, introduced exotic foods and clothing and amassed large collections of books and manuscripts which
have made the Hadramawt one of the richest areas in manuscripts in
the PDRY. These are now collected in the Yemeni Centre for Cultural
and Archaeological Research (Ahkaf Library in Tarim). The famous
school of Rabat in Tarim has influenced cultural thought within
the Hadramawt and, to a certain extent, the rest of South Yemen.
Its fame ran wide; a great number of learned people graduated
from this school and spread as teachers, *imams* of mosques,
judges, and so on. Apart from this school no other cultural activities
existed except what came into the country by way of travellers,

bringing Egyptian newspapers and books, or returning emigrants to the Hadramawt.

## The Western Aden Protectorate

The Western Aden Protectorate was less fortunate; it was kept as a buffer zone between the northern sector of Yemen and Aden. Primary schooling started after the Second World War. Foreign influence was restricted to British and Indian administrators, or a trickle of emigrants who came back from the United Kingdom and America with hardly any change in their attitudes towards modern society. The only part of the Western Aden Protectorate that developed culturally was Lahej: schools were opened here in the 1930s and in the same decade students were first sent abroad on scholarships for further studies. Its proximity to Aden guaranteed a flow of newspapers, magazines and regular contacts with foreign communities. A further factor was that some members of its ruling family were very well-educated: they travelled abroad, and tried to imitate the princely courts which they had visited in India and the Arab world.

A particularly outstanding member of the Abdali family who has influenced culture until the present day is the famous author, poet and musician, Ahmad Bin Fadl. In the 1930s he wrote his famous *Hadiyat al-Zaman fi Akhbar Muluk Lahaj wa Adan*, a brief history of Aden and Lahej up to 1930, including documents relating to Turkish rule in Lahej up to the First World War. Ahmad Bin Fadl was a musician in his own right: he wrote many songs that are still famous throughout the PDRY. He also wrote a pamphlet in praise of music, and a reply to his critics in religious circles who frowned at the excessive use of musical instruments and singing. Bin Fadl's influence on cultural developments in Lahej and the PDRY as a whole is unique. A man of breadth of vision, he was so impressed by a visit to India that he introduced gardening to Lahej for its aesthetic value, rather than as a means of growing vegetables; he also introduced certain foods and dress. It is due to his influence that the authorities encouraged schools and scholarships. He was also instrumental in opening a literary club in Aden, called the Arab Literary Club. Bin Fadl has inspired many poets and singers over the past four decades. A wealth of poetical work was published by another famous Lahej poet who was deeply affected by the work of Bin Fadl; this was Adbullah Hadi Subait, whose work is also sung.

**Aden up to the Second World War**

Aden was a different matter completely and perhaps some historical background would be helpful to an understanding of the cultural development of Aden between the two World Wars.

*The Cultural Environment*

During and after the First World War Crater was a docile, sleepy little town with a population of 10,000 together with it sisters, Ma'alla village and Tawahi. Sheikh Othman was a village, a rural hamlet for the gathering of caravans and visitors to Aden from the hinterland. The clouds of the First World War, although dispersed in the outside world, were still thick over Yemen. The Turkish Army and the British still waged war between Dala' and Sheikh Othman. A state of uneasy loyalties dominated the tribes, large Adeni families, *shaikhs* and ordinary people. Culture and education were the last things on the mind of the local ruler or the outside coloniser. No serious steps were taken to build schools or to introduce any kind of formal education. Education was the monopoly of the Indian elite, the Parsee businessmen, the Jewish community and the missionaries. The latter started formal education in Crater, Sheikh Othman, Tawahi and Ma'alla and dominated the educational system until the 1940s. In Crater it was a Danish Mission which opened a school (and also a bookshop). The Roman Catholic Mission opened the famous RCM school which continued until the 1970s. There were also the Keith Falconer Presbyterian Mission in Sheikh Othman and St Anthony's School in Steamer Point. The latter catered mainly for Anglo-Indian students coming from Goa, and for '*Kurstan*' (a corruption of 'Christian', and referring especially to recently converted or non-European Christians).

The government started the Residency School which ran parallel with the missionary work but was less efficiently run; not until the 1940s was Arabic introduced as a compulsory subject. During this period, the sole purpose of education was the learning of English. A student's cultural achievement was measured by the number of books by Michael West (*Reader for Indian Students*) that he had finished. A young man who had finished five books had a good chance of becoming a clerk in the Municipality. The aim was to earn a living; for that, the only important requirement was to learn English. Whatever else the student learnt, and it was little enough, was unimportant. It would betoken an indulgence on his part in matters that brought him no benefit.

Under these conditions the local Arab was at a loss. He was dominated by alien forces, political, cultural, social and economic. He was mainly the provider of services, clerical work, menial jobs. A wave of Indian culture dominated the country. Arabic songs were sung to Indian music, dresses were worn in Indian style. Government notices and warnings were written in English and translated into a form of Arabic that was predominantly Indian in grammar and text. A visitor to Aden at that period had the impression that Aden was an alien city in an Arab country — Amin al-Rihani wrote about the contrast between Aden's glorious Arab past and the state of affairs in 1924:

> Where, O Aden, is your wall which surrounded the island; where are your palaces, surpassing the palaces of Ibn Dhi Jadan . . . where are the works of your writers and poets, and those who marched proudly under your flag? Indeed, where is that language among the lingos and gibberish which infiltrated it from East and West? Where is that spirit, the spirit of Qahtan? And those noble qualities of Adnan? . . . Aden in those days was the Aden of the Arabs and of union. I do not mean the union of religion only, but of nationhood and language also. The unity of nationalism had already been fissured by a mixture of Indians who emigrated to this corner of the Arab world before the British occupied it. The Banyan [Indian merchants] were in Aden when the French mission came to it [in 1709] . . . The Zaidi Yemeni Arab was generous to them . . . he did not know that in the future his children would be their servants and the servants of those who would come from the West as well.[3]

The impression that one receives either from visitors or from Yemeni intellectuals during that period is that Aden compared extremely unfavourably with the India of the British Raj. A dread of government (*sirkal*[4]) institutions prevailed; thus government warning notices were obeyed to the letter and, in spite of poverty and lack of jobs, law and order reigned. It was a period of uncertainty both inside and outside Yemen: Italian occupation threatened from Ethiopia, Palestine was being dominated by the Jews, the Wahhabi state was created in Saudi Arabia, and the Indian struggle for independence was intensifying. It is also worth noting that Aden was dominated economically by non-Yemeni elements: the big commercial Parsee and Indian houses started in the early days of the British occupation. The influx of Indian administrators, teachers and engineers who were brought in by the British gave a sense of power to the Indian community. The Indian felt more at home than the local Yemeni and, with the exception of a few families long settled in Aden, the Yemeni resident saw Aden as a temporary base for his activities, whether labour or commerce, and had no intention of residing permanently in the town.

The prospect of any administrative change caused considerable concern to the Indians, who feared, quite correctly, that their position would be affected by a non-Indian administration. This factor, together with their confidence in their own domination of Aden, were such that they went so far as to attempt to persuade the local Yemenis to fight British plans to annex Aden as a British colony in favour of continued subjection to India within an independent India. But the majority of local Yemenis did not favour a further relationship with India and agreed to sign the document annexing Aden to the British Crown: this was signed by Sir Muhammad Abdulqadir Makkawi and others.[5]

*Influences on the Cultural Renaissance*

Although the above gives a picture of the general scene, the Yemenis in Aden began to look for their cultural ties beyond Yemen, India or Britain. They turned to their brothers in Iraq, Egypt and Syria, and even as far as Morocco. Events in the Arab world also helped to inspire a feeling of belonging to a larger, more educated and perhaps a freer Arabia. It was a period of search for an Arab identity, a period of great expectations of a united Arab world. A number of events were particularly influential in shaping cultural and, later, political and social thought in Aden and Lahej, and to a lesser degree the rest of South Yemen. A brief list of such events may help to measure their impact on the area during that period:

(1) The success of King Ibn Saud in ousting the Sherif of Mecca and the ascendancy of the Wahhabis had their effects in South Yemen: (a) a highly educated group of men, who migrated to Aden in the late 1920s, contributed a great deal to its cultural development. A prominent figure among them was Syed al-Dabbagh, a member of a Hijazi Hashimite family, who opened a school called al-Najjah where he introduced modern subjects and even started a music group. He was a great personality who affected people deeply and visited several parts of Southern

Yemen like Tarim and Yafa'. (b) The success of the Wahhabis created bitter religious divisions which lasted until the 1950s. There was much discussion about the prohibition on music, and about visiting saints and prayers to saints, discussions which, in a sense, indicated an awakening to the social changes which would affect the future of Aden in the 1950s. The Wahhabi movement was also an inspiration to some people to reform religion, as will be discussed below.

(2) In 1925 Aden was visited by Abdul Aziz al-Tha'alibi who was instrumental in suggesting the creation of the Arab Literary Club.

(3) The Palestinian revolution of 1936 fired the imagination of the local Adenis and thus sowed the seeds of political aspirations which culminated in 1948 in riots in Aden against the partition of Palestine, to which the people of Aden were strongly opposed. Visits by Palestinian dignitaries such as Tal'at al-Ghusain (who visited Aden in 1936) caused many Adeni intellectuals to rally round them and also cemented an already existing relationship. Another famous Palestinian, Muhammad Taher, published a newspaper in Egypt called *Al-Shura* which always discussed Yemeni affairs and published subjects relating to Aden. Taher had even represented Aden and the Adenis when they were prohibited from attending the General Islamic Conference held in Jerusalem in 1931.[6] Taher was a personal friend of two eminent authors, Muhammad Ali Luqman, founder of the Adeni newspaper *Fatat al-Jazira*, and Ahmad Sa'id al-Asnaj who wrote a book in 1931 (published by *Al-Shura* publishing house) called *Aden: its Share of the Cultural Movement*, a compendium of biographies and articles on cultural matters.

(4) Visits were made to Aden by various other dignitaries, such as Tawfiq Nuri al-Barqawi who fled from Libya in 1937–8 and arrived in Aden. He was a focus for intellectuals and after the independence of Libya started a magazine in Tripoli called *Al-Jabal al-Akhdar*; while in Aden he wrote a book called *Al-Yaqut fi Tar'ikh Hadramawt* (a brief history of the Hadramawt).[7]

### Cultural Renaissance in Aden

In 1929 the Arab Reform Club was formed in Steamer Point by Adeni intellectuals and men of culture. The following year, the Islamic Arab Reformation Club was formed in Crater and another branch opened in Sheikh Othman. The Reformation Club continued in one form or another well into the 1950s. Among its members were many would-be political journalists and it undoubtedly had an effect on thought in Aden for more than two decades. The Club encouraged its members to participate in all the major events in the Arab world, for example, by making collections for war victims or protesting at the Jewish colonisation of Palestine.

During this period three famous works were published. *Sa'id*, the first Yemeni novel, was written by Muhammad Ali Luqman. In 1932 the same author published *Why the West has Advanced*, a critical discussion of the causes of the backwardness of the East and the advance of the West. By the beginning of the Second World War, there was evidence of a cultural renaissance; the first Adeni newspaper in Arabic, *Fatat al-Jazira*, was published at this time.

An important literary circle called *Mukhayyam Abu al-Tayyib* (Abu al-Tayyib Camp), which held its meetings at the *Fatat al-Jazira* premises, was formed. By 1942 it had published its one and only literary work, *Aqlam Mukhayyam Abu al-Tayyib*, a collection of essays on subjects permitted by the British government during the war period, covering such topics as Boy Scouts, the Adeni fisherman, polygamy, youth in Aden, the famous eleventh-century poet Abu al-Tayyib al-Mutanabbi (from whom the circle took its name), and so on. One cannot help noticing two features of this period. First, there was a recognition of the lack of Arabic study; thus the first aim of the circle, as defined in the preface of *Aqlam*, was 'to encourage the learning of the Arabic language and its use, and the revival of Arabic literature'. Secondly, it was recognised that all literary work was either in imitation of or heavily dependent on Classical Arabic culture as a whole; there was little recognition of Yemeni culture as such.

Other circles were formed later on in the names of Karmat [vineyard of] Ibn Hani, an Andalusian poet, and Abu al-Ala al-Ma'arri, a twelfth-century poet and philosopher from Syria. These were the expression of the aspiration to belong to a wider Arab world, and to be distinguished from the alien community dominating both the cultural and the economic scene in Aden.

During the Second World War, life went on, threatened sporadically by the Italians bombarding Steamer Point and Shamsan mountain, and with the population concerned about the outcome of the war. There was strict rationing of foodstuffs and imported materials, creating a hardship not known during the pre-war years. One result was that clothes started to be smuggled from Dar Sa'ad to

Aden, providing the inspiration behind a famous novel by Abdullah Arslan which added a new word to the Adeni Arabic vocabulary. The book was called *Yawmiyat Mubarshat,* '*barshat*' being a corruption of the word 'parachute', used for smuggling. The word is still used for acquiring goods or money by illegal means.

During the war years formal secondary education began to be taken seriously; Arabic was introduced as a compulsory subject at this level, one to be taken in the Senior Cambridge School Certificate. Formal education was in English except for Religion, Arabic and Arabic literature. During those years and well into the 1960s, the text-book for Arabic literature was *Al-Muntakhab min Adab al-Arab* published in Egypt. The curious thing about this book is that it does not mention a single Yemeni poet or writer throughout Arab history. The closest to a mention of a Yemeni poet is that of Umara al-Yamani, and he is mentioned only because of his association with the Fatimids in Egypt. Students had never heard of Hamdani, Nashwan al-Himyari or other eminent Yemeni philosophers or writers. The quotations were all from al-Mutanabbi or Abu Nuwas, but never from Yemeni literature. From the point of view of an onlooker today, the cultural scene would have seemed very grim: voices arose now and then demanding that more importance be given to Arabic and more stress laid on learning Arab history, with special reference to Yemeni history and culture.

Outside Aden, where schools were non-existent and alien influence was minimal, the people expressed themselves in the traditional *humaini* poetry,[8] sung to the dance called *shabwaniya*. A little of this filtered to the towns, with visitors or families moving to the city, but nowhere did it appear to be written or published until independence, with perhaps the exception of the poetic works of Ahmad Bin Fadl. During the war two poetic works were published by Ali Luqman, son of the founder of *Fatat al-Jazira: Al-Watar al-Maghmur* was published in August 1944, and *Ash Jan fi'l-Lail* in September 1945.

**Post-war Developments**

After the Second World War it was evident that the wind of change that had swept the rest of the world would also bring change to Aden and South Arabia. Effective secondary education, with the aim of preparing students for further education abroad, was achieved. Well-to-do families sent their children abroad to school. The political parties encouraged further education and also helped to make bilateral agreements with sympathetic governments to accept students from South Yemen.

Two outstanding learned people who had studied at Al-Azhar University in Cairo dominated the religious and social scene in Aden in the 1950s; they were Ali Ahmad Bahamish and Muhammad Salim al-Baihani. The latter was associated with another learned person, Ahmad al-Abbadi, a prominent figure in Sheikh Othman. Al-Abbadi had written a book consisting of a poem of religious reformation called *Hidayat al-Murid ila Sabil al-Haqq wa'l-Tawhid* (published in Cairo in 1939), in which he advised against the visiting of tombs and an excessive belief in saints — advice which was considered by many as Wahhabi.

Al-Baihani was a student of al-Abbadi and was accused of having the same religious stand; his speeches and sermons were attacked by a group of learned people and mosque imams, led by Ali Bahamish. Between 1952 and the later 1960s, and parallel to the political labour discussions of the time, these religious groups fought a different war. The subjects discussed included the following:

(1) Should *'id* prayers be permitted on football grounds? Al-Baihani said yes, Bahamish no. This was followed by a three- or four-year argument until people accepted that prayers on a football ground were not against religion.
(2) Should offerings be given to saints? Al-Baihani said no, Bahamish yes. (It had been the custom for many people to seek health and success by praying at a saint's tomb and offering gifts to the person in charge of the tomb.)
(3) Should women give up purdah and be educated? In 1950 al-Baihani wrote a book called *Ustaz al-Mar'a*, advising that women should be educated in moderation but coming out firmly against the abandonment of purdah.
(4) There were also minor questions such as the sighting of the moon at the beginning of Ramadan, singing, dancing, films, and so on.

Al-Baihani later built a famous school (which remained open until 1967) called al-Ma'had Al-Islami, which provided education up to Secondary School Certificate level. Non-government schools were started all over Aden and finally the creation of two institutions, one educational and the other economic, had an ineradicable effect on the changing scene in Aden.

Aden College was built and opened in 1950; it was the first secondary grammar school to be organised on the British public-school system. Only a few students were accepted each year and the College was provided with the best teachers and equipment and ultra-modern laboratories. It was for a long time the focal point of education, not only for Aden, but for all the Protectorate and it even accepted scholarship students from Somaliland. It dominated the cultural and educational scene in Aden throughout the 1950s and most of the 1960s; it is worth noting that most of the intelligentsia, ministers and administrators of the pre- and post-independence periods were educated at this College. Cultural development in Aden and the Protectorate cannot be studied without mentioning the effect of this school.

The Aden refinery was built at about the same time, creating immense opportunities for work and demanding a huge labour force which Aden alone was unable to provide. Doors were opened for workers from the North, from the Protectorate and even from Somalia. For the first time emigration to work in the oilfields in Dhahran in Saudi Arabia, which had been popular in the 1940s, stopped. It was also the first time that, as a result of labour coming from the hinterland and the North, Aden developed a cosmopolitan nature, and Yemenis from all parts of Yemen accepted and developed an understanding of each other. This had hitherto been impossible because of the barriers and suspicions created by the different types of administration and the restrictions on movement during the 1930s and 1940s. In fact, the situation was full of hope for the future.

The 1950s and most of the 1960s, however, were years of total political and social confusion. It will be some time before a full analysis of the situation is possible. The occupation of Palestine by Israel shocked Yemen, as indeed it shocked the rest of Arabia, but it may have had a greater effect in Aden because of the South Yemenis' long-standing sympathy for the Palestinians. The revolutions and counter-revolutions in the northern sector of Yemen, Syria, Egypt and Iraq had their echo among the population of Aden and found sympathisers, and often followers, at every level of society. It was a period of many political parties and ideologies, the free importation of films, newspapers and books, and the absorption of the various influences that faced the local Yemeni at this time. In Mukalla the British were faced with a situation of semi-revolt when, in 1952, the people stormed the palace of the Sultan protesting against the appointment of a non-Hadrami Minister of State, something that had hitherto been accepted as a matter of course.

The 1948 revolution in North Yemen had profound echoes in the South, charging the atmosphere with the hope that a powerful administration in the North would make the British change their attitude and lead the way to self-government and, eventually, independence. The creation of the Federation of South Arabia was a clumsy step towards that end.

The writings published during the 1948–65 period were mostly political. A great deal of literature was written for and against various political stands; newspapers were started, only to stop publication a few months later. Despite this situation, a few cultural works appeared: poetry by Muhammad Abdu Ghanim and Lutfi Aman; *Al-Mustaqbal*, a magazine started in 1949 by Abdullah Badheeb and a group of young people with a vision of social reformation; *Jazirat al-Arab Tattahimu Hukama'aha* by Hashim Abdullah, a book which bitterly criticised contemporary Arab regimes; a play called *Khawatir* by Hamza Luqman; and a short story, *Sa'id al-Mudarris*, by Sa'id Miswat. Other writers and poets who became famous during the period were Idris Hanbala, Muhammad Sa'id Garada and Abdullah Hadi Subait.

A report published by the government of the Federation of South Arabia for the United Nations in 1964 summarises the cultural situation as follows: one museum, the Aden Society of Arts, the Aden Society of Music, the Aden Society of History and Archaeology, and the creation of a Department of Antiquities. The number of newspapers and magazines available at the end of 1964 was 25, and some of these continued to be published until independence in 1967.

**Developments since Independence**

On 30 November 1967, after a long and bitter struggle, the independence of the People's Republic of South Yemen was won. A new spirit of adventure in culture was created — hitherto non-existent because of political and religious inhibitions — resulting in new cultural horizons.

The First Three-Year Development Plan (1971/72–1973/74) was modest in its aims as far as culture was concerned. The foremost considerations in formulating the Plan's objectives in the cultural field were: '1. The necessity of providing for the increasing popular demand on cultural services of various kinds; 2. The state's financial possibilities.'[9] The Plan made modest provision, of 700,000 dinars (YD), for the following activities: the development of three museums, the protection and restoration of archaeological sites, the revival of craftsmanship and popular arts, three cultural centres and the building of a national theatre.

By 1975 substantial interest had been aroused in local arts and crafts and the study of ethnography. A few organisations were created (listed below) to propagate and popularise local culture. In a study of the history of the Yemeni revolution, the following position is taken:

> Attention is drawn to an important and delicate fact about the new and the old. Not all the old and the traditional is bad, and not all that is new is good. Scientific socialism makes use of all that is positive and fights all deviations. Ultimate refusal of the old culture does not express scientific understanding, for within the old culture the elements of national culture exist.[10]

Arising from this position, it is worth noting that a complete transformation has taken place, encouraged by a firm belief in the unity of Yemen as a whole and a humanistic approach to culture in general. These thoughts also led to an effort to make Yemeni culture better understood in relation to other cultures, and to give opportunities for it to be studied in various ways. The essential, important theme is the belief that national culture has to stem from the old and traditional, but must use modern means of study and analysis. A revival of extinct or hitherto unpopular arts existing in the countryside took place. A seemingly limitless amount of poetry, proverbs, literature and works on philology and dialects has been published and analysed, with the purpose of stressing the unity of culture in Yemen as a whole. This policy has already been successful in unifying cultural thought in the different parts of the PDRY and, indeed, throughout Yemen.

Recent archaeological excavations have revealed common factors in the civilisation, methods of building and building materials in Timna', Shabwa, Ghaibun and Wadi Hadramawt in South Yemen and those of Ma'rib and Sarwah in the North. Excavations have also shown a common denominator of cultural tradition and dialects throughout the history of these areas. Archaeological research is still in its infancy in Yemen but it already indicates, with intensive study of epigraphy, the unity and similarity of cultures in the area. As already mentioned, local culture was isolated from outside influences between the two World Wars and thus was preserved almost intact. It is important as source material for the study of archaeology and pre-Islamic languages like Mahri and Socotri. A joint study of Mahri is at present being made by the Universities of Aden and Paris; a similar study of Socotri is being undertaken by the Academy of Science in Leningrad in the USSR and the Yemeni Centre for Cultural Research. This Centre has also started the documentation of other local dialects, the study of customs and traditions, and a comparative philology of existing dialects related to Yemeni history.

The foregoing discussion of the inter-war period in cultural development has indicated a lack of any cultural intercourse between Aden and the hinterland. There was, in fact, a complete isolation of the arts and crafts, poetry, and so on. Although the town of Aden was affected by foreign and Arab newspapers, films and books, little of this filtered into the countryside. Independence, with the consequent change of attitude towards the countryside, has resulted in the recognition of a more original and unlimited source of cultural material.

During the seminar on humaini poetry held by the Yemeni Centre for Cultural Research in 1979, with the participation of poets from North Yemen, a great deal of poetry was recorded and has provoked discussion and analysis of social and historical matters. The amount of material gathered in the seminar is so large that it has taken a great deal of time to condense it to a size suitable for publication, which is scheduled to take place shortly.

Among the collections gathered by the Yemeni Centre are stories, proverbs and similar cultural works describing the use and manufacture of guns, tribal treaties, specialised expressions in tribal law, customs and traditions. Whereas culture in the towns was dominated by outside influences, the rural areas provided fresh and original material that is both fascinating and enjoyable.

In 1974 a massive search for manuscripts was initiated by the Centre, and many families were persuaded to give their documents to the Ahkaf Library in Tarim, which is at the moment the Central Library for manuscripts (a catalogue is to be issued). A worldwide search for Yemeni manuscripts is also taking place and a great number have been microfilmed and deposited in the National Library in Aden. The government of the PDRY has created this Centre with the role of taking full responsibility for collecting source materials for the history of Yemen and encouraging archaeological excavations, the creation of libraries and the documentation of local arts and crafts, and so on.

The Ministry of Culture in the PDRY has encouraged the creation of several unions to promote particular fields of interest, namely the Union of Writers, the Union of Artists, the Union of Musicians and the Union of Young Writers. It has also created the Fine Arts Institute, offering courses in music, fine arts, acrobatics, theatre and ballet. The Ministry has also created the Department of Translation and Publications, which has already published some 30 books by Yemeni writers in various fields. It is worth noting the spread of cinemas, which were previously concentrated in Aden; there is now one cinema in every major town, drawing large audiences. Moreover, the PDRY now has 25 regular publications.

In short, there is a popularisation of culture throughout the area, through government encouragement and through rewards and public honours for artists, poets and authors. In addition, a new revival in culture has been helped by the spread of education and the gradual eradication of illiteracy while, for the longer term, there remains a great deal of material worthy of classification and study.

## Notes

1. A. A. Bakathir, *Human aw fi Bilad al-Ahkaf* (n.p., Cairo, 1934), p. 18.

2. A. A. Saban, 'Al-Haraka al-Ummaliya wa Tatawwuruha fi Wadi Hadramawt', lecture submitted in Sai'un for 1 May celebrations (Yemeni Centre for Cultural Research, Aden, June 1982), p. 8.

3. Amin al-Rihani, *Muluk al-Arab* (Al-Matba'a al-Ilmiya, Beirut, 1924), p. 401 in the 1980 reprint by Al-Mu'assasa al-Arabiya li'l-Dirasat wa'l-Nashr, Beirut.

4. 'Sirkal' means 'the authorities' in corrupted Indian-Arabic.

5. Sultan Nagi, 'Education and the Cultural Situation in Aden during Indian Rule' in *Al-Iklil*, vol. 2, no. 1 (1982).

6. M. A. al-Taher, *Nadharat al-Shura Press* (Al-Shura Press, Cairo, 1932), p. 145.

7. The manuscript was presented to President Mu'ammar al-Qadhafi when he visited Aden in 1980, for future publication by the Libyan government.

8. Humaini is poetry written in the local dialect.

9. *Three-Year Development Plan 1971–73* (Aden, 1971), p. 72.

10. *Dirasat Ta'rikh al-Thawra al-Yamaniya* (no author, n.p., Aden, 1975).

# 19 THE CONSERVATION OF THE URBAN ARCHITECTURAL HERITAGE OF YEMEN

Ronald Lewcock

The opportunities for undertaking serious research in Yemen, which began after the end of the civil war in the North (1970), have been nowhere more significant than in architectural studies. Although only a limited time has passed since then, and architectural researchers are seriously handicapped by the early state of archaeological study and by the absence of classification of most of the documentation, the immense wealth of surviving buildings has made it possible to establish the main outline of building development for at least the last 300 years, and, in the case of mosques, for well over 1,000 years. It has proved possible subsequently in some areas to link this with early accounts of the country, so that the essential continuity of architectural design in urban areas can be asserted with some confidence for a period dating back almost to the beginning of Islam, and reasoned speculation can arguably take it back four centuries earlier.

The pride of the Yemeni in his traditional architecture is still evident, in spite of the recent acculturation. With good building materials readily to hand, especially stone, plaster and translucent gypsum, and with little alternative means of expression of his success in life besides building, the houses, mosques, minarets and some *samsaras* tended to grow in size and acquire decoration and rich finishes, whereas today such expression of the Yemeni's wealth is diverted to the acquisition of motor cars and relatively impermanent household gadgets. The stimulus given to the quality of architectural design and construction by the pride in owning fine buildings must have been a millennia-old phenomenon in Yemen, and explains the distinction attained by its architecture — which has led to it now being widely admired in the outside world.

With the recent appeals by both Yemeni governments to UNESCO to launch international campaigns to protect and conserve the old walled city of San'a' and the cultural heritage of the Hadramawt, in particular the old walled city of Shibam, attention has been focused on the problems of conservation of the urban heritage of Yemen. In addition, a number of buildings in urban areas are now the object of serious conservation efforts, in particular the Great Amiriya complex in Rada', the Ashrafiya complex in Ta'izz and the minaret of the old Friday Mosque in Aden. But these are only a few of the marvellous monuments of Yemen that urgently require conservation if they are to be preserved for posterity.

Yemen's rapidly growing cities have many problems in common with those of the rest of the developing world. Some of the problems are technical and are the direct result of the speed with which these towns and cities have expanded to four or five times their size only a few years ago. One of the most visible (and most serious) of these technical problems is the extent to which damp is rising to unprecedented levels in the walls of the buildings. This is due to the fact that, in every urban area, piped water has been made available to more people in greater quantities than ever before. The infrastructure for draining that water out of the central area has not been supplied, or, in the few cases where it has been, the drainage has not been adequate in size or in standards. Both the water supply pipes and the drainage pipes tend to be of low quality and are easily damaged by traffic. The result is that as water flows along the pipes, even the water supply of new systems, a good part is simply lost into the ground. The lack of necessary drainage and sewerage is therefore only one aspect of the problem; the other aspect is the inadequate water-supply system. The water-mains systems installed in the last ten years have been of a low standard — due to an insistence on economy by the many organisations funding the schemes. The pipes are of either asbestos or plastic, both materials which crack very easily under pressure and with the movement of vehicles and buildings: they are in many ways the source of the problem.

The water which drains into the ground forms a 'perched water table', that is, a water table which is retained in the top 3 or 4 m below ground level because of an impermeable layer of fine clays below it, thus stopping the water going through and draining into the main water table. After only a few years, these perched water tables become so full that the water emerges at ground level, where it frequently lies for long periods of time. In this way the water can easily rise by capillary attraction to quite high levels in the walls of the buildings. Not only are the foundations undermined and the clays dissolved below the stones of the building, but water rising through the walls causes tremendous damage: it dissolves the clays and mortars in the walls. If, as usually happens, the water is also polluted by excrement from broken sewer pipes, by urine, by chemicals which are part of the exhaust of motor vehicles and by industry, then this polluted water forms acids which readily attack the materials of the walls. Recent repairs are already under attack in many areas, and it is evident that the life of new building materials can be as short as five or ten years under such conditions.

These problems affect both the outsides of the buildings and their interiors. This is clearly, then, a major problem in upgrading any old area — because the cost of rectifying it represents something like a quarter to a third of the total cost of any programme of rehabilitation.

Shibam in South Yemen has the highest known mud buildings in the world; some of its houses are over 30 m high. But the very inadequate drainage systems are bringing the sewage down into the streets, where it usually soaks into the ground. Again, the contamination of the water in the ground by sewage and other factors has produced extraordinary problems, undermining the foundations and soaking up into the walls. Cracking might begin in one corner of a building at the bottom, but by the time it reaches the sixth floor it will run right through the entire structure in every direction — the major cracks will be approximately 4–5 cm across. In the old city of Shibam many of the buildings that have already collapsed are in the centre of town, where the water supply and drainage systems have leaked on a number of occasions, and produced collapses very close to where they run in circuit. The collapses or near-collapses which are threatening to produce major damage to the outside of the city are, to a large extent, produced by the lack of an effective water-mains system and drainage system around the periphery, further aggravated by flood damage. The cracking there is almost entirely due to the water-level in the ground and not to ground movement.

San'a' has high buildings too, but the attempt to introduce a piped water-supply there has caused more trouble than it has cured. As in many Third World cities, the piped water-supply was introduced without any complementary piped drainage system — the old city of San'a' still has no communal drains. The Minister of Water told the author that in the previous 18 months he had paid out just under $1 million in compensation for about 40 collapsed houses in the old city. In April 1983 five houses collapsed in one week while the author was there. Even if the entire building does not collapse, its fine old decoration will often be destroyed by the rising damp.

Electricity is another modern development that is ruining old cities in a number of ways. For example, the wiring can be extremely amateurish and dangerous, as well as unsightly. Main power lines run through the houses across window openings, and at low levels in areas where children play. From a visual point of view, the wires are simply festooned across the walls, or form spiders' webs at the tops of leaning poles in the narrow streets.

Another problem is posed by the roads. Like many of the old medieval town centres of Europe, those in the Middle East often had cobbled streets — this is difficult to detect nowadays, because all that one sees underfoot is earth. The cobbling has not been maintained, and the road-bed has become extremely uneven. In order to allow vehicular traffic into the area and to make it easier to walk, people have simply spread earth over the top of the cobbling. Whenever it rains the streets become both impassable and dangerous. The mud also adds to the problem of rubbish disposal and street cleaning, and thence to the pollution of the ground-water.

Yet another problem is traffic circulation. Although the *suqs* were always crowded, one could walk through them with relative ease. Vehicular traffic involved the use of very narrow carts that carried firewood, delivered goods and brought water; they were especially designed to pass easily through narrow streets, with huge wheels that went over ruts and through puddles, and did not obstruct the movement of people. Six or seven years ago bicycles and motorcycles began to appear among them. For a while even that mix of vehicles and people was tolerable. It became standard in the old cities in the Middle East, and it did not cause much nuisance or much danger to life and limb. Nowadays, however, the number of motorised vehicles has so increased that pedestrians are tyrannised and the streets of the markets have become very unpleasant. Cars and trucks are parked everywhere and block the passages. This raises the major issue of whether such a situation can be allowed to continue. If this is the logical route to modernisation, can one insist on segregation? San'a' Municipality is agonising over this question at present. It has tentatively decided to restrict traffic to a very limited number of streets in the old city and to segregate pedestrians. Access for traffic will be allowed only during restricted times, at night. Whether the Municipality will be able to enforce such policies is another matter.

In the old streets of Ta'izz one also finds an extraordinary mix, with cars moving at some 50 km an hour through crowded pedestrian streets. One of the questions raised — and one obviously worth considering in any discussion — is how to slow down traffic that includes pedestrians, horse-drawn vehicles, donkeys, and goats or sheep tethered outside, together with buses and delivery vans moving through at some 60 km an hour. Motor bicycles ought to be more suitable because they are smaller, but in fact they move faster and are therefore more dangerous. Moreover, Yemenis traditionally feel the right to use the street as a living and working space, as a place for children to play in, and for pedlars to make, repair and sell goods. This mix of activities poses tremendous problems.

Deterioration from lack of maintenance is yet another major problem. Buildings which were constructed in the traditional Islamic style were meant to be maintained every year. It was accepted that, after the rains, repainting and replastering would be necessary to repair any damage. If this is no longer undertaken every year, a building deteriorates remarkably rapidly. First the roof gives way, then the corners drop off because the walls have been damaged by the rains, and suddenly a fairly respectable multi-storey building becomes a ruined single-storey building! It remains a single-storey building, however, and is not allowed to collapse entirely, because the ground-floor tenants are often shopkeepers, and the rent they pay in most traditional environments, whether rent-controlled or not, represents the bulk of the profit on the building investment. It is then in everybody's interest, including the owner's, to maintain the ground floor. He waterproofs the floor of what was once the first storey (i.e. the ceiling of the ground floor) and that becomes the roof of the building.

This may sound far-fetched, but it is happening in nearly all old Middle Eastern cities. Nor is it limited to 'profit-making' buildings, where a grasping landlord purposely allows his buildings to decay because he considers the rents too low. It is happening to some of the major monuments of Islam. In Cairo probably 30 per cent of the *waqf* properties in the old city are shrinking storey by storey until they reach ground-floor level, with ghostly walls rising up three or four floors. (In Cairo there is a waqf property, the canvas-makers' suq near Bab Zuwaila, whose upper levels were once beautifully designed, comfortable houses, all of which have been allowed to decay. Yet conservationists have always regarded this as one of Cairo's major monuments.) The problem of building deterioration may be slightly further advanced in Cairo than in the rest of the Islamic world, but in San'a' the city wall repaired some eight years ago is already vanishing. In short, annual maintenance will have to be accepted as a basic principle in the preservation and upgrading of Islamic cities.

Another question is how to improve the standard of living for the people in these congested cities. In the minds of people today, 'improvement' includes open-air play spaces for children, but how could this be accomplished? Bahrain has instituted a policy of demolishing a couple of houses in the middle of each quarter for this purpose, yet this only destroys the continuity of the built fabric, banishes some families and creates an entirely new, unpredictable situation. Another major public-service problem is the provision of public lavatories. In the mid-1970s San'a' acquired the reputation of being a very smelly city. This was attributed to the lavatories in private houses, but they certainly did not cause this problem in the early days. Every mosque had its ablution area, and there are many mosques in the old city of San'a'. As the population density increased, the ablution areas — particularly those around the suq — were more and more frequently used as public lavatories. They were never intended for this purpose, needless to say, nor were they properly maintained for it.

Another problem which contributes to corrosion is the keeping of animals in the city. Animals have always been a part of life in the traditional Islamic household, but in most urban communities they were kept inside the house at night and taken out of town to the nearest open space during the day. Now they are no longer taken away, because hiring the herdsmen used to be a communal service provided by the *shaikh* of the quarter. He would arrange the appointment of someone to take the animals to graze early in the morning and bring them home late at night, when they were locked up in the houses for safe-keeping. In that way they rarely soiled the streets; now they do so all day long. This new situation has arisen only in the last five or six years in most parts of the Middle East, and it would be easily remedied if the Municipalities simply took over responsibility for hiring the herdsmen. Each time the author has suggested this idea to the municipal authorities, they have been surprised: clearly they have never even thought of it. In San'a' animals were always kept in the suq at public expense when they became old, injured, lame or unable to do any work. A pile of fodder was provided for strays to keep them alive and happy until they died a natural death. In that sense, there was some provision for animals to stay inside the city during the day, but it was of a very special kind.

Natural disasters pose more than just the obvious problems for urban upgrading, because there is a tendency to think only of immediate problems and ignore potential ones. For example, in many areas of the Middle East flooding is frequent but not usually very serious; it can be controlled by means of diversion dams. Once every 30, 50 or 100 years, however, there is a major flood. Although a city may have been washed away regularly once or twice a century for a thousand years, no action will have been taken to prevent this happening again. One of the very first priorities of any upgrading scheme, therefore, is to take steps to anticipate that problem. Although there has been no major earthquake for quite some time, history tells us that they are possible throughout the Middle East. Upgrading should surely take this into account.

In a recent flood in Shibam, not only the city walls, but a number of houses behind them, collapsed. This raises a related question, that of land tenure, which is very different in the Islamic world from the system in the West. One difference is that it was often the responsibility of the people who live immediately behind the city walls to see to the maintenance of the section of wall directly in front of them. Similarly, street-cleaning was traditionally done by the inhabitants of the abutting houses. These customs have rapidly been abandoned in the last twenty years, or in some places as recently as the last six or seven years. In Shibam the inhabitants say, 'We're now living in a modern state; we've got a powerful central government; why should we pay for repairing the town wall?' It is an extraordinary attitude, considering that when the walls fall the houses behind them crack and eventually collapse too.

Ownership is another problem. Even buildings regarded as national monuments may be privately owned, and private ownership may involve so many members of a family that the protection and maintenance of the monument can be ruined through their lack of agreement, or for want of a single person to take responsibility.

As is apparent from the repair of earthquake damage in Italy, the problem of providing against earthquakes in traditional constructions is extremely difficult, and quickly becomes very expensive. One technique is to take reinforcing through the structure and provide diagonal bracing; the other is to reinforce the outside skin. The second is, of course, not nearly as good; nor is it much cheaper. That the traditional builders thought of earthquake-proofing can easily be proved. There is evidence of it in houses in Jeddah as well as in San'a'. They have wooden beams right around them, very strongly jointed at the corners, all the way up the full height of the building, to give some lateral strength.

Inadequate material for repair is another problem. An excellent Islamic material, whose existence has almost been forgotten, is called by different names in different places. It is a very hard lime plaster made by pounding five, six or even seven layers, one after another. This extraordinary technique can also be used for decoration, although it takes considerable skill. It is extremely long-lasting: traditional builders say it will last for 200 years, but it is possible to date existing surfaces of it much further back. It is found at archaeological sites in the Islamic world both on recently excavated cisterns and on those long exposed to the elements: it is sometimes demonstrably more than a thousand years old. Thus the material is extremely strong. Although very hard, it does not crack, because lime expands and contracts with the weather. It has only one drawback — cement cannot be put next to it, because it usually has a low gypsum content which the cement will attack until it disintegrates. This point illustrates the danger of adopting a technology that is unfamiliar when upgrading traditional buildings.

Traditional building materials and techniques also add to the annual maintenance problem because to use them in repair work necessitates a high degree of skill. Building a house nearly 30 m high in earth requires extensive knowledge of the techniques of mud-brick building. Layered earth is another elaborate technique that involves, among other things, hammering the mud into place with a heavy block of wood for about an hour for each square metre. Given current rates for construction workers in the Middle East, the cost can be very high, and what appeared to be a cheap material turns out to be an extremely expensive one. So what can be done about annual maintenance, if repairing these buildings costs so much?

Using traditional materials has many other ramifications. The 30-m-high buildings in Shibam are built of apparently crude mud bricks with straw reinforcement. In the opinion of all the best builders, this mud must come from around the roots of a good, strong date-palm. If it does not come from the best arable land, then the building will not be strong. Chemical analysis shows why: the continual irrigation by flood waters increases the amount of fine clay so that there is a higher percentage of pure clay in this earth than in that taken from a non-agricultural or deserted area. It is also relatively free of salt, since continual watering allows the salt to sink to a very low level. But taking building material from arable land comes into direct conflict with attempts to improve agriculture. So what building materials should be used for maintenance if the traditional sources are forbidden? The Ministries ought obviously to be looking for alternative sources.

In addition to the problem of annual maintenance, there is the question of repair after damage. This, too, is a highly specialised and skilled business, not easily tackled by modern architects. A layer of mud added onto mud bricks or a mud wall will simply fall off again unless the laborious techniques of experienced master masons are used to make it stay on and fuse with the old wall. Alternative, inexpensive techniques to repair these buildings have yet to be found. In short, the traditional buildings of much of the Middle East may have been economical until seven or eight years ago, but they are now rapidly becoming expensive, mainly because of all the manual work involved.

Plumbing in the Islamic world was traditionally of a gravity type, with either a cesspit underneath the toilet or, in the case of high buildings, what is generally called a long drop — that is, a shaft that ran down through the building and carried the soil down to a masonry box at the bottom. In the long drop, the urine was separated away from the solid excrement, and the latter was allowed to dry in its masonry box (or else on a platform, where it was mixed with ash every morning and evening). After about six weeks the box was opened by a man whose hereditary occupation it was, and the contents were removed in sacks on donkey-back through the streets of the city. The tourists never noticed the burden of the donkeys they were brushing against, which is a good indication of how odourless the material had become. It was then dried off in the sun and burnt as fuel in the public baths; thus sterilised, the ash finally became fertiliser for the vegetable gardens inside the walls, to grow food which was eaten again by the inhabitants of the houses, thus completing the cycle. Most visitors to San'a' are not even aware these gardens exist because they cannot be seen beyond the high buildings along the narrow streets — which give the impression of an immensely urban environment. But for the knowledgeable, there are little doors between the houses that open onto these unusual market gardens. The inhabitants do not need to walk through the streets to get from one end of the city to the other; they can use the pleasant shaded quietness of the market gardens. They also provide convenient, overlooked areas where children can play.

From the bathrooms the separated urine and washing water ran down vertical drains on the outside walls of the houses to cesspits in the streets. Made of waterproof plaster, the drains were always clean because the inhabitants used to wash them down every time they used the bathroom by swilling the contents of the pottery water jar across the bathroom floor.

This sewage cycle, which was built into the entire urban design, is no longer as extensively used in San'a'. In about 1975 international advisers convinced the inhabitants to upgrade the lavatory system to water-borne sewerage, but the first stage of the upgrading that they advised was extremely ill-thought-out. They recommended putting in a type of collecting hopper at the outlet of the bathroom which is not (and cannot be) properly joined with any kind of a seal to the bathroom floor, so that it immediately leaks. Half the liquid falls into the hopper and down the pipe; the other half runs down between the pipe and the vertical drain on the face of the wall. Since the wall remains damp, moss grows, which has all sorts of effects on the structure and causes unpleasant smells and decay until eventually the building materials begin to disintegrate near the pipe, and ultimately the building may collapse.

In the traditional system, the water following the urine down the chute to clean it ran into a french drain leading to a cesspit in the street. That used to work well, as the french drains were kept cleaned out and there were no pipes to confuse the issue. Now, however, the system has broken down: the city of San'a' smells, major decay is attacking the buildings and the situation is serious. Although each house has its own rather inadequate cesspit, there is as yet no municipal drainage system in the old city in spite of international funding for the water supply and the external drainage pipes. Whether the situation would have deteriorated to the same extent without international intervention is impossible to say, but the same kinds of problems are unfortunately characteristic of much so-called development in other Islamic cities.

Finally, one should ask whether there are practical solutions to the problems raised here. One possible approach to the waterproofing of existing thick walls, in areas where underground, highly corrosive damp is causing major damage to structures, involves using a skin on the outside of the walls. The skin can be made of any number of materials that can seal in a waterproofing agent, but the technique presumes that there is a very solid stone foundation underneath the building. In most buildings in which the author was involved, there were large foundation stones which would hold in the bulk of any fluid. Liquids, silicone or stearate can then be gravity-injected to prevent damp from rising into the wall. (The membranes introduced on the sides are intended to stop the stearate or the silicone from running out into the soil, for the surfaces of these traditional walls are often very porous.)

In traditional construction in most Islamic buildings there is an outer skin, an inner skin and a much softer central core. The latter is usually a very soft stone that has become pulverised, rather like clay, and which reacts badly with water. This soft material spills out like a pile of sand if one tries to cut through a wall, and this makes it virtually impossible to put a solid sheet of damp-proofing material through the wall, necessitating some sort of alternative technique like that discussed above.

The advanced decay that is menacing the urban fabric of these cities is clearly of tremendous concern to everybody who admires the extraordinary expression of human achievement represented by traditional Islamic architecture.

# 20 THE ECONOMIC IMPORTANCE OF TOURISM IN YEMEN

Abdulhadi H. al-Hamdani

## Introduction

Tourism occupies a special position in the economic policy of most countries today. There is no doubt that it represents an important element in the development of several countries and peoples; and for many it is a basic source of national income.

It is no exaggeration to call tourism the most attractive and prosperous industry of our age; successful experiments in many countries emphasise this fact. Tourism is important to both developed and developing countries, yet it is more important to the latter because of its impact on economic development. This is primarily due to the high foreign-currency yield of tourism, and its direct contribution to employment and traditional industries.

We will consider here the economic importance of the tourist industry in the two parts of Yemen (North and South). As Yemen is classified among the less-developed countries in the world, the importance of tourism as a productive economic sector is clear from the outset. In addition to its economic importance, tourism brings other benefits of a social and political nature, reflected in internal tourism between North and South Yemen. This aspect is helpful in the two countries' attempts to achieve unity. Tourism falls within the economic complementarity of the two parts of Yemen and provides a practical way forward within the two governments' policy of taking steps towards achieving unity. The results of this policy are also seen in a number of other practical steps such as joint projects and economic establishments, of which the Yemen Tourism Company is among the first.

Choosing tourism as the first joint economic experiment between the two parts of Yemen can perhaps be referred to a number of considerations and advantages:

(1) Yemen's poverty and scarcity of resources put several obstacles in the way of any large investment plan to exploit its natural

226

resources such as minerals, petroleum, and so on. Tourism does not require such massive financial investment and, moreover, it secures a rapid and quite good return when compared to other fields of investment.

(2) While playing an important economic role, tourism has another role in promoting unity between the two parts of the country through human mobility and the strengthening of social relationships between the inhabitants of the two parts.

(3) Tourism will lead to the establishment of several important projects linked to tourist activities, thereby providing more employment opportunities and increased trade and investments.

Yemen's tourist potential is comparable to that of several developed countries. This chapter will consider Yemen as a tourist destination and describe its most important attractions, as well as the efforts made to improve them and other aspects of the development of a modern tourist industry in Yemen.

**Factors in the Potential of Yemeni Tourism**

Yemen has some major tourist attractions in its ancient civilisations, its wealth of monuments, its beautiful landscape embracing mountains, valleys, warm mineral springs and long coastlines, and its pleasant climate, as well as its colourful folkloric traditions, distinguished by variety and originality. We will consider briefly the most important of these elements.

*History*

The historical aspect of Yemen forms a powerful element of attraction for historians and students interested in human history and civilisations. For this reason, Yemen has been, and still is, the centre of interest for researchers all over the world. Historians agree that Yemen witnessed the rise of great civilisations comparable to those of the ancient world such as Egypt and Mesopotamia. Scriptures and scrolls found in Egypt reveal the existence of commercial relationships between Egypt and Yemen 3,000 years BC.

Archaeological discoveries prove that during the second millennium BC, Yemen witnessed the successive existence of three flourishing civilisations. The first was the civilisation of Ma'in that flourished in Jawf province; its capital was Qarnaw, known today as

Ma'in, after the Ma'ini state. Among the most famous cities of the Ma'ini state was Baraqish, its religious centre. Next came the Sheban state, with its capital first at Sirwah and then at Ma'rib. Sheba was famous for its agricultural and architectural achievements as well as for the development of a governmental system based upon consultation and collective decision-making. The Qur'an mentions the story of the people of Sheba, their Queen Bilqis and the wise King Solomon, King of Jerusalem. Among the most important features of Ma'rib are the famous Ma'rib Dam, the temple of the Moon God al-Maqa and the throne of Bilqis.

Finally came the Himyarite state, which fell around the middle of the sixth century AD and whose capital was Zafar. The last Yemeni kingdom before the advent of Islam, it was also the biggest Yemeni state as it dominated most areas of Greater Yemen. There were other secondary Yemeni civilisations such as the Qataban, whose capital was Timna'.

The most important economic foundations of these states were trade, agriculture and industry. The Yemenis were famous for their highly developed agricultural system based on a superb water control and distribution system, and terraced farmlands on the tops of high mountains. These terraces still exist today. Yemeni trade in those days depended on neighbouring markets and those of the Mediterranean Sea. Yemen was famous for the trade in incense, used in temples, which represented the most important export. But it was also famous for a number of important industries such as Yemeni swords, high-value textiles and jewellery. Contemporary historians have left detailed accounts of Yemen's prosperity in those days. Agatharchides, the Ancient Greek historian, said that the standard of living in Ma'rib was very high because of the progress in agricultural and construction activities. This wealth made the country the target of the greedy aspirations of many powerful countries. In 24 BC Augustus tried to invade Yemen but failed in his campaign. Then the Ethiopians succeeded in occupying the country for a short period, only to leave because of fierce Yemeni resistance. Yemen subsequently fell under the control of the Persians, who had come to help the Yemenis against the Ethiopians. When Islam came to Yemen, a new historical phase began in the life of the Yemeni community, because of the prominent role that the Yemenis played in support of Islam. That role was instrumental in pushing outwards the frontiers of the Islamic nation; Yemen provided the infant community of Islam with well-armed, trained fighters. Within Yemen itself a creative interaction began between the cultural heritage of the nation, and the new sublime Islamic values. All this gave the Yemenis a wider scope for the cultural creativeness which we find reflected in the artistic monuments of the Islamic/Arabic civilisation in Yemen. Yemen is still today, as it was in the past, one of the strongest citadels of Islam and one of its original homes.

Although Yemen's role was eclipsed by the Ottoman occupation in the North and then the British occupation in the South, and although the country suffered from divisive tribal struggles, it was nevertheless finally able to bring an end to foreign occupation and to overcome internal divisions. Yemen was able to break from its backwardness by means of two revolutions: the revolution of 26 September 1962 in the North which ended the rule of the Hamid al-Din family, and the revolution of 14 October 1964 in the South which won independence from British occupation.

During the last two decades, the country has made much progress in its development efforts aimed at changing social and economic conditions in order to catch up with the contemporary world.

## Monuments of Ancient Yemen

Yemen has one of the richest archaeological legacies in the world, despite the fact that few efforts have been made to excavate what is still buried. The archaeological treasures of Ma'rib have already been mentioned; the Ancient Greek historian Strabo described the city thus: 'Ma'rib is a wonderful city whose buildings are ornamented with gold and inlaid with ivory and precious stones, and it has great buildings that seize the heart.'

San'a', one of the oldest cities in the world, is a living archaeological and cultural museum which contains immortal monuments going back to very ancient periods of history. An example is the Palace of Ghamdan, said once to be 20 floors high. There are also old walls, Islamic mosques with high minarets and great palaces built in a unique style still to be seen today in San'a'.

There are, in fact, many important archaeological sites such as Baraqish, one of the capitals of Ma'in, whose monuments date back to the second millennium BC; Timna', capital of the Qataban state in the Baihan area; Shabwa, which lies between Ma'rib and the Hadramawt; Shibam, in the Hadramawt, which is famous for the first skyscrapers in the world, which still exist today; and Zafar, one of the capitals of the Himyarite state which lies to the south of San'a'. As for archaeological antiquities and precious relics,

Yemeni museums are full of them. The most important of these are
the National Museum in San'a', the Ta'izz Museum in the city of
Ta'izz and the Zafar Museum in Yarim. In the southern part of the
country, there is a similar number of museums which contain
historical relics, folkloric dresses, jewellery, swords, daggers,
handicrafts and cultural objects. All this represents the life of the
Yemeni community both past and present.

*Geography*

We can say, in general, that Nature itself is one of the most important tourist attractions in Yemen. The terrain varies from high
mountains, whose peaks rise to more than 3,650 m above sea-level,
to deep gorges and green valleys. The country extends from the
warm shores of the Red Sea to the utter silence of the Rub' al-Khali,
one of the world's hottest deserts. In addition, the many islands in
the Red and Arabian Seas are great tourist attractions. Moreover,
there are warm mineral springs and natural sauna baths for those
seeking to rejuvenate their health. Geographical variation has given
Yemen another advantage — its good climate, which varies from
one area to another. The areas of plateaus and high mountains have
the best climate, for the high altitude protects them from both the
humidity of the coast and the heat of the desert. The rains give life to
a marvellous variety of flora. The sun always shines.

**The Yemeni Community**

The Yemeni community is first and foremost agricultural. Therefore, unlike the rest of the Arabian Peninsula, it has always been
sedentary. This explains the highly developed systems of irrigation,
and the harnessing of flood water by means of dams. The Romans
described Yemen as 'Arabia Felix', meaning 'Fortunate Arabia'. To
this day, the Yemenis farm their agricultural terraces on the tops of
high mountains, and this has forged a bond throughout history
between man and his land. In Yemen, it is also evidence of the power
of man and his ability to face nature and overcome its obstacles and
hardships.

   Among the most important characteristics of the Yemeni community is that it is built upon very ancient customs and traditions, based
upon respect for the family and clan ties.

   Although emigration is one of the characteristics of the Yemeni community, this does not mean that it is an unstable community. Whereas there have been waves of emigration at various historical periods, they came as a response to catastrophes (as with the collapse of the Ma'rib Dam) or to economic pressures.

*Religion*

Islam is the religion of almost all Yemenis. There are very few adherents of other religions, in spite of the fact that Christianity and Judaism existed in Yemen prior to Islam. Yemen witnessed the bloody struggles between the two religions until the advent of Islam.

*Language*

The population of Yemen belongs to the Arab Qahtani race. Yemen is considered as the origin of the Arab nation, as most Arabs trace their origins to it. The language is classical Arabic, although some foreign words have crept in.

*Folklore*

Yemeni music is distinguished among the different kinds of Arab music for its varied and numerous tunes and rhythms. Yemeni folk dancing has its own gestures and movements which have their specific meanings, such as the dance of war, harvests, weddings, and so on. Dancing may be divided into two types: war and emotional. War dancing is characterised by the carrying of daggers, jumping and bending of the knees in rapid and sharp movements. But emotional dancing, in which women join, is monotonous and is usually danced in groups.

*The Phenomenon of Qat*

A prevalent social phenomenon in Yemen, *qat* is a kind of green leaf chewed and kept in the mouth for some hours during the period from noon to sunset. Comprehensive studies are currently under way to discover its economic, social and hygienic effects. Some preliminary studies show that, although qat is a stimulant, it contains no narcotic materials.

**Official Efforts to Develop Tourism in Yemen**

The tourist industry in Yemen is a recent social and economic activity, for Yemen itself is quite new to the process of cultural, social and economic development. Neither the Yemen Arab Republic (YAR) nor the People's Democratic Republic of Yemen (PDRY) is an exception to the general trend in all developing countries which are trying to achieve comprehensive development starting from very backward conditions. This means there is an increasing need for such countries to develop and increase their income from foreign sources. Tourism as a productive industry therefore represents a very important source of national income for such countries. But tourism cannot flourish without wider development, especially in infrastructure. Thus we see that the state's delay in giving serious attention to the development of tourism has been caused, above all, by the country's need to develop the basic services which are the necessary foundation for starting active tourism. Such services include the building of roads, public utilities, hotel services, airports, modern means of transport and communications, and so on. These efforts are surveyed below.

## Government Efforts in the YAR

The first Administration for Tourism was established by the Ministry of Mass Communication when the first Yemeni government was formed after the revolution of 26 September 1962. In view of the unexpected complications faced by the revolution, various programmes and development plans were not put into practice. Thus in tourism, as occurred in other fields, nothing happened before the 1970s, which can be considered the real beginning of Yemen's opening to the world, both economically and politically. This period also marks the beginning of tourism, with increasing numbers of tourists coming from all parts of the world. At that time a law was issued to establish the Administration of Summer and Winter Tourism to cope with the growing number of tourists. This Administration developed into the General Corporation for Tourism (GCT) in 1978, in order to cope with the increasing responsibility of promoting the tourist industry.

The period 1976–81 perhaps witnessed the most remarkable development in the Yemeni tourism sector. This period saw the achievement of many important tourist projects, as well as the development of basic utilities such as international and internal airports, roads, hotels and public administration. Expenditure on tourism marketing and mass media was about 10 million rials (YR), and 1,356 tourist projects were carried out, including hotels of various classes, tourist and travel agencies, parks, restaurants, buffets and workshops for handicrafts — all financed by private-sector invest-ment. The policy of economic expansion and the government's encouragement of the private sector through legislation, including Investment Law 18, perhaps played a major role in attracting such tourism-oriented investments.

The following data from the GCT show the growing numbers of foreign tourists who visited the YAR during the years 1978–81:

| Year | 1978 | 1979 | 1980 | 1981 |
|---|---|---|---|---|
| Number of tourists | 17,075 | 34,185 | 39,283 | 56,131 |

The expenditure on tourism for the years 1980–81 showed a similar rise:

| Year | Total expenditure (YR) |
|---|---|
| 1980 | 108,185,300 |
| 1981 | 154,584,774 |

Within the Second Five-Year Development Plan (1982–86), the sum of $98 million has been allocated to carry out the GCT plan to promote tourism through marketing, in-service training and pro-ducing qualified tourist-guides; the allocation also covers a tourism survey and the opening of new tourism bureaux, as well as the development of tourist sites.

During the period 1976–81 some successful efforts were made in the fields of the restoration and maintenance of monuments and building museums. Three museums were built in San'a', Ta'izz and Zafar, and some historic buildings were repaired. Manuscripts were collected and preserved, and two precious statues of King Zamar Ali and his brother were recently returned to Yemen after having been repaired in Germany. The latest stage of the efforts to develop tourism has been the joint efforts of the two governments. This has led to the establishment of the Yemen Tourism Company, whose objective is to promote internal and external tourism, and for which purpose a large capital backing has been authorised. Subsequently, the Supreme Council for Tourism was established under the chair-manship of the Prime Minister of the YAR.

## Government Efforts in the PDRY

The General Corporation for Tourism (GCT) was established in 1973, with the aim of providing and managing hotel services, as well as running parks, places of entertainment and tourist bureaux, and preparing plans and programmes for tourist activities. At the same time, the first survey was carried out to study the possibilities for tourism in the country. At the beginning of 1976 work started on building a number of public parks. Various tourism projects which had been completed earlier were repaired and maintained by the GCT. These include archaeological sites such as the al-Tawila cisterns in Aden and a number of museums. The state finances all development and tourism projects and the role of the private sector is therefore very limited. There are probably sufficient infrastructure, utilities and tourist services such as hotels, roads, and so on.

The available data concerning the number of foreign tourists visiting the PDRY during 1976–78 show a distinct fluctuation, as follows:

| Year | 1976 | 1977 | 1978 |
|---|---|---|---|
| Number of tourists | 28,867 | 37,988 | 32,740 |

Expenditure on tourism for the same period, however, maintained an upward trend:

| Year | 1976 | 1977 | 1978 |
|---|---|---|---|
| Expenditure (YD) | 378,668 | 538,226 | 542,918 |

### The Yemen Tourism Company

The establishment of the Yemen Tourism Company in 1980 was an important indication that Yemen's tourist industry has entered a new stage in its development and in its socio-economic role in the two parts of the country. The efforts of both governments now foster tourism in two ways: individually, through the GCTs belonging to each government; and jointly, through the Yemen Tourism Company. These agencies are now collectively responsible for developing the tourist industry in the entire country.

Let us consider some of the texts of the agreement establishing the Company as well as the objectives defined for it, and the guarantees and legal facilities stipulated to smooth the Company's work and investments in both parts of Yemen. The Preface to the agreement shows the importance of the Company's role and the reasons for establishing it:

Out of the desire of the two governments of the North and the South to deepen the spirit of complementarity between them; and in the light of their attempts to create more co-operation in the field of internal tourism between the two parts of the one country and international tourism; due to the two governments' awareness of the possibilities for tourism abounding in Yemen in its two parts, whose development will lead to cultural, social and economic benefits; and due to their belief that this development will not be realised without the support of the two governments for that sector; therefore it has been agreed to establish, according to this agreement, a Yemeni limited company called the Yemen Tourism Company.

Thus the establishment of the Company was in harmony with other steps towards unity taken by both governments.

## Objectives of the Company

In the light of the general objectives stated in the establishment agreement, we can examine the most important aspects which distinguish the Company as an independent institution in the field of tourist activity. It can tackle those issues which other official institutions cannot, whether at the level of internal or international tourism.

The establishment agreement stated the objectives of the Company as follows:

(1) Promoting internal tourism between the two parts of Yemen.
(2) Promoting international tourism to and from the two parts.
(3) Opening bureaux for tourism-marketing in both parts and abroad.
(4) Supplying means of transport for tourism whether by ownership or hiring.
(5) Establishing and managing hotels, tourist societies, resthouses, restaurants, motels and various health centres, as well as making use of natural spas.
(6) Encouraging traditional Yemeni industries and marketing their products.
(7) Printing tourist publications such as books, pamphlets, guides, maps, posters, films, and so on.

In order to enable the Company to achieve its objectives, the agreement incorporated a number of guarantees and advantages, the most important of which are the following:

(1) The contribution of the two governments is 70 per cent of the total capital of YR 130 million.
(2) Twenty per cent is for the public and mixed corporations.
(3) Ten per cent is for the private sector.
(4) The Company is a legal entity as well as having administrative and financial independence. The Company may own all kinds of assets.
(5) The Company will have, in both parts of the country, all the rights and necessary facilities to perform its duties and achieve its aims.
(6) The agreement gives the Company all kinds of legal and political protection.
(7) The Company's capital, in the two parts of Yemen, is not subject to nationalisation, confiscation, custody or seizure.
(8) The Company enjoys the benefits assigned to investments in the laws applied in both parts of Yemen.

In many ways the Company can carry out activities which the GCT in each country cannot. Chief among these are promoting internal and international tourism as well as establishing and managing tourist facilities. But some of the responsibilities of the company are also those of the national corporations. For instance, printing tourist publications, mass publicity and encouraging handicraft industries are all the responsibility of the national corporations.

## The Beginning of Company Activity

In attempting to evaluate the Company's achievements since its establishment, we must recognise that this period is very short, and that the establishment stage of any company requires great efforts to achieve what may be a distant success. Moreover, we must allow for shortages in many of the managerial and material requirements. The Company, however, has been able to carry out some of its objectives in the field of promoting tourism between the two parts of Yemen as well as international tourism. This has been done through efficient marketing, advertising, acquiring a fleet of buses for overland transportation and creating the nucleus of a qualified administrative personnel.

*Promoting Internal Tourism*

The Company pays particular attention to this aspect. Over the last few years, the Company has arranged group and family trips between the two parts of Yemen, especially on religious and national occasions. These trips were successful and such efforts were received with satisfaction and enthusiasm on the part of the people throughout Yemen.

*Promoting International Tourism*

The steps taken by the Company in this field are as follows:

(1) Making direct links with a number of institutions, agencies and tourism organisations to enable Yemen to participate in their programmes and tourist activities.
(2) Appointing officials who are specialists in the field of mass communication and tourism-marketing in Yemen through the different agencies.
(3) Participating in a number of conferences, symposia and international tourism fairs held in different countries.
(4) Printing tourist publications and distributing them all over the world, as well as publishing and broadcasting periodically articles and programmes about tourism in Yemen through international newspapers and radio and television stations.
(5) Producing the first international tourist film about Yemen. This is a documentary film incorporating various features, monuments and other aspects of tourist interest in Yemen. The film has been distributed to television stations around the world.
(6) Printing the first tourist book about Yemen in five foreign languages, as well as printing a comprehensive tourist guide, and a number of various picture postcards.
(7) Arranging several group visits through a number of tourist agencies around the world. Such visits have had useful consequences in strengthening the Company's relations in the field of tourism.

*Establishing Marketing Bureaux*

The Company's head office in San'a' has been equipped with the necessary facilities and the Company's chief branch in Aden has been similarly provided for.

*Means of Transport*

The Company has purchased a number of vehicles to facilitate travel
to the various sites. It has also bought accommodation facilities,
such as camps and tourist tents, to be used in the areas where accommodation is not available. An agreement has been signed with the
Land Transport Company in the YAR to arrange transport between
San'a' and the airport at reasonable rates.

*Establishing and Managing Hotels*

The Company runs two hotels in San'a' and two in Aden. These
hotels are a part of the contribution by the two governments to the
capital of the Company.

   The Company has set up a permanent exhibition centre for handicrafts and traditional industries in San'a' and signed a contract with
the Yemen Pottery Company to market its products in an effort to
encourage such crafts and industries. The exhibition contains a section for marketing traditional dresses and jewellery. In the future
the Company plans to establish a number of tourist hotels, resthouses, parks and restaurants at tourist sites.


**Conclusion**

The development of tourism in Yemen from the early 1970s until
today has gone through a number of stages. Official efforts to
develop it have been effective, but the results have been concentrated in small areas such as San'a', Aden or other main cities, which
has led to excess capacity, especially in hotels. Meanwhile, many
tourist destinations are suffering from the lack of essential facilities.
Future government efforts will have to be directed towards training
and qualifying administrative personnel and tour guides. Historical
monuments are still subject to damage, theft and neglect, and many
sites are suffering considerable deterioration in the face of modern
life.

   The establishment of the Yemen Tourism Company was thus a
natural response to the needs of the country. However, the Company will not be able to undertake its responsibilities properly unless
it obtains the full support and encouragement of the governments of
the two parts of Yemen.

   Tourism in Yemen does not lack the basic ingredients for success,
for Yemen is rich in its historical heritage and Nature. But this today

forms only one element of tourism, there are other considerations. Experts define the essential factors in tourism as: first, the sites (geographical location, weather, historical monuments, religious places to visit and natural scenery); second, the means of exploitation (the people involved in tourism, tourism consciousness, facilities and modern means of transport and communication); third, securing the markets where tourism services and possibilities are marketed.

In the light of these factors, it is necessary for the tourist industry in Yemen to assess its present tourist resources so as to define its potential. This requires a comprehensive tourist survey to specify all the possibilities available in the two parts of Yemen, and a comprehensive plan. The plan should include programmes to promote tourism in all its aspects. It is vital to concentrate on attracting and encouraging local Arab and foreign investments; and Yemen must benefit by the experience of developed countries in the field of tourism in order to extend its capacities. Priority should be given both to marketing at world level and to developing a comprehensive consciousness of tourism at local level.

# 21 TOURISM: A BLESSING OR A CURSE?

Michael Adams

**Historical Background**

Tourism in the Yemen Arab Republic (YAR) is a relatively new phenomenon — and for this there are very good reasons. Until the revolution of 1962 it was government policy — meaning in effect that it was the personal wish of the old Imam Ahmad, whose death precipitated the revolution — to keep the country in a state of almost total isolation from the outside world.

The circumstances in which he came to power, after the assassination of his father and with half the country in revolt, combined with his own suspicious nature to convince him that his own security and that of Yemen would be best served by excluding as far as possible all foreign influences from the country. By inclination reactionary, he did not, as is sometimes suggested, set his face against progress of any kind; like his father before him, he gave some encouragement to education and to agricultural development and he established post and telegraph offices throughout the country. Generally speaking, however, Imam Ahmad was extremely selective in the kind of progress he was prepared to countenance and he remained deeply suspicious of any development projects which did not serve his overriding aim of maintaining the tightest possible security in a realm over which his authority was never unchallenged.

In his obsession with security and his mistrust of foreign influences, Imam Ahmad was following well-established precedents. Although its early prosperity had been based on its advantageous situation astride one of the most important trade routes of the ancient world, Yemen's modern history has been one of determined seclusion, in which the attempts of foreigners to penetrate the country, whether peaceably or by conquest, were always resisted. The account of his journey given by Carsten Niebuhr, who led the Scandinavian expedition to Yemen in the middle of the eighteenth century graphically illustrates the difficulties encountered by the few enterprising travellers who tried to violate this seclusion; and the resistance offered to successive Turkish attempts to conquer the country reinforces the traditional image of Yemen as a kind of medieval redoubt firmly barricaded against the modern world.

This indeed was its character until 1962, when the revolution and the foreign intervention which followed it altered the picture. Even then, however, the country remained difficult of access for the ordinary traveller, since throughout the 1960s it remained a prey to civil war. It was only when royalists and republicans finally came to an understanding with each other in 1970 that the YAR opened its doors to the outside world and travel for its own sake — tourism — became a practical possibility.

**Laying the Foundations**

At that time, and in the wake of the civil war, there existed in Yemen virtually nothing of the necessary infrastructure for a tourist industry. The only surfaced road in the country was the one which Chinese engineers had not yet finished building between San'a' and the Red Sea port of Hodaida. Internal communications were primitive in the extreme, and in parts of the country any movement at all was subject to the whim of tribal leaders whose loyalty to the central government was at best uncertain. There were no modern hotels and few other of the amenities which all but the hardiest of twentieth-century travellers would require. Perhaps the most important consideration was a psychological one: here was a country which for centuries had been accustomed to keep the foreigner at bay. Could its inhabitants be expected in the twinkling of an eye to renounce the habit of xenophobia and to assume instead the collective smile of a people genuinely prepared to welcome into its midst those whom it had been taught to regard with enmity and mistrust?

The transformation that has been effected in little more than a decade is striking. As far as the material infrastructure is concerned, a network of excellent trunk-roads now links the main population centres of San'a', Ta'izz and Hodaida, and there are also first-class highways running north from San'a' to Sa'da, east to Ma'rib on the edge of the Rub' al-Khali and south-west from Ta'izz to the old port (now being reconstructed) of Mocha on the Red Sea.

A similar network of telecommunications, which has been constructed with remarkable rapidity, provides country-wide telephone and television services to regions separated from each other by some of the most rugged terrain in the world. There are first-class hotels — with first-class prices — in San'a' and Ta'izz, which will shortly be matched, when a modernisation programme is completed, by one in Hodaida. With the creation of the Yemen Tourism Company and of Yemenair, the national airline which operates domestic services between San'a' and the main regional cities, as well as overseas links with London, Paris and Frankfurt, a sound practical basis now exists for the development of tourism on a scale which only ten years ago would have been difficult to envisage.

As for the psychological uncertainty about the reception which the people of Yemen might be expected to give to inquisitive and often insensitive foreign visitors, it has simply evaporated. Perhaps because they are glad to be rid of their isolation, perhaps because they have never been colonised (or colonised others), the Yemenis have accepted with equanimity the small numbers of tourists who have so far come among them and they show no sign of resenting their presence. This is not necessarily to say that problems may not arise when the numbers increase and the presence becomes a more obtrusive one; however, what might have been an awkward threshold has been crossed with less effort than might have been expected.

**What Yemen Has to Offer**

Once these initial difficulties have been overcome, few countries enjoy more advantages, both natural and man-made, for the development of tourism. The climate of North Yemen is temperate and genial, the landscape remarkable by any standard, with variations which are unusual anywhere and unique in the Arab world, between coastal scenery, high mountain plateaus and the fringes of the great Arabian Desert. A long and rich history is reflected in monuments of exceptional interest and in a distinctive architectural tradition. A friendly and unaffected population, holding unself-consciously to its own particular habits of dress and life-style, adds a picturesque attraction to the scene. For the uninformed traveller — and that is what most tourists are — with a palate jaded by much journeying on more familiar ground, Yemen offers, as few other countries can do today, the prize of novelty. And for the visitor with an interest in the history and culture of the Arab world, what Dame Freya Stark wrote more than 40 years ago remains true today. Here in the Yemen, she wrote,

One sees neither the ancient desert world nor the modern world of the Arabian north; one climbs into mediaeval Arabia and the sort of life travellers found in Palestine or Syria from the Crusades and onward, until the Mediterranean lands became westernised at heart.[1]

## Pros and Cons of Tourism

With advantages such as these, the rapid expansion of tourism in North Yemen seems both natural and inevitable. Before accepting this assumption, however, it would be advisable to cast up a balance sheet and to compare the pros and cons of making — and perhaps making too fast — so radical a departure from recent tradition. The gains are easily perceived and seem alluring; but there will be losses too, less obvious but worth considering in the light of the experience of other countries whose example the Yemenis must now decide whether or not they wish to follow.

On the credit side there is, first, the opportunity to enter more fully into the mainstream of twentieth-century life, renouncing finally and for ever that goal of seclusion from influences both good and bad to which the Yemen of the Imams was dedicated. In the modern world of mass communications, such seclusion is no longer possible; but the interplay of diplomacy and commerce, through which Yemen is bound to be linked with its neighbours, will not by itself forge more than formal and impersonal connections. One of the arguments in favour of tourism, in Arabia as elsewhere in the world, is that it provides an opportunity for individuals to make contact which, since they are uninhibited by considerations of political or commercial advantage, can plant the seeds of true and disinterested co-operation and mutual understanding.

In this context there may be for the people of Yemen an added inducement in the thought that their history and their cultural traditions, varied and distinctive as they are, are almost unknown to the outside world, which the Imams were at such pains to keep at arm's length. Tourism, it is true, involves contacts which in themselves are all too often merely superficial. But, where understanding is the goal, some contact is better than none; even the most glancing acquaintance may set in train the desire for a deeper appreciation. If outsiders are to come to know and understand Yemen, they must start somewhere, and tourism offers at least a modest point of departure, with potential advantages for both parties to the undertaking.

Finally, there is the mundane consideration that tourism can provide a valuable source of income. The YAR has few natural resources and has been endowed by nature — as far as we know — with none of those raw materials for which the world is prepared to pay richly in foreign currency. As much as any people in the world, the Yemenis, if they are to stand on their own feet, must make the most of what they have. And what they have, in the context of tourism, is a rich heritage which, with judicious management, could be made to yield a valuable cash-crop. Moreover, it is not, in the economists' jargon, a wasting asset, but one whose worth can only increase as it becomes better known and attracts closer study and exploration.

And the disadvantages which should be placed in the opposite balance of the scales? What are they, and are they heavy enough to outweigh the potential gains? To assess them, we have only to look at other countries which have chosen to make capital out of what nature or man's ingenuity have left them as an endowment — and there are plenty of warnings. The polluted shores of the Mediterranean, the jostling crowds of sightseers in some of the world's most sacred shrines, the insensitivity on one side and the exploitation and petty racketeering on the other side of the tourist equation almost anywhere in the world: these constitute the blight that tourism too often, although not inevitably, carries with it. Equally damaging and more insidious is the vulgarisation that follows when cultural values are swamped by commercialisation; when what was natural and spontaneous becomes artificial and self-conscious; when the distinctive is transformed by over-exposure into the merely commonplace, a cliché for the tourist's camera.

These are the perils and to evade them calls for skill and determination, whether in Rome or in Rajasthan. But in two respects Yemen is better placed to resist them than are places more firmly established on the tourist map. First, in view of Yemen's geographical situation and its remoteness from the main sources of tourists, it must be many years before visitors will arrive in large numbers. Second, because Yemen comes late on the scene it can profit by the experience of others. If that experience can be wisely used while the numbers are still small, it should be possible to forestall many of the misjudgments that have marred the development of tourism elsewhere and to preserve what in many respects is an ideal climate for it in Yemen today.

The expansion of tourism is already under way and it seems unlikely that anything will now reverse the process. What is important is to ensure that the expansion is well planned and that, in carrying it out, the Yemenis make the best use of the assets they possess and are not misled by commercial interests into trying to emulate in Yemen the promoters of tourism in other and totally different environments.

**Assets**

*Climate*

Those assets are by any standard remarkable. Let us start with the climate. San'a' is situated further south than Rangoon or Timbuktu and not far north of the equator; but instead of jungle heat or a quivering horizon of desert sands, the visitor encounters here a succession of temperate days and cool nights, with only a modest variation through the seasons. The rain here in the highlands (for San'a' stands nearly 2,300 m above sea-level) falls in summer, when Yemen catches the tail end of the monsoon from the Indian Ocean, and is carefully husbanded on the contoured terraces which cling to every mountain-side. The rest of the year round, the sun shines out of a perennially blue sky and through an atmosphere as yet unthreatened by industrial pollution, marvellously invigorating to the refugee from lowland climates, whether in Arabia or in distant Europe.

*Architecture*

In this clarity and against the perpetual background of the mountains — which change from brown to grey to blue as the light shifts and plays on them through the day — the scattered towns and villages are at first dwarfed in the distance by the grandeur of their surroundings. Closer at hand, they reveal themselves as remarkably substantial, with a fortress character which bears witness to centuries of tribal warfare in which the first concern was always to ensure security against attack. Stone-built at the base and with the upper storeys of brick or beaten earth, the houses are tall and crowd closely together. In spirit these provincial towns of Yemen are reminiscent of the hill towns of central Italy, with their mountain setting and an air of self-assurance tempered by beauty of line and a lively feeling for decoration. Many of them are still surrounded by the walls through which the only access was by way of one of the fortified gates; and above them a citadel crowns an impregnable crag to which the defenders, if the town itself were to fall, could withdraw to stand siege (as many of them did as recently as 1962–70) and prepare their counter-attack.

*Cultural Tradition*

In their splendid setting these towns offer the visitor a vivid glimpse of the traditional pattern of Arab life before it was swamped and standardised, as it has been elsewhere, by the tide of modernism. The Yemenis are proud to be the guardians of the oldest cultural tradition in Arabia. In San'a' and outside the city of Ta'izz in the south there are mosques of an almost unrivalled antiquity; Zabid, near the Red Sea coast, is the home of an Islamic seminary which was famous in the Middle Ages; and where the mountains meet the desert in the eastern part of the country, reaching back more than a thousand years before the coming of Islam, there are the remains of an earlier civilisation vaguely identified (for the records are scanty) with that Kingdom of Sheba to which both the Bible and the Qur'an make reference — with a tantalising lack of precision. At Ma'rib, where the foothills shelve into the sands of the great Arabian Desert, stand the columns of a temple to the Moon God in what was once the capital of Saba, or Sheba, some five or six centuries before the birth of Christ.

*Archaeology*

Nearby, at the mouth of a deep wadi, are the remains of one of the great monuments of antiquity, the Ma'rib Dam, the vital base on which rested the fabled prosperity of Sheba. On either side of the wadi, where it opens out onto what is now a dusty plain, stand piers of well-cut stone, built onto the rock wall. Between the piers there extended, two thousand years ago, a series of sluices which controlled the flood waters coming down from the high mountain complex to the west. And below, where the plain is now empty and desolate, were fields and gardens irrigated by the flood water as it flowed through the sluices into channels criss-crossing what is now merely the edge of the desert.

Somewhere in the sixth century AD — nobody quite knows when, but the catastrophe resounds through the early history of Yemen — the dam broke and the civilisation which depended on it was swept away in a sudden violent flood. The echoes of the disaster spread far and wide and it set on foot a wave of migration which altered the demographic picture in the whole of the Arabian Peninsula. For the visitor, what remains of this pioneering system of flood control and land reclamation constitutes an extraordinarily evocative sight. Moreover, the possibility exists, if present plans are brought to fruition, that an ambitious project of reconstruction may restore to Ma'rib something of its original prosperity. The government of the United Arab Emirates has offered to finance the project and a Swiss firm has undertaken the survey work, with a view to rebuilding the system of sluices. If that can be done and the ancient irrigation system can be re-created, not only will the plain be green again, with waving crops and fruit trees and fresh water flashing in the sunlight, but visitors to Yemen will be able to see in operation at Ma'rib a reconstruction of one of the most significant examples of early technology. Not many tourist authorities anywhere in the world could rival that.

*Natural History*

Apart from its historical interest, Yemen has much to offer to the visitor whose preferences lie in other directions. The overlapping between the Red Sea and the Rub' al-Khali of three distinct biogeographical regions makes of Yemen an interesting transition zone in which coexist some of the flora and fauna of Europe, Africa and Asia. There is fascination here for the botanist (who should refer to Hugh Scott's *In the High Yemen*[2]), the geologist and the birdwatcher, as well as for the simple traveller who enjoys mountain scenery on the scale of the Alps or the Rockies.

**Room for Improvement**

To make the most of these assets will require in Yemen, as it requires elsewhere, effort and imagination: the effort to maintain what is good and to protect it against moral as well as material deterioration; and the imagination to present it in such a way as to attract as well as interest the traveller. (Every tourist thinks of himself as a traveller and it does no harm to humour him — or her.) With this in mind, as well as the experience gained in conducting two groups of well-travelled tourists to Yemen, the author would offer a few suggestions which might further improve the prospects for the expansion of tourism in the country.

(1) Immigration and customs procedures need to be drastically overhauled. Only at San'a' airport, it seems, does the traditional Yemeni suspicion of foreigners survive — but first impressions can be lasting ones. It would be a sound investment to institute a training programme for immigration officers which would include a grounding in at least one foreign language. It would also be inexpensive and time-saving to provide baggage trolleys.

(2) A recent experiment in Ta'izz has shown that it is possible to win the co-operation of the Yemeni public in the collection and disposal of refuse. By extending the experiment to other towns and cities, and eventually to the countryside, the authorities would dispose, at a stroke, of the criticism most widely voiced by foreign visitors to the country.

(3) In the matter of hotels, the wealthy traveller and the businessman with a lavish expense account are now well provided for in the main cities of Yemen (although not elsewhere). If the younger and more adventurous are to be encouraged to visit the country — and it is their good opinion which will be worth winning for the future — the need is now for more modest hostelries. The chain of tourist inns which have helped the Turkish authorities to build a flourishing and successful tourist industry provide a model worth emulating.

(4) If life in Yemen could be made less expensive altogether for the foreigner, either through an alteration in the exchange rate or by instituting a special rate for the tourist, many Europeans who at present cannot afford to do so would be able to visit the country and help to establish connections with it.

(5) To those who do come and who travel about the country by road, as most of them are likely to do, it would come as a great relief to know that new and stringent standards had been established for the issuing of driving licences. As a corollary to this, it would surely be wise to remove the carcases of vehicles of all kinds which have come to grief on the mountain roads and which at present remain by the roadside, perhaps as a warning — certainly a most alarming one — to others to be more careful.

**The Future**

In conclusion, it can be said that Yemen is exceptionally well endowed for the development of a successful tourist industry and that over the past ten years a good start has been made in providing the necessary infrastructure.

Further expansion should not be difficult, but before undertaking it the authorities in Yemen would be wise to look closely at the experience of other countries. They are likely to conclude that, if harmful side-effects (both material and psychological) are to be avoided, the expansion should not be too rapid.

If the decision to expand is taken, and since the tourist industry will have to compete with other sectors of the economy for its share of scarce governmental resources, it will be desirable to create a Ministry of Tourism. The Ministry should consider and propose administrative and economic measures to deal with remaining shortcomings.

To maintain the present good relationship between the population and the foreign tourists is vital, and it will not necessarily be easy when the number of tourists increases. A public information campaign, directed at both sides (separately) by means of leaflets, posters and television programmes, could usefully be undertaken to meet this important need.

If the problems involved are tackled with energy, tact and imagination, there is every reason to expect the successful development of tourism in Yemen, with benefit both to the economy of the country and to the strengthening of its relations with the outside world.

## Notes

1. Freya Stark, *East is West* (John Murray, London, 1945), p. 23.
2. Hugh Scott, *In the High Yemen* (John Murray, London, 1947).

## GLOSSARY OF ARABIC WORDS NOT EXPLAINED ON FIRST APPEARANCE

*dhurra*    millet or sorghum.

*dukhn*    pearl millet.

*fiqh*    Islamic jurisprudence.

*hadith*    a tradition relating the actions of the Prophet Muhammad.

*'id*    Islamic festival or holy day.

*imam*    in this context, one of the hereditary rulers of North Yemen up to the 1962 revolution; their powers were both religious and secular.

*jabal*    (plural *jibal*) hill, mountain.

*qadi*    a judge, operating in the field of Islamic law.

*qat*    *Catha edulis* — a shrub whose leaves are mildly stimulant when chewed.

*samsara*    caravanserai.

*shaikh*    tribal leader; scholar in a traditional Islamic science; old man.

*suq*    market, bazaar.

*waqf*    in Islam, a pious and inalienable endowment for charitable purposes.

## CONTRIBUTORS

*Ahmad Ali Abdulsadiq* works in the Ministry of Planning, Aden.

*Michael Adams* is Editor-in-Chief of *Middle East International* and a writer on Arab affairs.

*Mohamed A. Alkhader* is Deputy Dean of the Faculty of Education at San'a' University.

*Ueli Brunner* is a member of the Department of Geography in Zürich University.

*Peter Clark* was until recently the British Council Representative in San'a'.

*Abdulhadi H. al-Hamdani* is Chairman of the Yemen Tourism Company.

*Nigel Harvey* is an economist and staff writer for the *Middle East Economic Digest*.

*Horia Mohammad al-Iryani* is Principal of al-Furat Primary School in San'a'.

*Ahmed al-Kasir* is from Egypt and is Lecturer in Sociology at San'a' University.

*Horst Kopp* is Professor in the Department of Geography at Tübingen University and scientific co-ordinator of the Tübingen Atlas of the Middle East (TAVO).

*Ronald Lewcock*, who is both architect and historian, is Professor at Clare Hall, Cambridge University and co-editor of *San'a': an Arabian Islamic City*.

*Günter Meyer* is in the Department of Geography at the University of Erlangen-Nuremberg.

*Abdullah Ahmed Muheirez* is Director-General of the Yemeni Centre for Cultural and Archaeological Research in Aden.

*Martha Mundy* is Lecturer in the Department of Humanities and Social Studies at Yarmouk University, Jordan.

*Cynthia Myntti* is Program Officer with the Ford Foundation, Cairo.

*V. V. Naumkin* is Professor in the Afro-Asian Institute of Moscow University.

*Taher A. Rajab* is General Manager of the Yemen Bank for Development and Reconstruction in San'a'.

*Abdulaziz Y. Saqqaf* is Chairman of the Department of Economics in San'a' University and Adviser to the YAR government.

*Günther Schweizer* is Professor of Human Geography and Head of the Geography Department at Cologne University.

*Jon C. Swanson* works in the International Consulting Division of Chemonics and is a writer on Yemeni affairs.

*Shelagh Weir* is Assistant Keeper of the Museum of Mankind (the Ethnography Department of the British Museum, London).

# INDEX

*NB.* All entries, except proper names, refer to the Yemen Arab Republic (YAR), unless otherwise stated.

al-Abbadi, Ahmad 209
Aden
  cultural development in 203-11
  *see also* Western Aden Protectorate
Aden College 210
agrarian society
  Bani Awwam district (Hajja) 134-5, 142-3
  Ma'rib region 59
  Razih province ( Sa'da) 65-8, 73-81
  Tihama 31-5
agriculture (PDRY) 5-6, 9, 13, 16
  and Second Five-Year Plan 17-18
  resource base 12
agriculture (YAR)
  crop production 32, 47, 57-8, 124-6; Razih province (Sa'da) 66, 72, 75-7
  decline of 34, 104, 105
  impact of emigration on 77, 123-7
  Ma'rib region 51-62; current practice 56-9; development plan 59-61; Sabaean period 54-5, 61
  mechanisation 32, 33, 34, 35, 58; *see also* pumping equipment
  Razih province (Sa'da) 65-7, 75-7; qat cultivation 67-8, 72-3
  resource base 42-3
  Tihama 22-39, 77; modernisation proposals 35-9; pump farming 30-2, 39-40n8, 47; traditional techniques 23-9
Agricultural Credit Bank 100
Ahkaf Library (Tarim) 201, 213
archaeology
  PDRY 212-13
  YAR 229-30, 246-7
architecture 128, 215, 245-6
Arslan, Abdullah 208
al-Asnaj, Ahmad Sa'id 206

Bahamish, Ali Ahmad 209
al-Baihani, Muhammad Salim 209
  Bakathir, Ali Ahmad 200-1
balance of payments
  PDRY 17
  YAR 84, 102-4, 105, 106, 148
banana plants 66, 68-9, 76-7

Bani Awwam district (Hajja) 133, 134-6, 137, 143
Bank Misr 84
banking 96-101, 139
barley 56, 66, 76
al-Barqawi, Tawfiq Nuri 206
basin irrigation 26, 27, 47
Bin Fadl, Ahmad 202
bond issues 92, 105, 140
budget
  PDRY 10
  YAR 84, 85-94; deficit 90-1, 92-3; expenditure 85-8, 92; revenue 87, 88-90, 94
building materials 69, 80, 215, 222
building sector 148-9, 151-2, 153-63
  labour force in 148-9; housing patterns in San'a' 163; integration in urban society 161-2; migration patterns 154-61; place of origin 151-2, 153
buildings, traditional 216-17, 221-5

cash-crops 76, 125
  coffee 66, 74, 75, 135
  cotton and sesame 26, 29, 30, 32
Central Bank of Yemen 85, 92, 98, 99, 105
central places 109, 114, 118
Central Planning Organisation 85
Central Statistical Office (PDRY) 14
child-rearing 104, 166, 171
Civil Registration Office (PDRY) 14-15
climate 42-3, 51, 134, 245
  *see also* rainfall
coffee 66, 73-5, 102, 126, 135, 146n7
Confederation of Yemeni Development Associations 133, 138, 145, 146n15
conservation *see* urban renewal
construction industry 148, 149, 150
consumerism 104, 134, 136
consumption 102-6
co-operatives, rural *see* Local Development Associations
cotton 26, 29, 30, 32, 102
  decline in production 124, 125

Printed in the United States
by Baker & Taylor Publisher Services